AF522537

Bhavan's Book University

MAHABHARATA

in Comics

Scriptwriter: Kamala Chandrakant
Illustrator: P.B. Kavadi

2018
Bharatiya Vidya Bhavan
Kulapati Munshi Marg
Mumbai 400 007

Place of Publication : Mumbai

First Edition 2018

Price : ₹ 895/-

ISBN : 978-81-7276-595-8

PRINTED IN INDIA
by Parksons Graphics,
15, Shah Industrial Estate, Off Veera Desai Road, Andheri (W), Mumbai 400 053

Foreword

Rendering of the Mahabharata into comics format was a daunting task that sorely tested the dedication and creativity of the various comics professionals who worked on the project. The script was written by Kamala Chandrakant, former associate editor of Amar Chitra Katha and the superb graphics were provided by P.B. Kavadi, one of the pioneers of comics art in India. Using old world prose to match the mood of the great epic, Kamala Chandrakant takes us through scenes of intrigue, deceit, adventure, heroism and chicanery as she unravels layer after layer of this timeless tale to finally uncover the centrepiece – the great war that finally establishes the supremacy of Dharma. There is thunder and storm and passion and tenderness as the fascinating story of the rivalry between the Pandavas and the Kauravas gradually unfolds and moves inexorably into the realms of war and annihilation.

This is a work that should be read by all – young and old, rich and poor, Hindu and non-Hindu, Indian and non-Indian as it explores the human condition in situations that can be universally understood. Reading it in times of ease and comfort gives joy and insight into human nature; reading it in times of adversity gives solace and peace of mind.

P. N. Santhanagopal
Director
Bharatiya Vidya Bhavan

THE MAHABHARATA

SCRIPT:
KAMALA CHANDRAKANT

ILLUSTRATIONS:
P. B. KAVADI

AS THE BOAT REACHED AN ISLAND IN THE RIVER, A FOG GATHERED TURNING DAY INTO NIGHT...

WHEN THE FOG CLEARED THE SAGE WAS GONE. VYASA, WHO WOULD LATER TELL THIS GREAT STORY WAS BORN OUT OF THIS UNION.

AS SOON AS HE WAS BORN, VYASA WILLED HIS BODY TO GAIN ITS FULL STATURE.

VYASA LEFT LEAVING HIS YOUNG UNWED MOTHER WONDERING WHAT THE FUTURE HELD FOR HER.

HASTINAPURA WAS RULED BY THE FORTY-YEAR-OLD KURU KING, SHANTANU. HE HAD ONE SON, DEVAVRATA, BORN TO HIM OF GANGA.
BUT, IN KEEPING THE SON, SHANTANU HAD LOST HIS CELESTIAL WIFE.

THEN ONE DAY, ON THE BANKS OF THE YAMUNA, HE CAME ACROSS SATYAVATI.

FOR THE LONELY KURU KING, IT WAS LOVE AT FIRST SIGHT.
O LOVELY MAIDEN, WHO ARE YOU?
I AM SATYAVATI, DAUGHTER OF THE FISHERMEN'S CHIEF.

THEN I WILL SEEK HIS CONSENT TO MAKE YOU MY WIFE.

WHEN SHANTANU WENT WITH HIS PROPOSAL TO THE FISHERMAN –
...PROMISE ME THAT THE CHILD BORN TO YOU WILL BE THE HEIR TO YOUR THRONE.

SHANTANU WAS STUNNED BY THE FISHERMAN'S DEMAND.
MAKE THE CHILD BORN TO SATYAVATI MY HEIR! HOW CAN I?

I HAVE PROCLAIMED DEVAVRATA AS MY HEIR.

AND THE RIGHT IS HIS; YET... I CANNOT LIVE WITHOUT SATYAVATI.

WHEN DEVAVRATA SAW SHANTANU, HE GUESSED AT ONCE THAT SOMETHING WAS WRONG.

I KNOW THAT ALL IS WELL WITH THE KINGDOM. THEN WHY IS MY FATHER DEJECTED?

THE MINISTER, HIS CONFIDANT, SHOULD KNOW.

THE MINISTER TOLD DEVAVRATA ABOUT SATYAVATI AND HER FATHER'S DEMAND.

KEEN TO KEEP HIS FATHER HAPPY, DEVAVRATA WENT TO THE FISHERMAN'S HUT WITH A FEW KURU CHIEFS.

THERE WILL BE NO CHILDREN.

I VOW TO REMAIN A CELIBATE. A BRAHMACHARI.

THIS TERRIBLE VOW FROM A PRINCE ASTOUNDED THE VERY CELESTIALS.
BHEESHMA! BHEESHMA!
AND FROM THEN ON DEVARATA, THE ONLY CHILD OF SHANTANU, CAME TO BE CALLED BHEESHMA WHICH MEANS 'HE OF THE TERRIBLE OATH'.

BHEESHMA TURNED TO SATYAVATI.
COME, MOTHER, LET US HASTEN TO HASTINAPURA.

AT HASTINAPURA-

SHANTANU WAS TOUCHED AND AMAZED.
YOU SHALL LIVE AS YOU DESIRE. DEATH SHALL DARE COME TO YOU AT YOUR WILL ALONE, BHEESHMA.

SATYAVATI AND SHANTANU HAD TWO SONS, CHITRANGADA AND VICHITRAVEERYA.

WHEN SHANTANU DIED, BHEESHMA CROWNED CHITRANGADA KING.

CHITRANGADA, HOWEVER, DIED IN A COMBAT WITH A GANDHARVA KING.

BHEESHMA THEN PLACED YOUNG VICHITRAVEERYA ON THE THRONE AND ACTED AS HIS REGENT.

WHEN VICHITRAVEERYA CAME OF AGE...
MOTHER, THE KING OF KASHI IS HOLDING A SWAYAMVARA FOR HIS THREE DAUGHTERS.

PERMIT ME TO GO AND WIN THEM FOR MY BROTHER.
GO, MY SON.
BHEESHMA LEFT FOR KASHI.

DRIVING INTO THE SWAYAMVARA ENCLOSURE AT KASHI...

...BHEESHMA GATHERED THE THREE PRINCESSES INTO HIS CHARIOT...

...AND DROVE AWAY.
I AM TAKING THESE BRIDES FOR MY BROTHER. STOP ME IF YOU CAN!

THE COTERIE OF KINGS AT THE SWAYAMVARA IN KASHI TOOK UP BHEESHMA'S CHALLENGE.

A FIERCE BATTLE FOLLOWED...

...IN WHICH BHEESHMA EMERGED THE VICTOR.

AS BHEESHMA RACED TOWARDS HASTINAPURA, SHALVA, THE KING OF SAUBHA, ATTACKED HIM.

BHEESHMA SLEW SHALVA'S STEEDS BUT SPARED HIS LIFE...

...AND SPED WITH THE BRIDES TO HASTINAPURA.

HOWEVER, WHEN BHEESHMA REACHED HASTINAPURA WITH THE BRIDES -
I LOVE THE KING OF SAUBHA AND HE LOVES ME.

IT WAS AMBA THE ELDEST OF THE THREE BRIDES.
KNOWING THIS, DO AS YOU SEE FIT.

BHEESHMA PONDERED ON THE MATTER FOR A WHILE. THEN -
YOU ARE FREE TO STAY OR GO WITH OUR BLESSINGS.
AMBA CHOSE TO GO AND LEFT FOR SAUBHA.

AMBIKA AND AMBALIKA WERE GIVEN IN MARRIAGE TO VICHITRAVEERYA.

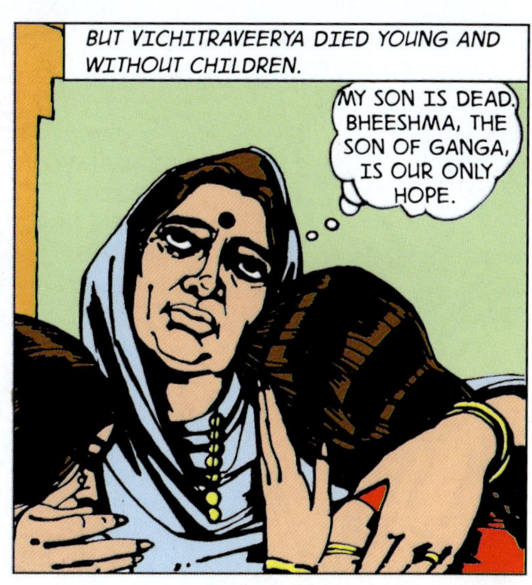
BUT VICHITRAVEERYA DIED YOUNG AND WITHOUT CHILDREN.
MY SON IS DEAD. BHEESHMA, THE SON OF GANGA, IS OUR ONLY HOPE.

AFTER THE FUNERAL RITES WERE OVER -
I MUST INSTALL BHEESHMA ON THE THRONE.

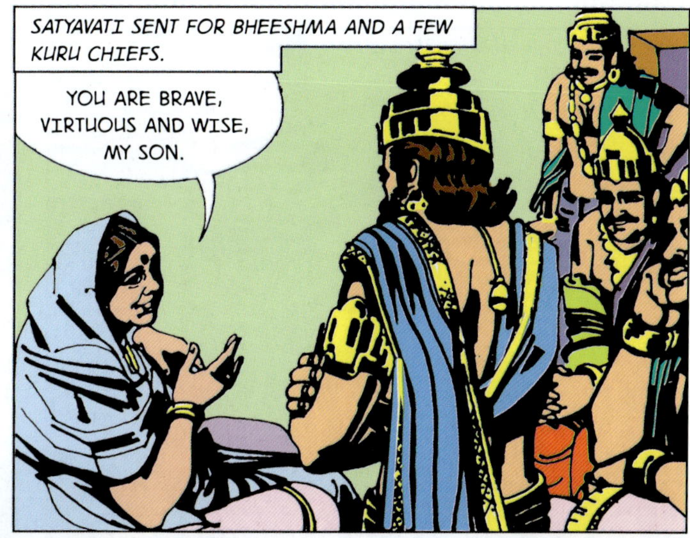
SATYAVATI SENT FOR BHEESHMA AND A FEW KURU CHIEFS.
YOU ARE BRAVE, VIRTUOUS AND WISE, MY SON.

ONLY YOU CAN CARRY FORWARD YOUR FATHER'S DYNASTY AND HIS GLORY.

WED AMBIKA AND AMBALIKA AND BEGET CHILDREN. ASCEND THE THRONE AND RULE THE KINGDOM.

BHEESHMA, HOWEVER, TURNED DOWN SATYAVATI'S PROPOSAL.
I CAN NEITHER WED NOR BEGET CHILDREN, NOR BE KING.

THE OATH I TOOK WAS IN YOUR PRESENCE AND IS WELL KNOWN.

UPON THIS THE KURU CHIEFS LEFT THE CHAMBER.

SATYAVATI DID NOT GIVE UP.
O BHEESHMA, I HAVE SOMETHING TO TELL YOU.

AND SHE TOLD HIM OF HER SON, VYASA, AND HIS MARVELLOUS BIRTH.
IF YOU APPROVE, HE WILL COME HERE...

...AND GRACE OUR DYNASTY WITH THE CHILDREN WE DESIRE.

BHEESHMA AGREED AND SATYAVATI THOUGHT OF HER SON, VYASA...

THE SAGE WHO WAS DEEP IN MEDITATION DIVINED THAT HE WAS NEEDED BY HIS MOTHER AND...

...HE CAME TO HER AT ONCE - AS HE HAD PROMISED WHEN THEY HAD PARTED.

SATYAVATI WEPT AT THE SIGHT OF HER FIRST-BORN.
I AM HERE, MOTHER, TO CARRY OUT YOUR WISHES.

O VYASA, FOR THE SAKE OF VICHITRAVEERYA YOUR BROTHER AND FOR OUR DYNASTY AND FOR THE KURU PEOPLE...

...GRACE AMBIKA AND AMBALIKA WITH CHILDREN.

SINCE AMBIKA CLOSED HER EYES AS LONG AS THE SAGE REMAINED WITH HER, SHE GAVE BIRTH TO A BLIND SON WHO WAS NAMED DHRITARASHTRA.

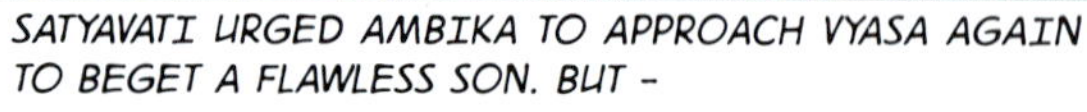

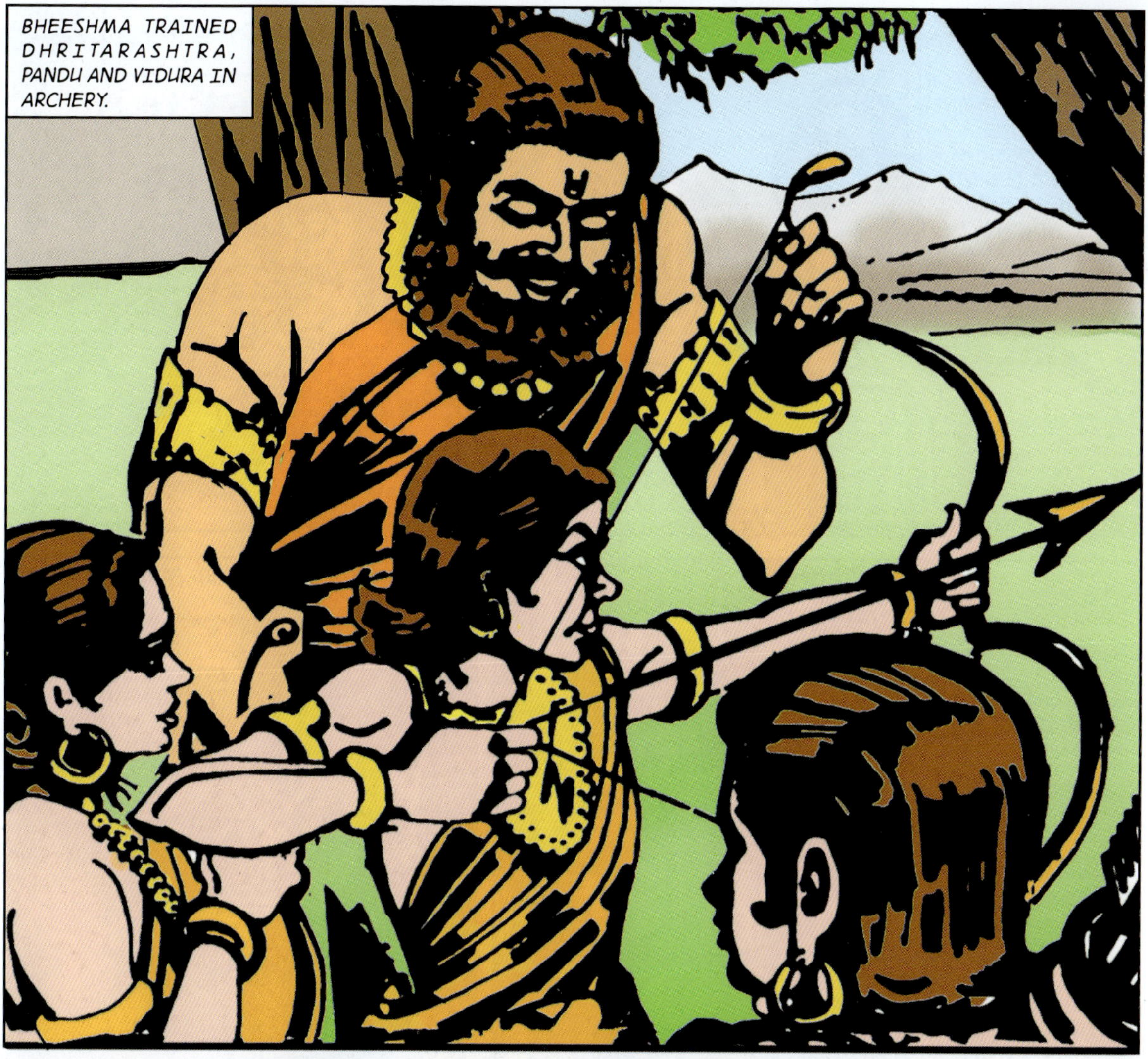

BHEESHMA TRAINED DHRITARASHTRA, PANDU AND VIDURA IN ARCHERY.

BHEESHMA STARTED LOOKING FOR SUITABLE BRIDES FOR THE PRINCES. WHEN GANDHARI, THE PRINCESS OF GANDHARA LEARNT SHE WAS CHOSEN FOR THE BLIND PRINCE DHRITARASHTRA -
TAKE THIS AND BLINDFOLD MY EYES LEST MY VISION MAKE ME BLIND.

AND SO DID GANDHARI WED DHRITARASHTRA.

IN A SWAYAMVARA, YADAVA PRINCESS KUNTI CHOSE PANDU AS HER HUSBAND.

BHEESHMA THEN DECIDED PANDU SHOULD HAVE A SECOND WIFE.
THE MADRA DYNASTY SHARES OUR STRENGTH AND STATURE. AN ALLIANCE BETWEEN THE TWO CLANS WOULD BE PRUDENT.

BHEESHMA APPROACHED MADRA KING SHALYA WITH FABULOUS GIFTS TO SEEK HIS SISTER MADRI'S HAND FOR PANDU...

...AND BROUGHT THE BEDECKED MADRI HOME TO HASTINAPURA FOR PANDU.

AFTER SPENDING BUT THIRTY DAYS WITH KUNTI AND MADRI, PANDU SET OUT ON A CAMPAIGN OF CONQUEST WHICH MADE HIM THE SOVEREIGN RULER OF THE EASTERN WORLD.

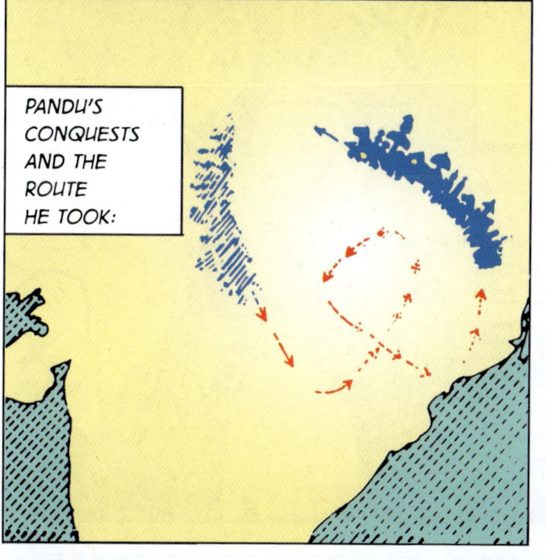
PANDU'S CONQUESTS AND THE ROUTE HE TOOK:

THE CONQUEROR RETURNED TO HASTINAPURA BRINGING UNTOLD WEALTH AND GLORY TO THE KURUS.
PANDU IS TRULY THE MONARCH OF THE WORLD!

AT DHRITARASHTRA'S COMMAND, PANDU GAVE AWAY THE WEALTH TO BHEESHMA, SATYAVATI, AMBIKA, AMBALIKA AND VIDURA...

...AND LEFT WITH HIS WIVES FOR A SOJOURN IN THE FORESTS.

HE CHOSE A SYLVAN RETREAT IN THE HIMALAYAS WHERE HE SPENT HIS DAYS HUNTING DEER.

ON ONE SUCH HUNT, HE SHOT DOWN A DEER ENGAGED IN THE ACT OF MATING.
O PANDU! HOW COULD YOU DO THIS TO ME AT SUCH A TIME!

YOU SHALL DROP DEAD THE MOMENT YOU TOUCH YOUR WIFE IN DESIRE.

THE DYING DEER'S FATAL CURSE LEFT PANDU BUT ONE OPTION - CELIBACY.
I WILL FORSAKE MY WIVES, AND LEAD THE LIFE OF A WANDERING ASCETIC.

KUNTI AND MADRI, HOWEVER, WOULD NOT BE FORSAKEN.
WE WILL GO WITH YOU. BUT AS COMRADES IN ASCETICISM.

THEN, TOGETHER WE SHALL RENOUNCE THE WORLD TILL I PASS AWAY.

PANDU GAVE AWAY ALL THE ORNAMENTS AND ROBES HE AND HIS WIVES HAD...

...AND SENT HIS ATTENDANTS TO HASTINAPURA.
PANDU AND HIS WIVES HAVE RENOUNCED THE WORLD AND HAVE GONE TO THE FORESTS.

O PANDU, WHY HAVE YOU ABANDONED US IN THIS MANNER?

THEN ONE DAY VYASA CAME TO THE PALACE. HE WAS WEARY AND HUNGRY AND GANDHARI LOOKED AFTER HIM WELL.

WHAT DO YOU DESIRE MOST?
A HUNDRED SONS - ALL AS MIGHTY AS MY HUSBAND.

YOU SHALL HAVE THEM.
AND IN DUE COURSE GANDHARI CONCEIVED.

MEANWHILE, AFTER A LONG TREK OVER THE CHAITRARATHA RANGE AND BEYOND, PANDU, KUNTI AND MADRI REACHED GANDHAMADANA. FROM THERE THEY WENT ON TO LAKE INDRADYUMNA. AFTERWARDS, THEY CROSSED THE MOUNTAINS AND ARRIVED AT THE SHATASHRINGA RANGE WHERE THEY STAYED.

AT THIS HOLY PLACE THEY RAN INTO SAGES -

PANDU PONDERED ON THE WORDS OF THE HOLY MEN AND THEN SPOKE TO KUNTI.

YOU ALSO KNOW, KUNTI, HOW OUR DYNASTY WAS FOSTERED BY SAGE VYASA. SO...

... DO AS I SAY. LET ONE WHO HAS REALIZED BRAHMAN BEGET A CHILD FOR US THROUGH YOU.

PANDU'S REQUEST FORCED KUNTI BACK INTO A PAST WHEN SHE HAD WAITED UPON THE STERN SEER, DURVASA, FOR A WHOLE LONG YEAR.
YOU ARE PATIENT AND HOSPITABLE. I SHALL TEACH YOU A POTENT MANTRA.

THIS MANTRA WILL EMPOWER YOU TO SUMMON ANY CELESTIAL OF YOUR CHOICE TO BEGET YOUR CHILDREN.

AND DURVASA TAUGHT HER THE MANTRA...
...AND LEFT.

LET ME TEST THE MANTRA. I SHALL SUMMON LORD SURYA.

THE MANTRA WORKED. LORD SURYA CAME...
...AND ALL TOO SOON SHE FOUND HERSELF WITH A SON...

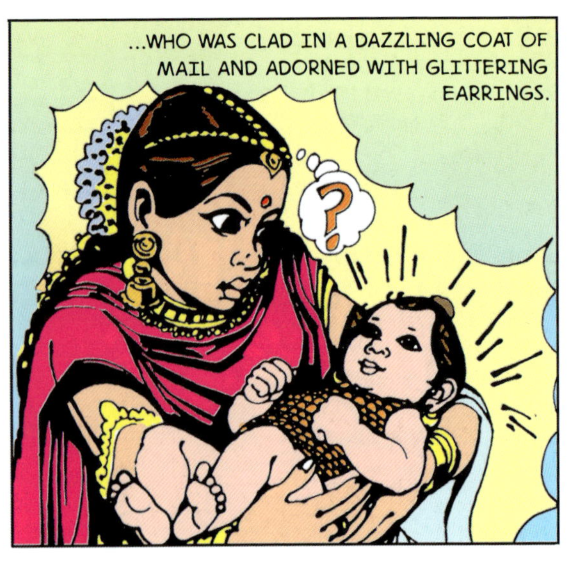
...WHO WAS CLAD IN A DAZZLING COAT OF MAIL AND ADORNED WITH GLITTERING EARRINGS.
?

I AM UNWED. WHAT WILL MY RELATIVES SAY?

AND THEN SHE, PRINCESS KUNTI, WHO WOULD ONE DAY HAVE TO BEAR HEIRS TO A THRONE...

...STEELED HER HEART AND...

WHY ARE YOU SILENT, KUNTI?
PANDU'S ANXIOUS QUERY BROUGHT HER BACK TO THE PRESENT.

KUNTI TOLD PANDU OF THE MANTRA. THEN -
WHICH DEITY SHOULD I SUMMON?

SUMMON DHARMA, THE DEITY OF RIGHTEOUSNESS. OUR COURSE WILL THEN BE BLAMELESS...

...AND THE SON BORN TO YOU, THE MOST RIGHTEOUS OF THE KURUS.

KUNTI CHANTED THE MANTRA.

DRAWN BY ITS POWER THE DEITY, DHARMA, CAME....
...AND GRACED HER WITH A SON WHOM THE CELESTIALS THEMSELVES NAMED YUDHISHTHIRA.

THIS PANDAVA SHALL BE YUDHISHTHIRA. AS KING, HE SHALL BE FAMOUS FOR HIS HONESTY AND RIGHTEOUSNESS.

GANDHARI SOON HEARD ABOUT IT.
A BRILLIANT SON HAS BEEN BORN TO PANDU AND KUNTI.

WOE AM I!
TWO YEARS HAVE GONE BY SINCE I CONCEIVED.
WHY HAVE I NOT YET DELIVERED?

THEN, BLINDED BY ENVY, SHE STRUCK HERSELF IMPATIENTLY AND VIOLENTLY.

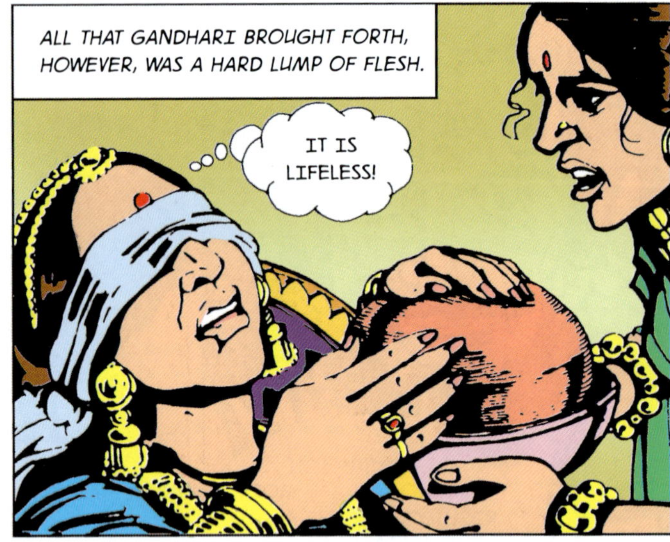
ALL THAT GANDHARI BROUGHT FORTH, HOWEVER, WAS A HARD LUMP OF FLESH.
IT IS LIFELESS!

THROW IT AWAY!

JUST THEN VYASA APPEARED.
WAIT!

VYASA PREPARED A HUNDRED POTS OF GHEE IN A SECRET PLACE. THEN...

...HE BEGAN PLACING A THUMB-SIZED PORTION FROM THE LUMP INTO EACH JAR.

WERE I TO HAVE BUT ONE DAUGHTER, TOO, I WOULD BE OVERJOYED.

THE SAGE KNEW GANDHARI'S MIND.
THE HUNDRED JARS ARE FILLED WITH A PORTION EACH OF THE FLESH YOU BROUGHT FORTH.

THIS PORTION THAT REMAINS SHALL BECOME THE DAUGHTER YOU DESIRE.

AND VYASA PLACED IT IN ANOTHER POT OF GHEE.

MEANWHILE AT SHATASHRINGA-
A KSHATRIYA IS DISTINGUISHED BY PHYSICAL STRENGTH. NOW BRING FORTH A MIGHTY SON, KUNTI.
TO FULFIL PANDU'S DESIRE...

...KUNTI INVOKED THE POWERFUL DEITY OF THE WIND, VAYU...

... WHO GRACED HER WITH A SON OF EQUAL STRENGTH. HE WAS NAMED BHEEMA.
THIS PANDAVA SHALL BE THE MIGHTIEST OF THE MIGHTY.

AS SOON AS BHEEMA WAS BORN...

...THE GROWL OF A TIGER STARTLED KUNTI AND HE WAS THROWN OFF HER LAP.
GRRRR

MIGHTY BHEEMA WAS UNHURT, BUT THE ROCK WAS SMASHED TO SMITHEREENS.

THAT SAME DAY, WHILE STORMY WINDS BLEW AND FOREST FIRES BLAZED OVER HASTINAPURA...

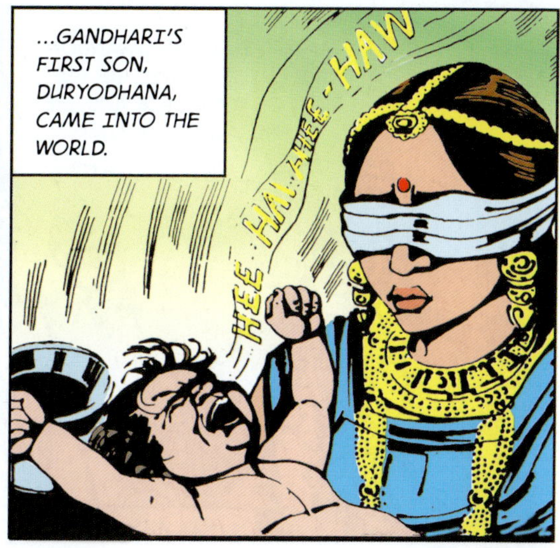
...GANDHARI'S FIRST SON, DURYODHANA, CAME INTO THE WORLD.
HEE HA... HEE-HAW

HIS LOUD, INSISTENT BRAY BROUGHT FORTH ANSWERING CRIES FROM THE BIRDS, THE JACKALS, THE VULTURES AND THE CROWS OF THE LAND.

DHRITARASHTRA SENT FOR BHEESHMA AND VIDURA.
AS THE FIRST-BORN PRINCE, YUDHISHTHIRA WILL RULE THE LAND.

BUT AFTER HIM, WILL THIS SON OF MINE BECOME KING?

WEIRD HOWLS RENT THE AIR EVEN AS THE QUESTION WAS ASKED.
GR-R-R
Y-E-O-O-O-W

MARK THE OMENS! ABANDON THE CHILD. HE WILL BE THE RUIN OF YOUR RACE AND THE LAND. ABANDON HIM!
THIS WAS VIDURA'S ADVICE.

BUT DHRITARASHTRA IGNORED IT.
HOW CAN I ABANDON MY SON? MY ELDEST SON?

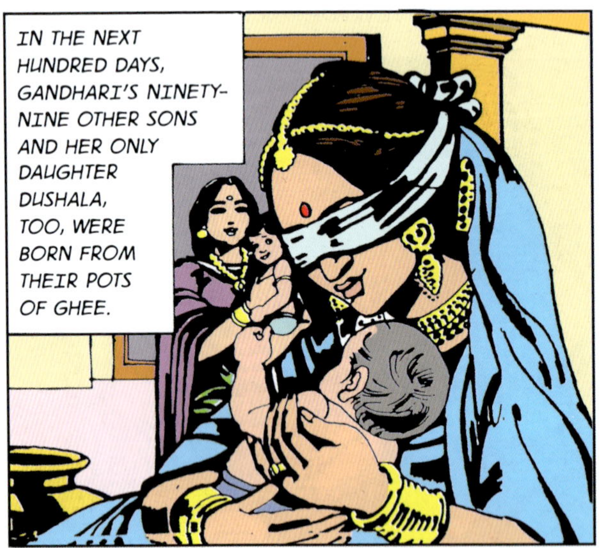
IN THE NEXT HUNDRED DAYS, GANDHARI'S NINETY-NINE OTHER SONS AND HER ONLY DAUGHTER DUSHALA, TOO, WERE BORN FROM THEIR POTS OF GHEE.

MEANWHILE, AT SHATASHRINGA, PANDU DESIRED A THIRD SON.
A SON WHO WILL BE SUPERIOR TO ALL...WHO WILL BE THE MOST POTENT AND GLORIOUS AMONG MEN.

A SON WHOM THE WHOLE WORLD WILL ADMIRE...

SO HE PUT HIMSELF AND KUNTI THROUGH A YEAR LONG PERIOD OF STRICT SPIRITUAL DISCIPLINE TO OBTAIN SUCH A SON.

THE DEITY KUNTI INVOKED WAS INDRA AND THE SON SHE CONCEIVED, ARJUNA.
THIS CHILD WILL MAKE YOU FAMOUS. BY HIS VALOUR HE WILL RESTORE THE GLORY OF THE KURUS...

...THE VERY CELESTIALS CROWDED THE SKIES TO ADORE HIM WITH DIVINE MUSIC AND A CASCADE OF FLOWERS.

WHEN PANDU WANTED YET ANOTHER SON, HOWEVER –
YOU KNOW WHAT IS ORDAINED IN THE SHASTRAS.

A FOURTH PREGNANCY IS FORBIDDEN...

...EVEN IN TIMES OF CALAMITY.
AND KUNTI REFUSED TO COMPLY.

PANDU THEN REQUESTED KUNTI TO HELP MADRI TO BECOME A MOTHER.

KUNTI AGREED AND WITH HER HELP, MADRI INVOKED THE TWIN DEITIES, THE **ASHWINS...**

...AND BROUGHT FORTH THE TWINS **NAKULA** AND **SAHADEVA.**
THESE PANDAVAS SHALL EXCEL ALL IN VIGOUR AND BEAUTY.

THE FIVE SONS OF PANDU CAME TO BE KNOWN AS **PANDAVAS**.

NURTURED UNDER THE MIGHTY ARM OF PANDU, THE FIVE PANDAVAS, **YUDHISHTHIRA, BHEEMA, ARJUNA, NAKULA** AND **SAHADEVA** GREW INTO STRAPPING YOUNG LADS OF UNUSUAL ABILITY.

THEN ONE DAY IN SPRING AS PANDU AND MADRI STROLLED THROUGH THE WOODS...

...PANDU FORGOT HIMSELF.

THE CURSE CAME TRUE AND HE FELL DEAD.

SEVENTEEN DAYS LATER, THE RISHIS OF SHATASHRINGA STOOD AT THE GATES OF HASTINAPURA WITH KUNTI AND THE FIVE PANDAVAS.
INFORM THE KING OF OUR ARRIVAL.

WHEN BHEESHMA, DHRITARASHTRA, VIDURA, SATYAVATI, AMBIKA, AMBALIKA, GANDHARI AND THE SONS OF DHRITARASHTRA CAME OUT -
PANDU, THE SOVEREIGN OF THE KURUS, DIED AT SHATASHRINGA, SEVENTEEN DAYS AGO.

BURNING WITH GRIEF, MADRI TOO SUCCUMBED TO DEATH. LET THE ORDAINED FUNERAL RITES BE PERFORMED FOR PANDU AND MADRI.

LET KUNTI AND THE FIVE SONS OF PANDU RECEIVE ALL THE HONOURS DUE TO THEM.

AND THE RISHI AND HIS ENTOURAGE VANISHED.

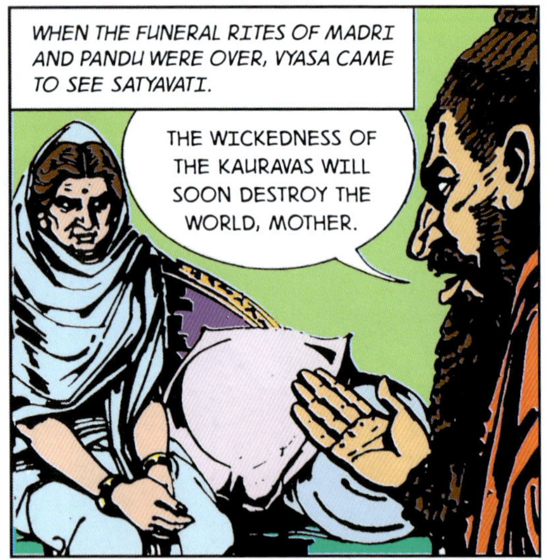
WHEN THE FUNERAL RITES OF MADRI AND PANDU WERE OVER, VYASA CAME TO SEE SATYAVATI.
THE WICKEDNESS OF THE KAURAVAS WILL SOON DESTROY THE WORLD, MOTHER.

RETIRE TO THE FOREST AND SEEK YOUR PEACE IN YOGA.
SO, ALONG WITH AMBIKA AND AMBALIKA, SATYAVATI LEFT FOR THE FOREST.

AND THERE IN DUE TIME THE WOMEN ATTAINED MUKTI THROUGH MEDITATION.

MEANWHILE AT HASTINAPURA, THE KAURAVAS SOON REALIZED THAT ARJUNA AND YUDHISHTHIRA WERE SUPERIOR TO THEM AND BHEEMA BEAT THEM ALL- BE IT IN WRESTLING...

...RUNNING...

...OR SHEER LUNG POWER.

AND DURYODHANA, THE ELDEST OF THE KAURAVAS, SOON REALIZED THAT BHEEMA WAS BECOMING MORE THAN A RIVAL - A THREAT.
IF I AM TO REIGN AS THE UNDISPUTED KING ONE DAY...

...I'LL HAVE TO GET RID OF HIM NOW...

...BY CUNNING IF NEED BE.

ACCORDINGLY, DURYODHANA ARRANGED AN OUTING TO THE GANGA. AND THERE AS THE PRINCES FEASTED AND MADE MERRY...

...HE FED BHEEMA WHO HAD A VORACIOUS APPETITE WITH POISONED FOOD.

THE PRINCES ENTERED THE RIVER TO AMUSE THEMSELVES. THE OTHERS SOON TIRED AND WENT BACK TO THE CAMP. BUT BHEEMA AND DURYODHANA STAYED ON.

AT LAST THEY, TOO, WERE EXHAUSTED AND FLUNG THEMSELVES ON THE BANK. AS THE STRONG POISON AND GENTLE RIVER BREEZE LULLED MIGHTY BHEEMA INTO A COMA...

...DURYODHANA SPRANG INTO ACTION. HE BOUND BHEEMA'S ARMS AND LEGS AND ROLLED HIM DOWN INTO THE WATER.

STILL UNCONSCIOUS, BHEEMA SANK DEEP, DEEP DOWN TO THE NAGA KINGDOM ON THE BED OF THE OCEAN.

THE NAGAS MERCILESSLY BIT THE INTRUDER. BUT THEIR DEADLY POISON...

...MEANT TO KILL, TURNED OUT TO BE AN ANTIDOTE...

...THAT SLOWLY BROUGHT THE POISONED BHEEMA BACK TO CONSCIOUSNESS.

AS HE FULLY REGAINED HIS SENSES, BHEEMA SNAPPED HIS BONDS...

...SEIZED THE SNAKES...
...AND DASHED THEM TO DEATH...

...ON THE FLOOR OF THE OCEAN.
THOSE THAT ESCAPED FLED TO THEIR KING, VASUKI.

MEANWHILE, AS THE PANDAVAS AND KAURAVAS WERE LEAVING, YUDHISHTHIRA FOUND BHEEMA MISSING.
DURYODHANA, WHERE IS BHEEMA?

HE WAS SLEEPING ON THE BANK WHEN I CAME BACK TO THE CAMP.

HE MUST HAVE WOKEN UP AND GONE AHEAD OF US.
YUDHISHTHIRA BELIEVED HIM.

WHEN THEY REACHED THE PALACE. YUDHISHTHIRA WENT STRAIGHT TO KUNTI.
WHERE IS BHEEMA? HAVE YOU SENT HIM ON AN ERRAND?
NO.

I HAVE NOT SEEN HIM.
BUT WE WERE TOLD HE WAS HERE. HE WAS FAST ASLEEP WHEN...

OR WAS IT SLEEP? COULD IT BE...?

AN ANXIOUS KUNTI SENT AT ONCE FOR VIDURA.
BHEEMA IS MISSING. DURYODHANA HATES HIM AND COVETS THE THRONE.

COULD HE HAVE MURDERED MY SON?
HUSH, GOOD WOMAN. DO NOT ACCUSE DURYODHANA LEST HE TURN ON THE OTHER PANDAVAS.

A LONG LIFE IS PREDICTED FOR YOUR SONS. BHEEMA WILL RETURN.
BUT KUNTI WAS NOT SO SURE.

FOR EIGHT LONG DAYS, KUNTI AND THE PANDAVAS WAITED FOR BHEEMA. AT LAST -
BHEEMA!

WHERE WERE YOU, BHEEMA?
IN THE KINGDOM OF THE NAGAS.

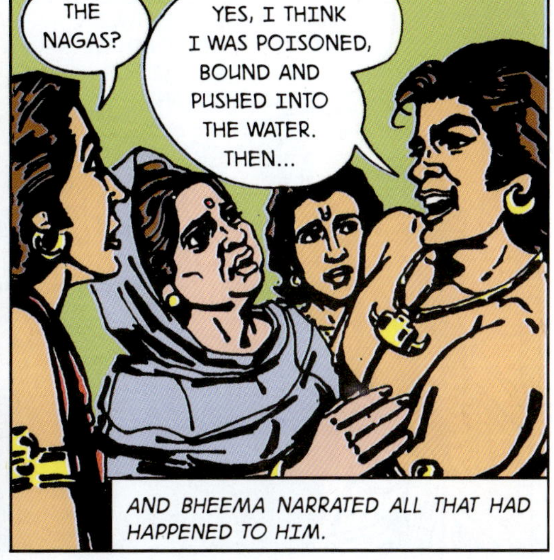
THE NAGAS?
YES, I THINK I WAS POISONED, BOUND AND PUSHED INTO THE WATER. THEN...
AND BHEEMA NARRATED ALL THAT HAD HAPPENED TO HIM.

"THE SNAKES THAT ESCAPED CAME BACK WITH VASUKI THEIR KING...

"...WHO OFFERED ME A MIGHT-POTION WHICH WOULD GIVE ME THE STRENGTH OF THOUSANDS OF ELEPHANTS. I HAD EIGHT FULL JARS OF IT.

THEN I SLEPT. WHEN I WOKE UP, THE NAGAS GUIDED ME TO THE SURFACE. AND HERE I AM.
AND SO BHEEMA ENDED HIS TALE.

BHEEMA WAS SAFE. ALL THE SAME YUDHISHTHIRA WAS WORRIED.
BHEEMA, DO NOT SPEAK OF THIS TO ANYONE.

LET IT REMAIN BETWEEN US. BUT HENCEFORTH WE SHOULD BE WARY OF DURYODHANA.

AND THE PANDAVAS BEHAVED AS IF NOTHING HAD HAPPENED.

MEANWHILE DHRITARASHTRA WAS TROUBLED.
MY SONS ARE WHILING AWAY THEIR TIME IN IDLE PURSUITS.

HE SPOKE TO BHEESHMA.
LET KRIPACHARYA TEACH THE PRINCES THE SCIENCE OF WEAPONS.

SO THE PRINCES BEGAN THEIR MARTIAL TRAINING UNDER KRIPACHARYA.

KRIPA, THE SON OF RISHI GAUTAMA, HAD A TWIN SISTER CALLED KRIPI...

...WHO WAS MARRIED TO DRONA, THE SON OF RISHI BHARADWAJA.

THE COUPLE HAD A SON WHOM THE CELESTIALS NAMED ASHWATTHAMA.

DRONA HAD LEARNT THE SECRETS OF THE FIERY AGNEYA MISSILE FROM RISHI AGNIVESHA...

...AND RISHI PARASHURAMA HAD GIVEN HIM HIS UNIQUE WEAPONS AND THEIR SECRETS.
RICH WITH THIS MARTIAL WEALTH...

...DRONA HAD REMEMBERED HIS CHILDHOOD FRIEND, DRUPADA.
WHEN I BECOME KING, ALL MY WEALTH SHALL BE YOURS.

TAKING DRUPADA AT HIS WORD, DRONA HAD GONE TO PANCHALA TO MEET HIM.
DRUPADA, MY FRIEND!

O BRAHMANA, I AM A KING NOW. AND GREAT KINGS CAN NEVER BE FRIENDS WITH POOR WRETCHES LIKE YOU.
!

ONE WHO IS NOT A KING CAN NEVER HAVE A KING FOR A FRIEND.

I AM A GREAT KING NOW! GREAT KINGS CAN NEVER BE FRIENDS WITH POOR WRETCHES!
INDEED!

ONE WHO IS NOT A KING CAN NEVER HAVE A KING FOR A FRIEND!
INDEED! INDEED!

RAGING OVER THE INSULTS THAT DRUPADA HAD HURLED AT HIM...
...DRONA HAD MADE HIS WAY TO HASTINAPURA, THE CAPITAL OF THE KURUS.

AT HASTINAPURA, DRONA HAD LIVED IN SECLUSION IN KRIPA'S HOUSE FOR MANY YEARS...

...TEACHING HIS SON THE MARTIAL ARTS...

...AND VEDIC LORE...
...EVEN AS HE CAREFULLY PLOTTED HIS REVENGE.

THEN ONE DAY THE PRINCES WERE PLAYING VITI DANDU WHEN -
YOU HAVE HIT IT INTO THE WELL!

HOW DO WE GET IT OUT NOW?
I WILL RETRIEVE IT FOR YOU.

IT WAS DRONA. HE WAS BUSY PULLING THE REEDS GROWING NEAR THE WELL.

DRONA PIERCED ONE REED INTO ANOTHER...

...AND WITH THAT REED CHAIN...

...PULLED UP THE VITI FROM THE WELL.

THE PRINCES WERE ASTOUNDED.
THAT WAS A RARE FEAT, INDEED, SIR.

WHO ARE YOU? WHAT COULD WE DO FOR YOU?

DRONA WAS READY WITH HIS ANSWER.
GO TO BHEESHMA TELL HIM WHAT YOU HAVE SEEN.

WHEN BHEESHMA HEARD FROM THE PRINCES ABOUT THE WONDROUS FEAT -
THE ARCHER COULD BE NONE BUT DRONA, THE SON OF RISHI BHARADWAJA.

AND HE WOULD MAKE A BETTER GURU - NAY THE BEST GURU FOR THE SCIONS OF OUR HOUSE.

I WILL GO AND MEET HIM.

BHEESHMA MET DRONA AND LED HIM TO THE PALACE.
WHAT BRINGS YOU HERE, O SON OF BHARADWAJA?

SPURNED BY MY CHILDHOOD FRIEND, DRUPADA OF PANCHALA...

...I HAVE COME TO THE KURUS IN SEARCH OF LOYAL DISCIPLES.
THAT WAS ALL BHEESHMA NEEDED TO HEAR.

THE KURUS WILL EVER STAND BY YOU. CONSIDER YOUR WISH AS FULFILLED. INDEED, YOUR ARRIVAL HERE IS A BLESSING, O DRONA.

BHEESHMA GAVE HIM A WELL-STOCKED HOUSE AND MUCH WEALTH...

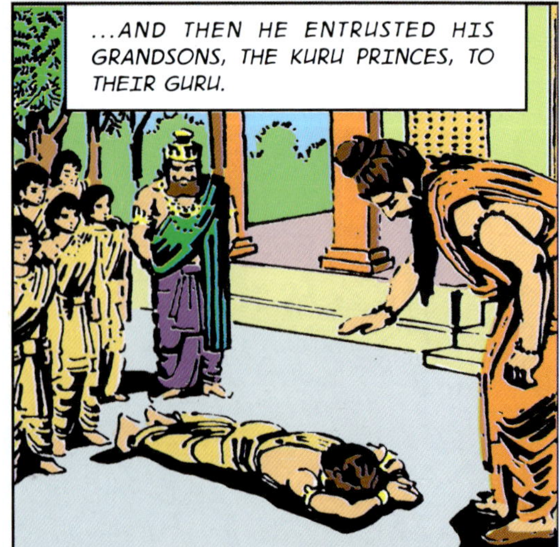
...AND THEN HE ENTRUSTED HIS GRANDSONS, THE KURU PRINCES, TO THEIR GURU.

DRONA FORMALLY ACCEPTED THE PRINCES AS HIS DISCIPLES. THEN -
PROMISE ME THAT YOU WILL ACCOMPLISH A CERTAIN DEED FOR ME, AFTER I HAVE TURNED YOU INTO EXPERT WARRIORS.

FOR A MOMENT ALL THE PRINCES REMAINED SILENT. THEN -
I WILL DO WHAT YOU WANT DONE.
IT WAS ARJUNA, THE PANDAVA.

DRONA HELD HIM CLOSE AND DRENCHED HIM WITH TEARS OF JOY.
I AM SURE YOU WILL, O SON OF PANDU. I AM CONFIDENT.

WHEN DRONA BEGAN TEACHING THE KURU PRINCES...

...MANY FLOCKED TO HIM TO BECOME HIS PUPILS.

AMONG THEM WAS KARNA, THE FOSTER-SON OF ADHIRATHA, THE CHARIOTEER.

GRADUALLY DRONA'S PUPILS BEGAN TO SHINE IN THEIR SPECIAL FIELDS. HIS SON, ASHWATTHAMA IN MYSTERIOUS WEAPONS, DURYODHANA THE KAURAVA AND BHEEMA THE PANDAVA IN MACE-FIGHTING...

DRONA REWARDED HIS DISCIPLE HANDSOMELY -
KEEP YOUR BODY AND MIND IN CONTROL AND RECEIVE THIS BRAHMASHIRAS MISSILE, ARJUNA.

THIS WEAPON IS UNIQUE. IT MAY ONLY BE USED AGAINST DEADLY, INHUMAN FOES. IF USED AGAINST ORDINARY ENEMIES IT WILL SET ABLAZE THE VERY UNIVERSE.

THEN DRONA BLESSED ARJUNA...
YOU WILL REMAIN UNEQUALLED AS AN ARCHER. YOUR VALOUR SHALL MAKE YOU FAMOUS.
...AND TAUGHT HIM THE SECRETS OF THE BRAHMASHIRAS MISSILE.

AT LAST THE PROUD GURU STOOD BEFORE DHRITARASHTRA AND THE KURU ELDERS.
AT YOUR COMMAND, THE PRINCES SHALL EXHIBIT THEIR SKILLS, O KING OF THE KURUS. THEY HAVE COMPLETED THEIR STUDIES.

AS YOU HAVE ACHIEVED THIS, DRONA, YOU CHOOSE THE TIME AND THE PLACE FOR THE TOURNAMENT.

AND I SHALL BE PLEASED IF YOU, LEARNED VIDURA, WOULD CARRY OUT THE PLANS OF DRONA.

IF BHEEMA AND DURYODHANA ACQUITTED THEMSELVES WELL AT THE TOURNAMENT...

...ARJUNA WAS THE HERO OF THE DAY. WITH THE AGNEYA MISSILE HE STARTED A FIRE...

...AND WITH THE VARUNA MISSILE HE PUT IT OUT.

WITH THE BHAUMA MISSILE ARJUNA BORED HIS WAY INTO THE EARTH...

...AND WITH THE PARVATA MISSILE HE SET UP MOUNTAINS.

THEN WITH THE ANTARDHANA MISSILE HE MADE HIMSELF INVISIBLE.

ARJUNA DISPLAYED ALL THE COMPLEX MOVES OF MACE-FIGHTING AND OF SWORD-FIGHTING.

HE SHOT FIVE ARROWS AT ONCE INTO THE MOUTH OF A REVOLVING WOODEN BOAR...

ARJUNA, THE SON OF INDRA IS THE LORD OF THE MARTIAL ARTS AND VISHNU'S EQUAL IN VALOUR!

O ARJUNA, I CAN MATCH ALL THOSE FEATS AND MORE! SO DO NOT GLOAT OVER THEM!
KARNA, THE CHARIOTEER'S FOSTER SON HAD COME TO CHALLENGE ARJUNA.

DURYODHANA WAS PLEASED, ARJUNA EMBARRASSED.
WELCOME, MIGHTY WARRIOR. THE KINGDOM OF THE KURUS AND I ARE AT YOUR COMMAND.

SHARE THE GOOD LIFE WITH US AND TRAMPLE YOUR ENEMIES.
IT IS DONE!

I YEARN FOR A COMBAT WITH ARJUNA...

THEN YOU YEARN FOR DEATH, KARNA. I SHALL SLAY YOU AND HELP YOU ATTAIN THE REALMS RESERVED FOR TRESPASSERS AND BRAGGARTS.

DON'T SPAR WITH WORDS LIKE THE FEEBLE. SPEAK WITH ARROWS AND I SHALL SEVER YOUR HEEL UNDER THE VERY EYES OF THE GURU.

ARJUNA SOUGHT HIS GURU'S PERMISSION....

...EMBRACED HIS BROTHERS...

...AND STOOD READY FOR THE FIGHT.

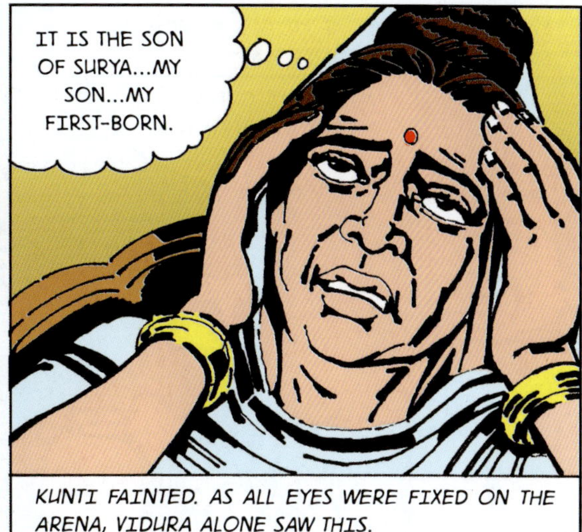

AND HE QUIETLY REVIVED HER WITH THE HELP OF HER MAIDS, WITH NO ONE ANY THE WISER.

MEANWHILE KRIPA, AN EXPERT ON THE PROTOCOL OF DUELS, STEPPED BETWEEN KARNA AND ARJUNA.

ARJUNA IS THE SON OF KUNTI AND A SCION OF THE KURU LINE.

KARNA'S FACE FELL AT KRIPA'S WORDS, BUT DURYODHANA GAVE IT A ROYAL LIFT.
MEN OF VALOUR MAY ASPIRE TO KINGSHIP, SAY THE LEARNED.

IF KARNA MUST BE A KING BEFORE ARJUNA WILL TAKE HIM ON, I CONFER THE KINGSHIP OF ANGA ON VALIANT KARNA.

AND RIGHT THERE IN THAT ARENA, DURYODHANA CROWNED KARNA WHILE THE SPECTATORS CHEERED.

AFTER HIS CORONATION, KARNA TURNED TO DURYODHANA.
NOW WHAT GIFT CAN I GIVE YOU IN RETURN, DURYODHANA?

YOUR FRIENDSHIP.... YOUR UNSWERVING LOYALTY AND FRIENDSHIP.

IT IS YOURS, MY FRIEND.

THEN, AS KARNA PICKED UP HIS WEAPONS, HIS FOSTER-FATHER, ADHIRATHA CAME THERE.
KARNA DROPPED THE WEAPONS...

...AND EMBRACED THE OLD MAN.
MY SON!
FATHER!
BHEEMA HEARD THIS.

THE GREAT KING OF ANGA IS A HUMBLE CHARIOTEER'S SON!

YOU ARE NOT WORTHY OF DEATH AT ARJUNA'S HANDS, YOU SON OF A CHARIOTEER! NEITHER ARE YOU WORTHY OF RULING ANGA.

GO, TAKE THE WHIP, KARNA, AND PURSUE YOUR TRUE CALLING!
BHEEMA'S WORDS OF SCORN CUT DEEP INTO KARNA'S HEART.

WHO BEGOT ME AND THROUGH WHOM? HOW I WISH I KNEW!

YET AGAIN AN ENRAGED DURYODHANA SPOKE OUT IN KARNA'S DEFENCE.
THE ORIGIN OF OUR GURU, DRONA, IS TRACED TO A WATER-POT AND THAT OF KRIPA TO A CLUMP OF REED AND I KNOW, BHEEMA, THE STORY OF YOUR OWN BIRTH!

DOES THAT DETRACT FROM THE MIGHT OF ANY OF YOU? IF MIGHT IS THE PRIME VIRTUE OF KSHATRIYAS....

...KARNA DESERVES TO REIGN NOT ONLY OVER ANGA BUT OVER THE WHOLE WORLD.

THEN DURYODHANA THREW A CHALLENGE TO THE ASSEMBLY AT LARGE.
MOUNT YOUR CHARIOTS, BEND YOUR BOWS AND FIGHT ME, IF YOU CANNOT SEE THE KING IN KARNA.

WHEN THIS CHALLENGE WAS MET WITH A SUBDUED MURMUR OF APPROVAL...

...DURYODHANA TOOK KARNA BY THE HAND AND LED HIM AWAY FROM THE ARENA.

THE HAPPENINGS AT THE TOURNAMENT LEFT YUDHISHTHIRA WORRIED...
KARNA IS AN ACE ARCHER AND HE HAS SWORN LOYALTY TO DURYODHANA.

BUT DURYODHANA WAS HAPPY.
WITH KARNA ON MY SIDE, ARJUNA NO LONGER REMAINS A THREAT TO ME.

KUNTI WAS SECRETLY PLEASED.
MY SON, MY FIRST BORN, IS THE KING OF ANGA!

AS FOR DRONA, HE WAS ELATED. THE DAY HE HAD PATIENTLY WAITED FOR HAD COME.
THE PRINCES ARE COMPLETE WARRIORS. I MAY NOW DEMAND MY DUES.

THE FEE I DEMAND IS DRUPADA, THE KING OF PANCHALA.

ATTACK HIS KINGDOM. CAPTURE HIM AND BRING HIM TO ME.

ALONG WITH DRONA, THE KURU PRINCES MARCHED OUT OF HASTINAPURA...

...FOUGHT THE PANCHALAS GUARDING THE OUTSKIRTS OF THE KINGDOM...

...AND SURROUNDED THE CAPITAL.

WHILE DURYODHANA, KARNA AND YUYUTSU, THE SON OF DHRITARASHTRA AND A VAISHYA WOMAN, VIED WITH ONE ANOTHER TO LEAD THE ATTACK...

...ARJUNA PLANNED HIS STRATEGY.
THEY WILL NOT BE ABLE TO OVERCOME DRUPADA. WE WILL MOVE IN...

...WHEN THEY RETREAT.
AND ARJUNA AND THE OTHER PANDAVAS WAITED.

DRUPADA, THE PANCHALA KING, SAW THE ADVANCING ARMIES OF THE KAURAVAS.

HE CHARGED OUT OF HIS PALACE...

...AND ATTACKED THEM WITH A VOLLEY OF ARROWS.

THOUGH DRUPADA FOUGHT SINGLE-HANDED, HIS ARROWS CAME SO FAST AND FIERCE...

...THAT THE TERROR-STRICKEN KAURAVAS WERE SOON ROUTED.

BEFORE LONG THEY CAME WAILING BACK TO THE PANDAVAS.

THE PANDAVAS SALUTED DRONA...
...AND MOUNTED THEIR CHARIOTS. ARJUNA KEPT YUDHISHTHIRA, THE ELDEST OF THEM, OUT OF THE BATTLE.

THEN WITH BHEEMA IN THE FOREFRONT...
...AND NAKULA AND SAHADEVA GUARDING HIS CHARIOT WHEELS...

...ARJUNA HIMSELF LED THE CHARGE.

THERE WAS COMMOTION AND CHAOS IN THE PANCHALA RANKS. BHEEMA SLEW THEIR ELEPHANTS LEFT AND RIGHT WITH HIS MACE...

...WHILE ARJUNA STEADILY MOVED IN TOWARDS DRUPADA BEHIND HIS STEADY STREAM OF ARROWS.

SOON ARJUNA'S ARROWS CUT THE PANCHALA KING'S BOW AND FLAGSTAFF INTO TWO, AND FELLED HIS HORSES AND CHARIOTEER.

THEN ARJUNA DREW OUT HIS SWORD, SPRANG OUT OF HIS CHARIOT AND INTO DRUPADA'S AND TOOK HIM CAPTIVE.

ARJUNA HAD PROVED HIS MIGHT TO THE WORLD AND HIS LOYALTY TO HIS GURU, DRONA.

THE GURU EYED THE CAPTIVE KING FOR A WHILE. THEN -

AND DRONA OFFERED DRUPADA THE TERRITORY SOUTH OF THE GANGA AND KEPT THAT TO THE NORTH FOR HIMSELF.

DRUPADA SHOWED A SMILING FACE BUT HE WAS SEETHING WITHIN.

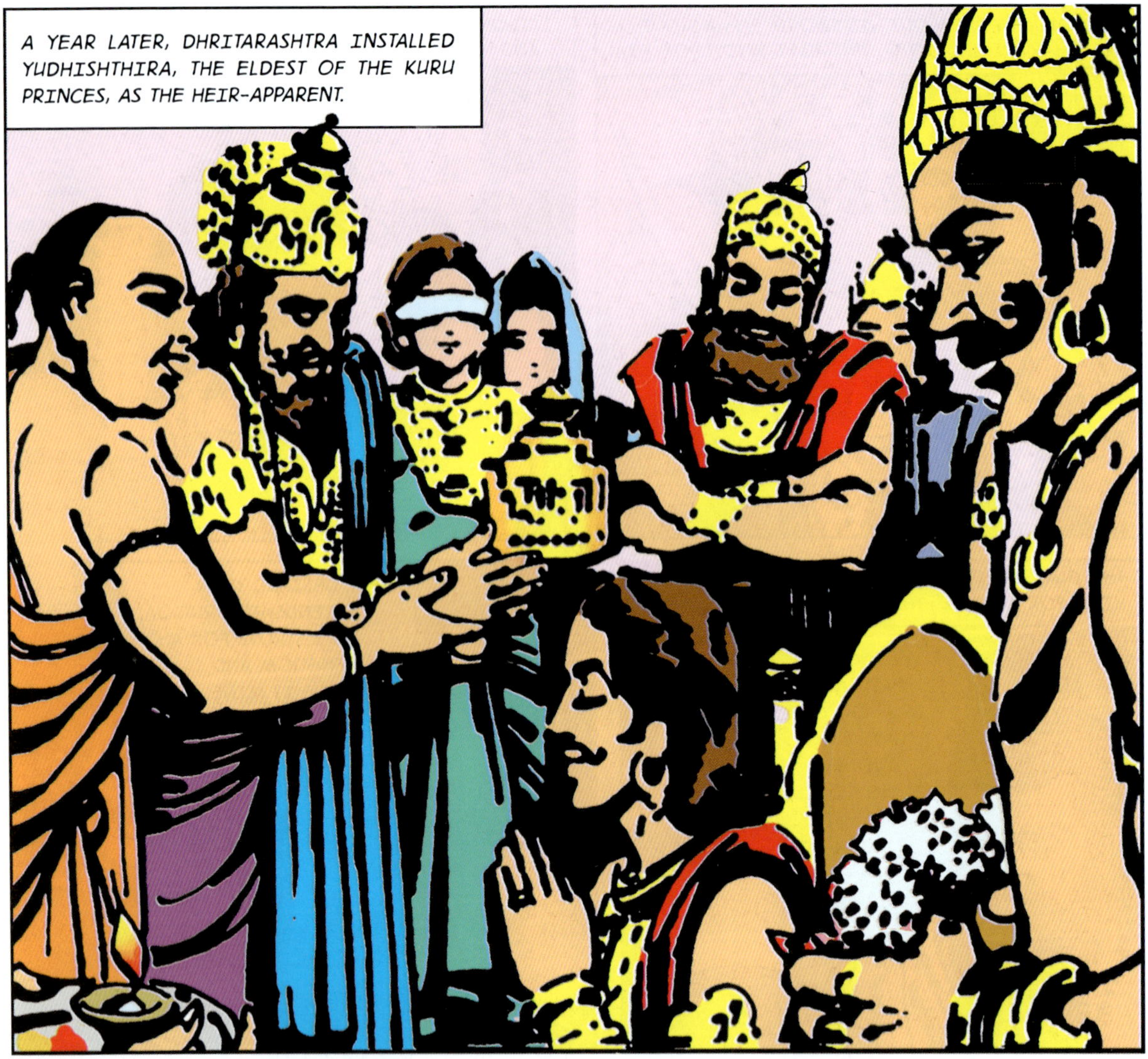

A YEAR LATER, DHRITARASHTRA INSTALLED YUDHISHTHIRA, THE ELDEST OF THE KURU PRINCES, AS THE HEIR-APPARENT.

THE BLIND KING SENT FOR KANIKA, HIS SHREWD COUNSELLOR.
THE ACHIEVEMENTS OF THE PANDAVAS DISTURB ME. I ENVY THEM. SHOULD I SEE THEM AS RIVALS OR AS ALLIES?

THE PANDAVAS ARE MEN OF MIGHT. PROTECT YOURSELF AND YOUR CHILDREN FROM THEM. ACT SO THAT YOU DO NOT HAVE TO REPENT.
SUCH WAS THE ASTUTE KANIKA'S COUNSEL TO THE BLIND KING.

MEANWHILE THE PANDAVAS WERE GAINING POPULARITY WITH THE PEOPLE.
HASTINAPURA HAS NEVER KNOWN SUCH GLORY SINCE THE DAYS OF PANDU.

THEN LET US INSTALL THE ELDEST PANDAVA ON THE THRONE. HE IS YOUNG, TRUTHFUL AND OBEDIENT.
MANY SUCH REMARKS REACHED THE EARS OF DURYODHANA.

JEALOUS AND PERTURBED, DURYODHANA, THE ELDEST KAURAVA, CAME TO HIS BLIND FATHER.
THE CITIZENS ARE OUT TO DISPOSSESS US OF THE THRONE. THEY WOULD SET YOU AND BHEESHMA ASIDE...

...AND HAVE YUDHISHTHIRA FOR THEIR KING.

IF PANDU'S SON BECOMES KING, THE SONS BORN TO HIM WILL CLAIM THE THRONE. WE AND OUR SONS WILL FOREVER REMAIN THE LOWLY ONES IN THE KURU LINE.

YOUR RULE, O KING, MUST SPARE US THE HELL OF LIFELONG DEPENDENCE ON THE CHARITY OF OTHERS.
DHRITARASHTRA HEARD DURYODHANA OUT...

...AND HE RECALLED KANIKA'S COUNSEL.
THE PANDAVAS ARE MEN OF MIGHT. PROTECT YOURSELF AND YOUR CHILDREN FROM THEM.

MEANWHILE, DURYODHANA CONSPIRED WITH SHAKUNI HIS MATERNAL UNCLE, DUSHASANA HIS BROTHER, AND KARNA HIS FRIEND...

...AND RETURNED TO DHRITARASHTRA.
IF YOU SEND THE PANDAVAS AWAY TO VARANAVATA UNDER SOME PRETEXT....

...WE SHALL BE FREE OF THE FEAR OF THEM.

DHRITARASHTRA WAS NOT SO SURE.
PANDU WAS EVER GENEROUS, PANDU'S SON IS EQUALLY GENEROUS.

HE HAS MANY ALLIES. MOST OF THEM PANDU'S MEN OR THE SONS OF PANDU'S MEN.

BUT DURYODHANA HAD ALREADY TAKEN CARE OF THAT.
I HAVE WON OVER THE POWERFUL AMONG THEM. AND WE NOW CONTROL THE TREASURY AND THE COUNSELLORS.

WHEN MY HOLD OVER THE DOMINION IS COMPLETE, THE PANDAVAS AND KUNTI COULD BE BROUGHT BACK TO HASTINAPURA.
DURYODHANA'S SCHEME SEEMED PERFECT.

BUT NOT TO DHRITARASHTRA.
BHEESHMA, DRONA, VIDURA AND KRIPA LOOK WITH EQUAL AFFECTION UPON US AND THE PANDAVAS.

THEY WILL NOT HEAR OF SENDING THEM AWAY.

DURYODHANA WAS NOT PERTURBED.
MIGHTY BHEESHMA IS EVER NEUTRAL. DRONA WILL BE WHERE HIS SON IS. AND HIS SON, ASHWATTHAMA, IS WITH ME.

KRIPA, WILL BE WHERE THESE TWO ARE.
AND THOUGH VIDURA FAVOURS THE PANDAVAS, HE IS DEPENDENT ON US.

HE CAN OFFER THEM NOTHING BUT MORAL SUPPORT.
THE BLIND KING WAS CONVINCED.

AFTER CONVINCING THE BLIND KING, DURYODHANA CALLED PUROCHANA.
DHRITARASHTRA WILL BE SENDING MY FOES, THE PANDAVAS, TO VARANAVATA.

REACH THERE BEFORE THEY DO AND HAVE A SPECIAL MANSION BUILT FOR THEM... WITH INFLAMMABLE MATERIALS. THEN WAIT FOR THE RIGHT MOMENT AND SET FIRE TO IT.

PEOPLE CANNOT BLAME US IF THE PANDAVAS ARE FOUND DEAD IN A FIRE.
PUROCHANA SET OUT AT ONCE FOR VARANAVATA.

MEANWHILE DHRITARASHTRA DID HIS BIT.
O PANDAVAS, THE FESTIVAL OF PASHUPATI IS TO BE HELD AT VARANAVATA.

GO THERE WITH YOUR FRIENDS, ENJOY THE FESTIVAL, AND COME BACK.

YUDHISHTHIRA WAS NOT DECEIVED BUT –
I AM POWERLESS.
SO BE IT. WE SHALL GO.

LEFT WITH NO CHOICE BUT TO OBEY, THE DISTRAUGHT PRINCES TOOK LEAVE OF THE ELDERS.
LET NOTHING UNTOWARD BEFALL YOU.

AS THE PANDAVAS DROVE OUT OF HASTINAPURA WITH VIDURA LEADING THEM –
VARANAVATA IS A NONDESCRIPT PLACE. HOW COULD BHEESHMA ALLOW THE PANDAVAS TO BE SENT THERE?

LET US ABANDON HASTINAPURA AND GO WHERE YUDHISHTHIRA GOES.
AND THE CITIZENS FOLLOWED THE PANDAVAS.

YUDHISHTHIRA, HOWEVER, STOPPED OUTSIDE THE GATES OF THE CITY AND COUNSELLED THEM.
FRIENDS, IT IS OUR DUTY TO OBEY THE KING WHO IS REVERED AS THE FATHER AND PROTECTOR.

SEE US OFF NOW WITH YOUR GOODWILL AND YOUR BLESSINGS AND...

...AT THE OPPORTUNE MOMENT, DO FOR US WHATEVER IS BENEFICIAL TO ALL.

SO THE CITIZENS QUIETLY, BUT SADLY, LEFT FOR THEIR HOMES.

WHEN THE CITIZENS HAD GONE BACK, VIDURA SPOKE TO YUDHISHTHIRA IN A SECRET LANGUAGE.
ONE WHO IS FOREWARNED SHOULD BE FOREARMED.

ONE WHO IS AWARE THAT LETHAL WEAPONS ARE NOT ALWAYS MADE OF METAL REMAINS SAFE. HE WHO MAKES USE OF A BURROW WITH MANY EXITS..

...CAN ESCAPE FROM FIRE.
I HAVE UNDERSTOOD.

THE PANDAVAS ENTERED THE MANSION AT VARANAVATA ARMED WITH THE COUNSEL OF VIDURA.
THE UNMISTAKABLE SMELL OF GHEE, AND TALLOW AND LACQUER!

YET, IF WE FLEE THIS PLACE, DURYODHANA WILL STALK US TO DEATH.

HE HAS RANK, ALLIES AND A FULL TREASURY. WE HAVE NONE OF THE THREE.
SO IN CONSULTATION WITH BHEEMA, YUDHSHTHIRA DECIDED TO PLAY INNOCENT FOR A WHILE.

THE PANDAVAS SPENT THE NEXT FEW DAYS PRETENDING TO ROAM THE FORESTS AND HUNT BUT, IN FACT, STUDYING THE ESCAPE ROUTES OPEN TO THEM.
THIS IS THE SAFEST ONE.

YUDHISHTHIRA WENT TO BHEEMA'S SIDE.
WE WILL SECRETLY HAVE AN OUTLET DUG FROM THE PALACE TO THIS PATH.

ONCE WE DO THAT NO FIRE CAN KILL US.
PUROCHANA, DURYODHANA'S COUNSELLOR, OF COURSE, WAS BLISSFULLY UNAWARE OF THEIR PLANS.

BEFORE LONG, A FRIEND OF VIDURA'S CAME IN SECRET TO THE PANDAVAS.
I AM AN EXPERT MINER. VIDURA HAS SENT ME TO HELP YOU.

AT YUDHISHTHIRA'S COMMAND, HE DUG A TUNNEL FROM THE CENTRAL HALL OF THE MANSION...

...TO THE ESCAPE ROUTE OUTSIDE.

THE ENTRANCE TO THE TUNNEL FROM THE MANSION, WAS LEVEL WITH THE FLOOR...

...AND WAS COVERED AND CONCEALED.

YUDHISHTHIRA THEN SPELLED OUT THEIR NEXT MOVE.
AT NIGHT WHEN THE STRONG WINDS BLOW, YOU BHEEMA, WILL SEND THE MANSION AND PUROCHANA TO A FIERY END.

THAT NIGHT WITH THE FIRST GUST OF WIND...

...BHEEMA SET TO WORK.

WHEN THE MANSION WAS ALL AND WELL ABLAZE, THE PANDAVAS AND KUNTI ENTERED THE TUNNEL.

THE RAGING FIRE AND THE ROARING FLAMES SOON WOKE UP THE CITIZENS OF VARANAVATA.

THEY GATHERED AROUND THE BURNING MANSION WAILING LOUDLY.
THIS WAS DONE BY DURYODHANA TO DESTROY THE HEIRS OF PANDU. ALAS! ALAS!
IT IS DONE WITH THE KNOWLEDGE OF DHRITARASHTRA. AS IF THEY WERE HIS FOES. ALAS! ALAS!
ALAS! ALAS! BHEESHMA, DRONA AND KRIPA HAVE BEEN BLIND TO THEIR DUTY!

THE PANDAVAS ESCAPED FROM THE HOUSE OF DEATH. THEY TRUDGED WEARILY THROUGH THE DANK TUNNEL...

...TILL TIRED AND TERRIFIED THEY COULD NOT WALK ANY FARTHER. SEEING THIS...

...THE INDEFATIGABLE BHEEMA CARRIED THEM ON HIS ARMS AND SHOULDERS AND WALKED ON.

MIGHTY BHEEMA PUSHED HIS WAY THROUGH THE DARKNESS WITH HIS LOAD...

...FELLING THE TREES WITH HIS CHEST AND SHAKING THE EARTH UNDER HIS FOOTFALLS.

AT LAST THEY CAME IN SIGHT OF THE BANKS OF THE GANGA.

THERE AT THE BANKS, A MAN STOOD READY WITH A BOAT –
VIDURA SENT ME. I AM HERE TO FERRY YOU ACROSS.

VIDURA SAYS YOU MUST CAST OFF YOUR GLOOM AND MOVE ON WITH CONFIDENCE.

WHEN THEY REACHED THE OPPOSITE BANK, THE PANDAVAS AND KUNTI GOT OFF...
...AND VIDURA'S MAN WENT BACK IN THE SAME BOAT.

WHEN NEWS OF THE PANDAVAS' DEATH REACHED DHRITARASHTRA –
ALAS! I SUFFER TODAY THE AGONY I SUFFERED WHEN PANDU DIED. OUR LOSS IS GREAT INDEED!

LATER, ALONG WITH HIS KINSFOLK HE MADE OFFERINGS FOR THE DEPARTED SOULS.
OH, YUDHISHTHIRA! YUVARAJA OF THE KURUS!
OH, KUNTI!

AND THOUGH WISE VIDURA KNEW THE TRUTH, HE JOINED THEM IN THEIR MOURNING.

MEANWHILE GUIDED BY THE STARS, THE PANDAVAS TRUDGED SOUTHWARDS TILL THEY REACHED A THICK FOREST. THERE –
I AM THE MOTHER OF FIVE SONS AND YET I AM RACKED BY THIRST.

KUNTI'S WORDS PIERCED BHEEMA'S HEART. THEN SUDDENLY –
THE CALL OF WATERBIRDS. THERE MUST BE WATER NEAR BY!

HE SET HIS MOTHER AND BROTHERS DOWN BELOW A SPREADING BANYAN TREE.
YOU REST HERE WHILE I GO IN SEARCH OF WATER.
AND BHEEMA SET OUT.

FOLLOWING THE CALL OF THE WATERBIRDS, BHEEMA SOON CAME UPON A LAKE.
HE QUENCHED HIS THIRST, SOAKED HIS UPPER GARMENT WITH WATER FOR HIS MOTHER...

...AND SPED BACK...

...TO FIND HER AND HIS BROTHERS FAST ASLEEP ON THE BARE GROUND.

THE SIGHT FILLED MIGHTY BHEEMA WITH GRIEF AND ANGER.
WHAT CAN BE MORE PAINFUL THAN THIS?

O DURYODHANA, IF YOU ARE ALIVE IT IS ONLY BECAUSE YUDHISHTHIRA DOES NOT COMMAND ME TO KILL YOU.

I WOULD SEND NOT ONLY YOU BUT YOUR BROTHERS AND KARNA AND SHAKUNI TO THE REGIONS OF THE DEAD.
AND BHEEMA SAT THERE ALONE, AWAKE, WAITING FOR THE REST TO GET UP.

UNKNOWN TO BHEEMA, HIDIMBA, A RAKSHASA WHO LIVED ON A TREE NEAR BY HAD SPOTTED THEM.
MAN, MY FAVOURITE FOOD!

HE TURNED TO HIS SISTER, HIDIMBAA.
GO KILL THOSE TRESPASSERS AND BRING THEM TO ME. WE SHALL FEAST ON THEM AND THEN DANCE.

THE RAKSHASI SLITHERED DOWN THE TREE...
...AND CREPT STEALTHILY UP TO BHEEMA.

BUT WHEN THE RAKSHASI SAW BHEEMA-
THIS MIGHTY MAN IS FIT TO BE MY HUSBAND!

I WILL NOT OBEY MY BROTHER'S CRUEL COMMAND.
SHE TOOK ON THE FORM OF A BEAUTIFUL BEDECKED, BEJEWELLED DAMSEL...

...AND APPROACHED BHEEMA WITH A SMILE.
I AM HIDIMBAA, A RAKSHASI. I STAY IN THIS FOREST WITH HIDIMBA, MY BROTHER.

HIDIMBA SENT ME HERE TO KILL YOU FOR HIS EVENING MEAL. BUT...

...THE MOMENT I SET EYES ON YOU, I WANTED YOU AS MY HUSBAND.

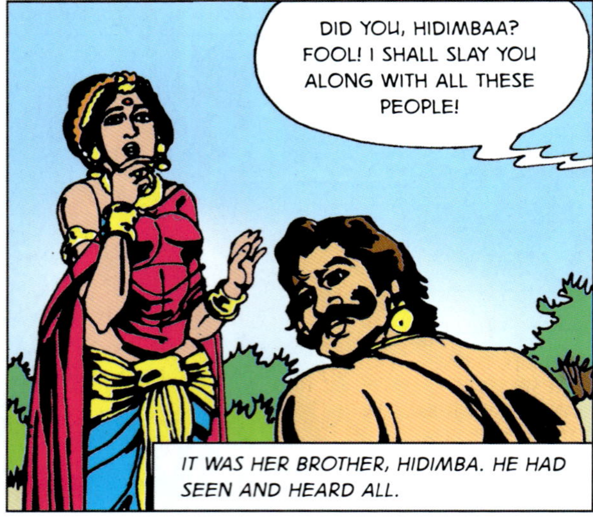
DID YOU, HIDIMBAA? FOOL! I SHALL SLAY YOU ALONG WITH ALL THESE PEOPLE!
IT WAS HER BROTHER, HIDIMBA. HE HAD SEEN AND HEARD ALL.

GNASHING HIS TEETH, HIDIMBA RUSHED TOWARDS HIDIMBAA TO KILL HER! BUT BHEEMA WAS ALERT.
STOP, HIDIMBA!

YOU WICKED WRETCH! ATTACK ME, YOU VILLAIN!

LET YOUR SISTER WATCH ME DRAG YOU ON THE GROUND LIKE A LION DRAGS THE MOUNTAINOUS ELEPHANT.

HIDIMBA RUSHED AT BHEEMA WITH HIS ARMS RAISED TO CRUSH HIM.

BUT BHEEMA PLAYFULLY GRIPPED HIS OUTSTRETCHED HANDS.

TAKEN BY SURPRISE THE RAKSHASA LET OUT A YELL OF FURY.
E-E-E-AH...
I'D BETTER DRAG HIM AWAY LEST HE DISTURB MY MOTHER'S SLEEP.

AND BHEEMA DRAGGED HIDIMBA AWAY FROM THE BANYAN TREE.

THE TWO GRAPPLED AND STRUGGLED AND ROARED.
E-A-A-H
GR-R-R-R

THE SOUNDS WOKE UP THE SLEEPING PANDAVAS AND KUNTI. THEY SAT UP WITH A START AND SAW HIDIMBAA.
THEY GAZED AT HER IN WONDER.

AT LAST KUNTI SPOKE.
WHO ARE YOU? ARE YOU AN APSARA? WHAT BRINGS YOU HERE?

HIDIMBAA TOLD HER ALL. THEN –
THERE THEY ARE! THE MIGHTY MAN AND THE CANNIBAL RAKSHASA!

THE FOUR PANDAVAS STOOD UP AT ONCE AND SAW THE ROARING RIVALS THROUGH THE CLOUD OF DUST THEY RAISED AS THEY TRIED TO OVERPOWER EACH OTHER.

AT LAST BHEEMA LIFTED THE RAKSHASA, HELD HIM ALOFT, WHIRLED HIM ROUND A HUNDRED TIMES...

...AND HURLED HIM...

...TO HIS DEATH.
EEE
THE FORESTS SHOOK WITH THE ROAR OF THE DYING RAKSHASA.

HIDIMBAA TURNED TO KUNTI.
O NOBLE LADY, FORSAKING MY BROTHER AND MY TRADITIONS, I HAVE CHOSEN BHEEMA AS MY HUSBAND.

SO UNITE ME WITH HIM OR KEEP ME AS YOUR MAID. IF YOU DENY ME I WILL NOT LIVE.

AND IT IS ONE'S DHARMA TO SUSTAIN LIFE.

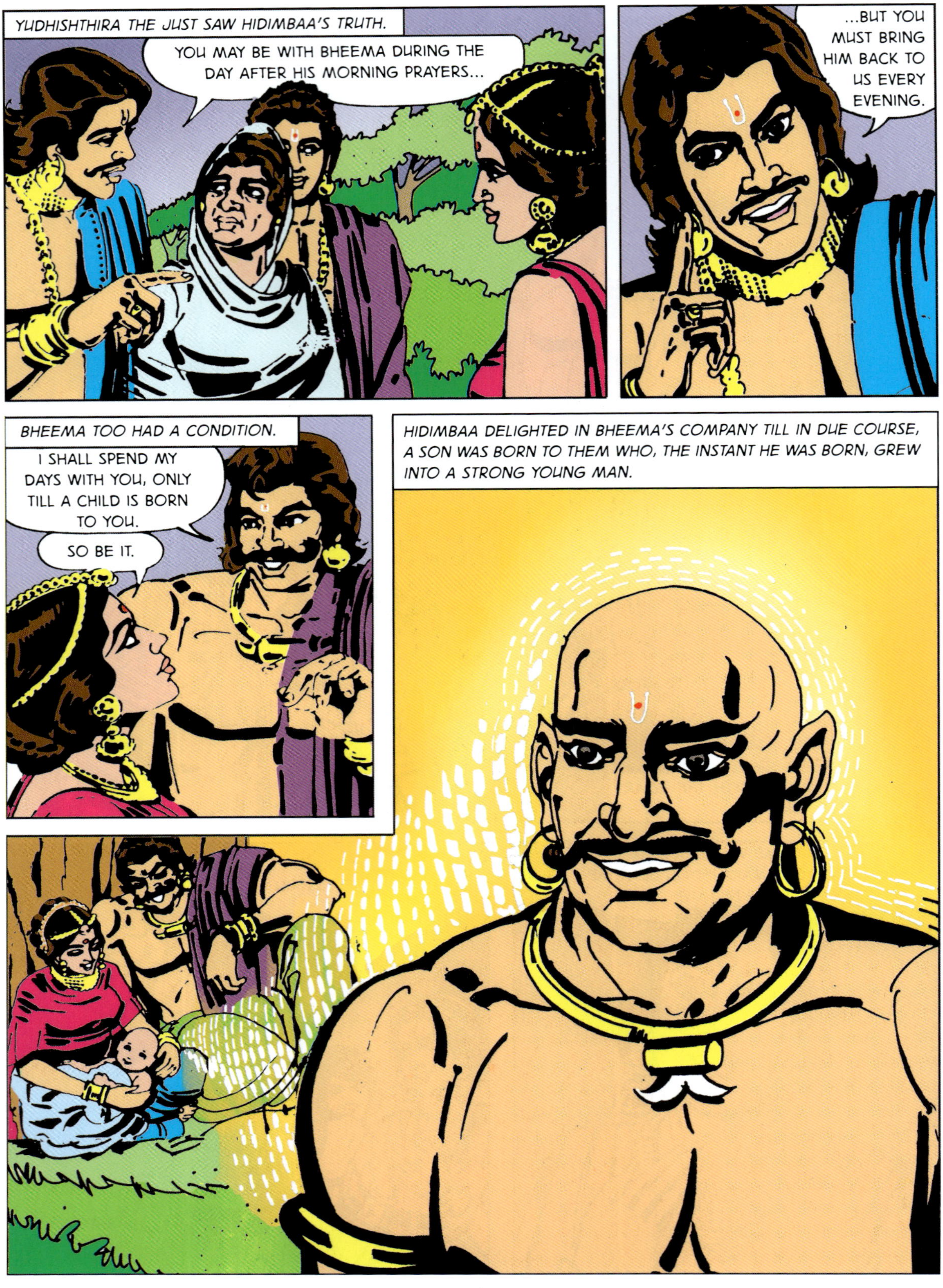

HIDIMBAA DELIGHTED IN BHEEMA'S COMPANY TILL IN DUE COURSE, A SON WAS BORN TO THEM WHO, THE INSTANT HE WAS BORN, GREW INTO A STRONG YOUNG MAN.

SINCE HIS HEAD IS AS SMOOTH AS A WATER POT, LET US NAME HIM GHATOTKACHA.
THEN, HONOURING HER PACT WITH BHEEMA, HIDIMBAA WENT HER WAY.

GHATOTKACHA STAYED ON WITH THE PANDAVAS AND MASTERED THE SECRETS OF WIELDING WEAPONS OF ALL KINDS.

HE WON THE AFFECTION OF THE PANDAVAS AND BECAME ONE AMONG THEM. THEN ONE DAY -
I WILL GO AWAY NOW. BUT...

...I SHALL REACH YOU WHENEVER YOU NEED ME.
AND HE, TOO, WENT HIS WAY.

AFTER GHATOTKACHA LEFT, THE PANDAVAS CLAD THEMSELVES IN BARK AND HIDE...

...MEDITATED ON THE VEDAS AND UPANISHADS AND PONDERED OVER THE PRINCIPLES OF ETHICS.

THEN ONE DAY RISHI VYASA CAME TO THEM.
THE KAURAVAS HAVE BEEN UNFAIR TO YOU. BUT DO NOT GRIEVE.

I SHALL TAKE YOU TO EKACHAKRA, A DELIGHTFUL TOWN NEAR BY.

AS HE LED THE WAY, VYASA CONSOLED KUNTI.
DO NOT BE ANXIOUS. YOUR VALIANT SONS WILL SUBDUE THE EARTH...

...AND LIVE IN REGAL SPLENDOUR. THEY WILL RULE OVER HASTINAPURA PROTECTING THEIR FRIENDS AND THEIR KINSMEN.

VYASA THEN LED KUNTI AND THE PANDAVAS TO A BRAHMANA'S HOUSE AT EKACHAKRA.
STAY HERE AND AWAIT MY RETURN.

YOUR STAY HERE WILL BE HAPPY, IF YOUR ACTIONS ARE JUDICIOUS AND TIMELY.

THE RISHI THEN WENT HIS WAY...
...AND THE PANDAVAS STAYED ON AT EKACHAKRA, COLLECTING ALMS FOR A LIVING.

DURING THEIR SHORT STAY AT EKACHAKRA BHEEMA ENCOURAGED BY HIS MOTHER, CHALLENGED...

...AND SLEW THE CANNIBAL RAKSHASA BAKA...
...AND DELIVERED HIS HOST...

...AND THE RESIDENTS OF EKACHAKRA FROM THE CLUTCHES OF THE TYRANT.

AFTER THE SLAYING OF BAKA, THE PANDAVAS CONTINUED TO LIVE AT THE BRAHMANA'S HOUSE AWAITING THE RETURN OF VYASA. ONE DAY, THEY HAD VISITORS.

ONE OF THE NEWCOMERS REGALED THEM ALL WITH WONDERFUL TALES OF VARIOUS PILGRIM CENTRES, AND CITIES AND KINGS.
BUT NONE OF THESE COMPARE WITH THE MARVELLOUS BIRTHS OF...

...DHRISHTADYUMNA AND DRAUPADI AT DRUPADA'S UNIQUE YAGNA.

THE CURIOSITY OF THE PANDAVAS WAS AROUSED AT THE MENTION OF DRUPADA.
WHY AND HOW DID THIS EXTRAORDINARY BIRTH TAKE PLACE, O BRAHMANA?

THE VISITOR TOLD THEM ABOUT THE EVENTS THAT LED TO DRONA'S HUMBLING OF DRUPADA -
BENT ON TAKING REVENGE, DRUPADA SEARCHED HARD AND LONG...

...FOR A BRAHMANA WHO COULD ACHIEVE ANY DESIRED GOAL BY POTENT RITES.

AT LAST DRUPADA CAME UPON YAJA IN AN ASHRAMA ON THE BANKS OF THE GANGA AND YAMUNA AND SAID TO HIM:
O YAJA, I AM CONSUMED WITH HATRED FOR DRONA, THE GURU OF THE KURUS.

NO MAN ON EARTH CAN DEFEAT THAT EXPERT SCHOLAR OF THE VEDAS AND WIELDER OF THE BRAHMASHIRAS MISSILE.

PROCURE A SON FOR ME WHO WILL SLAY HIM AND I WILL GIVE YOU 10,000 COWS.

THE VISITOR CONTINUED HIS TALE.
YAJA AGREED AND BEGAN A YAGNA. WHEN THE RITES WERE NEARING COMPLETION, HE POURED THE SACRIFICIAL OFFERING INTO THE SACRED FIRE...

...AND LO! THERE SPRANG FROM IT A SPLENDIDLY ARRAYED, RADIANT YOUTH OF CELESTIAL BEARING.
THIS PRINCE IS BORN TO SLAY DRONA, END THE SORROW OF THE KING AND BRING GLORY TO THE PANCHALAS.

AND THEN THERE CAME A DAUGHTER, TOO, FOR THE PANCHALA KING.
THIS DARK GIRL, THE MOST EXCELLENT OF WOMEN, WILL BE THE CAUSE OF THE FALL OF THE KAURAVAS.

YAJA NAMED THE BOY DHRISHTADYUMNA AND THE GIRL KRISHNAA BECAUSE SHE WAS DARK.

SOON AFTER THE YAGNA, DRONA TOOK DRUPADA'S SON, DHRISHTADYUMNA, ON AS HIS PUPIL AND INSTRUCTED HIM IN THE SCIENCE OF ARMS.

KRISHNAA THE PEERLESS BEAUTY OF DARK LONG EYES AND DARK LONG HAIR...

...LIVES AT KAMPILYA, THE PANCHALA CAPITAL, WITH HER FATHER KING DRUPADA.
SMITTEN BY WHAT THEY HAD HEARD, THE PANDAVAS BECAME RESTLESS.

THEN, VYASA RETURNED AS HE HAD PROMISED AND TOLD THEM ANOTHER STRANGE TALE.
THE DAUGHTER OF A RISHI PERFORMED AUSTERITIES TO OBTAIN A GOOD HUSBAND.

SHIVA APPEARED BEFORE HER AND SHE REPEATEDLY REQUESTED HIM TO GIVE HER A VIRTUOUS HUSBAND.

SINCE SHE REPEATED HER REQUEST FIVE TIMES SHIVA PRONOUNCED THAT SHE WOULD HAVE FIVE HUSBANDS IN HER NEXT LIFE.

VYASA CONTINUED HIS TALE.
THAT ACCOMPLISHED GIRL, NOW BORN IN THE HOUSE OF DRUPADA, IS DESTINED TO BE YOUR WIFE.

GO TO PANCHALA. YOU WILL BEYOND DOUBT WIN HER AND MUCH HAPPINESS.
VYASA THEN WENT HIS WAY...

...AND TAKING LEAVE OF THEIR HOST, THE PANDAVAS AND KUNTI SET OUT.

ON THEIR WAY TO PANCHALA, THE PANDAVAS HAD AN ENCOUNTER WITH THE KING OF THE GANDHARVAS, WHICH TURNED OUT TO BE FORTUNATE FOR THEM.
LET US REMAIN FRIENDS FOREVER.

THE GANDHARVA TOLD THEM THE STORY OF RISHI VASISHTHA WITH WHOSE GUIDANCE KING SAMVARNA HAD REGAINED HIS LOST KINGDOM AND WON TAPTI, THE DAUGHTER OF SURYA, FOR A BRIDE.
FRIEND, WHOM SHOULD WE CHOOSE AS OUR PRIEST.
LET RISHI DHOUMYA WHO MEDITATES IN THIS FOREST BE YOUR PRIEST.

WITH DHOUMYA AS THEIR PRIEST, THE PANDAVAS AND THEIR MOTHER WALKED ON TO PANCHALA.

WHEN THEY FINALLY REACHED DRUPADA'S CAPITAL...

...THEY STAYED THERE, UNRECOGNIZED, IN THE HOUSE OF A POTTER.

DRUPADA NURTURED SECRET HOPES OF GIVING HIS DAUGHTER DRAUPADI, NAMED KRISHNAA, TO ARJUNA IN MARRIAGE.

HE HAD A STIFF BOW MADE WHICH COULD BE WIELDED ONLY BY ONE SKILLED IN ARCHERY. HE ALSO HAD A TARGET SET UP HIGH IN THE SKY WITH A GAP IN THE MECHANISM. THE TARGET HAD TO BE HIT BY FIVE ARROWS SHOT SIMULTANEOUSLY THROUGH THIS GAP.

HEARING OF THE GRAND SWAYAMVARA, MANY SAGES AND BRAHMANAS CAME TO WATCH THE PERFORMING ARTISTES AND RECEIVE DONATIONS FROM THE ROYAL SUITORS ASSEMBLED THERE.

THE PANDAVAS TOOK THEIR PLACE AMONG THESE BRAHMANAS AROUND THE ARENA AND WAITED FOR THE GREAT DAY.

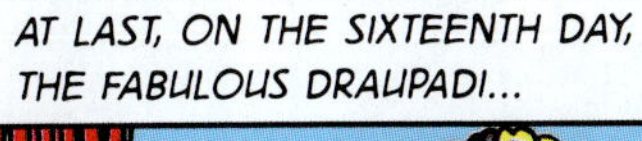

AFTER ACQUAINTING THE ASSEMBLED SUITORS WITH THE RULES OF THE SWAYAMVARA, DHRISHTADYUMNA TURNED TO DRAUPADI.

AS THE KINGS ENTERED THE ARENA, KRISHNA, THE YADAVA, NOTICED THE FIVE BRAHMANAS EYEING DRAUPADI WITH LONGING LOOKS.

HE TURNED TO BALARAMA.
THAT IS YUDHISHTHIRA! THAT IS BHEEMA AND THAT IS ARJUNA. NEXT TO THEM ARE THE TWINS.

I HEARD THEY ESCAPED THE BURNING HOUSE OF LACQUER.

MEANWHILE, MANY KINGS TRIED TO STRING THE BOW AND FAILED MISERABLY. WATCHING THEIR PLIGHT...
...KARNA PICKED UP THE BOW, STRUNG IT WITH EASE, THEN PICKED UP THE FIVE ARROWS...

...AND TOOK AIM. BUT AT THAT MOMENT DRAUPADI'S VOICE RANG OUT LOUDLY AND CLEARLY -
I WILL NOT WED A SOOTA*!
KARNA SHOT A GLANCE AT THE SUN, FLUNG AWAY THE BOW IN ANGER AND WITHDREW.

* CHARIOTEER

AFTER THAT, SHISHUPALA KING OF THE CHEDIS, MIGHTY JARASANDHA THE MAGADHAN KING, SHALYA THE KING OF MADRA, ALL TRIED...
...BUT FAILED AND WITHDREW.

AND THEN, A YOUNG BRAHMANA STOOD UP.
IT WAS ARJUNA.

AS HE STRODE TOWARDS THE BOW A CLAMOUR WENT UP.
STOP HIM! HOW CAN A MENDICANT BRAHMANA HANDLE A BOW WHICH MIGHTY KSHATRIYAS COULD NOT STRING!

IF HE FAILS, THE BRAHMANA WILL FOREVER BE THE BUTT OF ROYAL RIDICULE. STOP HIM!
ARJUNA, MEANWHILE, APPROACHED THE BOW, PICKED IT UP....

...AND STRUNG IT.

THEN TAKING AIM WITH ALL FIVE ARROWS...

...HE SHOT THE TARGET...

...AND BROUGHT IT CRASHING TO THE GROUND.

DRAUPADI GARLANDED THE HERO.

THE OUTRAGED KINGS CRIED OUT IN SHOCK.
THE SWAYAMVARA IS ONLY FOR KSHATRIYAS!
YET, DRUPADA WOULD GIVE AWAY THIS PEERLESS WOMAN TO A BRAHMANA AND HUMILIATE US.

THE SHOCK SOON TURNED INTO ANGER.
WE MUST PUT A STOP TO ANY SUCH HUMILIATION.
WE MUST.

WE MAY NOT SLAY A BRAHMANA. SO LET US SLAY DRUPADA AND DHRITSHTADYUMNA...
...AND FLING DRAUPADI INTO THE FIRE.

ARJUNA AND THE PANDAVAS HEARD THIS.

ARJUNA MADE READY HIS BOW AND BHEEMA UPROOTED A TREE.

AS THE THWARTED KINGS CHARGED, ARJUNA TOOK ON KARNA...

...AND BHEEMA TOOK ON SHALYA.

KARNA AND ARJUNA FOUGHT LONG AND HARD AND EACH FOUGHT TO WIN.
OBSERVE THE MIGHT OF MY ARMS!
FIGHT THIS, MY COUNTER MOVE!

SOON KARNA, REALIZED HIS RIVAL'S SKILL AND COULD NOT BUT ADMIRE HIM.
O BRAHMANA, ARE YOU THE SCIENCE OF ARCHERY ITSELF?

ARE YOU VISHNU? OR INDRA? OR ONE OF THE TWO COME HERE IN THE GUISE OF A BRAHMANA?

I AM NEITHER, KARNA. I AM JUST A BRAHMANA WHO HAS MASTERED THE BRAHMA MISSILE AND IS HERE TO TRUMPH OVER YOU. BEWARE!
EVEN AS ARJUNA'S ANSWER FRIGHTENED KARNA INTO BEATING A RETREAT...

...BHEEMA HELD SHALYA ALOFT...

...AND FLUNG HIM TO THE GROUND.

THE COTERIE OF KINGS WAS ALARMED.
TILL NOW, NONE SAVE ARJUNA WAS ABLE TO CHALLENGE KARNA!
AND SHALYA?

THE ONLY ONE WHO COULD OVERPOWER HIM WAS BHEEMA.
AMAZED AND PERPLEXED, THE KINGS AND WARRIORS...

...WISELY WITHDREW FROM FURTHER FIGHTING AND LEFT FOR THEIR RESPECTIVE CAPITALS.

ARJUNA WON THE CONTEST AND DRAUPADI WENT WITH ARJUNA AND HIS BROTHERS.

AS THEY WENDED THEIR WAY TO THE POTTER'S HOUSE, DHRISHTADYUMNA SECRETLY FOLLOWED THEM.

BHEEMA ENTERED THE HOUSE AND PLAYFULLY ANNOUNCING THAT THEY HAD RETURNED WITH ALMS.
SHARE IT AMONGST YOU.
LITTLE DID KUNTI DREAM THAT THE ALMS WAS DRAUPADI!

WHEN SHE SAW THE PANCHALA PRINCESS, KUNTI WAS AGHAST.
WHAT HAVE I SAID!

O YUDHISHTHIRA, HOW SHALL WE KEEP MY WORDS TRUE AND YET, SAVE DRAUPADI THE ANGUISH OF DILEMMA AND ETERNAL RUIN?

AFTER MUCH DELIBERATION, AND REMEMBERING VYASA'S WORDS, YUDHISHTHIRA MADE A DECISION.
THE DAUGHTER OF DRUPADA SHALL BE THE WIFE OF ALL OF US.

THAT EVENING, KRISHNA AND BALARAMA, KUNTI'S BROTHER'S SONS, CAME THERE.
I AM KRISHNA!

HOW DID YOU FIND US OUT? WE ARE HERE IN DISGUISE, IN SECRECY.
A SHROUD CANNOT HIDE THE GLOW OF A FLAME!

WHO BUT THE PANDAVAS COULD DISPLAY SUCH MIGHT, SUCH SKILL?

THEN KRISHNA DISCUSSED THE FIRE AT VARANAVATA.
IT IS FORTUNATE THAT YOU ESCAPED, THAT THEY FAILED IN THEIR ATTEMPT.

WE HAD BETTER RETURN TO OUR CAMP LEST OUR PRESENCE HERE REVEAL YOUR IDENTITY. FARE YOU WELL.

AND KRISHNA AND BALARAMA LEFT.

DHRISHTADYUMNA MEANWHILE POSTED HIMSELF AT A WINDOW AND OBSERVED ALL THAT WENT ON WITHIN THE POTTER'S HOUSE THAT NIGHT.

AFTER A CONGENIAL MEAL, THE PANDAVAS, KUNTI AND DRAUPADI LAY DOWN ON BEDS OF KUSHA GRASS COVERED WITH DEER-SKINS.

THEN THE HEROES CHATTED AMONGST THEMESELVES TILL LATE INTO THE NIGHT.
BRAHMANAS TALKING WITH AUTHORITY ON SWORDS, MACES, BATTLE-AXES, ELEPHANTS, CHARIOTS, CELESTIAL MISSILES. WELL...!

DHRISHTADYUMNA HASTENED TO DRUPADA AND TOLD HIM ALL THAT HE HAD SEEN AND HEARD.
ARE THE PANDAVAS ALIVE? WAS IT ARJUNA WHO HIT THE MARK AND BROUGHT IT DOWN?

ALL THAT I OBSERVED AND HEARD PROVES THEM TO BE THE PANDAVAS WANDERING IN DISGUISE.

THEY DID NOT PERISH WHEN THEIR HOUSE MADE OF LACQUER WENT UP IN FLAMES.

TO TEST THE IDENTITY OF THE PANDAVAS, DRUPADA INVITED THEM TO THE PALACE ON THE PRETEXT OF HONOURING THE GROOM AND HIS KINSFOLK IN STYLE AND WHEN THEY ARRIVED THE KING AND HIS SON KEENLY OBSERVED THEIR EVERY MOVE.
THEY CARRY THEMSELVES LIKE WARRIORS!

OF ALL THE ITEMS ON DISPLAY IT IS THE MARTIAL EQUIPMENT THAT INTERESTS THEM.

DRUPADA WAS OVERCOME BY JOY.
THEY ARE INDEED THE PANDAVAS!

HE WENT OVER TO YUDHISHTHIRA.
ARE YOU BRAHMANAS OR KSHASTRIYAS? FOR WHICH RITES SHOULD I MAKE PREPARATIONS?

WE ARE THE SONS OF PANDU. I AM THE ELDEST OF KUNTI'S SONS.
AS YUDHISHTHIRA TOLD HIM HOW THEY HAD ESCAPED FROM VARANAVATA...

...DRUPADA TREMBLED WITH SUPPRESSED JOY.
THEN LET ARJUNA WED MY DAUGHTER ACCORDING TO KSHATRIYA RITES ON THIS AUSPICIOUS DAY.

DRAUPADI SHALL BE WIFE TO US ALL.
DRUPADA WAS APPALLED TO HEAR THIS.

RISHI VYASA CAME UP TO THEM JUST THEN -
FIVE HUSBANDS?!

THIS PRACTICE IS NOW OBSOLETE, I AGREE. BUT YOUR DAUGHTER WAS DESTINED BY SHIVA TO HAVE FIVE HUSBANDS.
THIS WAS ENOUGH TO ALLAY DRUPADA'S QUALMS.

SO, THE FIVE PANDAVAS MARRIED DRAUPADI ON FIVE CONSECUTIVE DAYS WITH DHOUMYA AS THE OFFICIATING PRIEST AND THE FIRE AS WITNESS.
THEN DRUPADA PRESENTED THEM WITH....

...CHARIOTS, HORSES, ELEPHANTS, COSTLY ROBES, GOLD, ORNAMENTS AND JEWELS.
WITH A PEERLESS BRIDE, AND ALL THIS WEALTH AND POWER, THE PANDAVAS SPENT MANY A HAPPY DAY AT PANCHALA.

AT HASTINAPURA, AS DHRITARASHTRA ANXIOUSLY WAITED FOR NEWS OF THE OUTCOME OF DRAUPADI'S SWAYAMVARA, VIDURA CAME IN FULL OF JOY.
FORTUNE SMILES ON THE KURUS!
THE PANCHALA PRINCESS HAS CHOSEN DURYODHANA!

HAVE EXQUISITE ORNAMENTS MADE FOR DRAUPADI! HAVE HER BROUGHT HERE BY DURYODHANA.
WHEN VIDURA TOLD HIM THAT THE PANDAVAS WERE THE CHOSEN ONES...

...THE BLIND KING FEIGNED JOY.
PANDU'S CHILDREN ARE AS DEAR TO ME AS THEY WERE TO HIM. NAY MORE! THEY HAVE MADE DRUPADA A KINSMAN AND AN ALLY!

AFTER VIDURA LEFT, KARNA AND DURYODHANA GAVE VENT TO THEIR FEELINGS.
O KING, WHAT YOU DID WAS NOT WHAT YOU OUGHT TO HAVE DONE.
O FATHER, WE SHOULD MAKE EVERY EFFORT TO WEAKEN THE PANDAVAS.

YET YOU PRAISE THEM BEFORE VIDURA.
IT WAS ONLY TO CONCEAL MY INTENTIONS FROM HIM.

AND THEY ARE THE SAME AS YOURS. NOW YOU TELL ME WHAT IS TO BE DONE.

DURYODHANA WAS ALL FOR USING BRIBES AND CUNNING TO BRING ABOUT THE FALL OF THE PANDAVAS.
...AND WE MUST STRIKE FAST BEFORE THEIR TIES WITH DRUPADA BECOME FIRM.

BUT KARNA WAS SCEPTICAL ABOUT DURYODHANA'S SCHEMES.
FORCE IS THE PRIME WEAPON OF THE BRAVE. WE SHOULD USE FORCE. ATTACK DRUPADA!

VANQUISH HIM, IMPRISON THE PANDAVAS AND REIGN SUPREME OVER THE WHOLE WORLD.

AND THIS MUST BE DONE BEFORE KRISHNA AND HIS YADAVA ARMIES REACH PANCHALA.

YOU ARE A GREAT WARRIOR, KARNA, AND WISE. YOU WOULD EXTOL THE VIRTUES OF FORCE AND RIGHTLY SO. BUT...

...LET US SEE WHAT BHEESHMA, DRONA AND VIDURA HAVE TO SAY AND THEN ACT.
AND DHRITARASHTRA SUMMONED THESE ELDERS FOR THEIR COUNSEL.

BHEESHMA, THE FIRST TO SPEAK, WAS ALL FOR A JUST TRUCE.
THE REAPPEARANCE OF THE PANDAVAS CLEANSES YOUR REPUTATION, DURYODHANA.

FOR THE SAKE OF DHARMA AND THE WELFARE OF ALL, GIVE THEM HALF THE KINGDOM, THEIR INHERITANCE WITH GRACE.

IF YOU DO NOT, EVIL WILL BEFALL US AND INFAMY WILL BE YOUR LOT.

DRONA CONCURRED WITH BHEESHMA.
LET A COURTEOUS MESSENGER GO TO DRUPADA WITH PRECIOUS GIFTS FOR THE PANDAVAS AND DRAUPADI.

LET HIM CONVEY YOUR ELATION AT THE ALLIANCE, YOUR JOY AT THE TURN OF EVENTS...

...AND YOUR DESIRE FOR THE RETURN OF THE PANDAVAS. AND WHEN THEY COME HERE, WELCOME THEM AND INSTALL THEM ON THEIR ANCESTRAL THRONE.

THAT SHOULD BE YOUR ATTITUDE TO YOUR SONS AND THE SONS OF PANDU.
IT WOULD BE IN KEEPING WITH THE WISHES OF THE PEOPLE.
THIS WAS THE LAST STRAW FOR KARNA.

HE SPRANG TO HIS FEET.
IS IT NOT STRANGE THAT BHEESHMA AND DRONA WHOM YOU HAVE ALWAYS HONOURED AND RESPECTED SHOULD COUNSEL AGAINST YOU?

HOW CAN THE ADVICE OF FRIENDS WHOSE INTENTS ARE EVIL BE PURE? HOW CAN GOOD BE WROUGHT BY SUCH COUNSELLORS?

MY COUNSEL IS FOR THE GOOD OF THE KURUS. IF YOU GO AGAINST IT, THE KAURAVAS WILL SOON COME TO RUIN.

AT THIS, VIDURA ROSE TO SPEAK.
O KING, WHAT DRONA AND BHEESHMA, RIPE IN AGE, EXPERIENCE AND WISDOM, SAY IS FOR YOUR GOOD. NO ONE I CAN THINK OF IS A BETTER FRIEND TO YOU THAN EITHER OF THESE MEN.

DURYODHANA, KARNA, AND SHAKUNI ARE YOUNG, INEXPERIENCED, MISCHIEVOUS MISCREANTS. DO NOT LISTEN TO THEM.

I HAD WARNED YOU LONG AGO THAT DURYODHANA WOULD BE THE RUIN OF YOUR RACE.

DHRITARASHTRA REMEMBERED HIS WORDS.
MARK THE OMENS. HE WILL BE THE RUIN OF YOUR RACE AND THE LAND. **ABANDON HIM.**

WISE BHEESHMA, DRONACHARYA AND YOU, VIDURA, SPEAK FOR MY GOOD. AND YOU SPEAK THE TRUTH. THE SONS OF PANDU HAVE THE SAME RIGHT TO THIS KINGDOM AS MY SONS.

GO VIDURA, AND BRING THE PANDAVAS, THEIR MOTHER AND DRAUPADI HERE WITH DUE HONOURS.
VIDURA LEFT FOR PANCHALA...

...WHERE HE WAS FORMALLY WELCOMED BY DRUPADA...

...AND LOVINGLY EMBRACED BY THE PANDAVAS AND KRISHNA WHO WAS ALREADY THERE WITH THEM.

AND THEN VIDURA TURNED TO DRUPADA.
DHRITARASHTRA, BHEESHMA AND DRONA ARE PLEASED WITH THE ALLIANCE, AND SEND THEIR BEST WISHES.

ALL AT HASTINAPURA ARE EAGER TO SEE THE SONS OF PANDU AND THE PANCHALA PRINCESS.

SO PERMIT THEM, O KING, TO SET OUT FOR THEIR CITY WITHOUT DELAY.

DRUPADA HAD NO OBJECTION.
IT IS ONLY PROPER THAT THEY RETURN TO THEIR CITY. BUT...

...SINCE THE PANDAVAS ARE AS DEAR TO KRISHNA AS TO ME, I WOULD SEEK HIS VIEWS.
I THINK THEY SHOULD RETURN.

SO THE PANDAVAS, KUNTI AND DRAUPADI, ACCOMAPANIED BY KRISHNA, LEFT FOR HASTINAPURA WITH VIDURA.

WHEN THEY ENTERED HASTINAPURA, THE VALIANT HEROES WERE WELCOMED BY THE PEOPLE WITH GREAT JOY.
MAY THE PANDAVAS BE WITH US FOR A HUNDRED YEARS!

THEN, AFTER THEY HAD RESTED FOR A WHILE, DHRITARASHTRA SENT FOR THEM.
LET THERE BE NO FURTHER DISSENSION.

TAKE HALF THE KINGDOM AND RULE IT FROM KHANDAVAPRASTHA.

WITH KRISHNA'S HELP AND VYASA'S GUIDANCE, THE PANDAVAS HAD A SPLENDID PALACE BUILT AT KHANDAVAPRASTHA WHICH FOR ITS CELESTIAL DECOR CAME TO BE KNOWN AS INDRAPRASTHA.

LEARNED BRAHMANAS, MERCHANTS, AND ARTISANS FLOCKED THERE, INCREASING ITS PROSPERITY DAY BY DAY.

THEN, HAVING ESTABLISHED THE PANDAVAS RIGHT ROYALLY, KRISHNA LEFT FOR DWARAKA, HIS CITY.

WHILE THE PANDAVAS WERE IN THIS STATE OF EARTHLY BLISS, SAGE NARADA VISITED THEM...

...AND SAW DRAUPADI.

AND HE WAS CONCERNED.

LATER, WHEN ALONE WITH THE BROTHERS, THE SAGE SPOKE HIS FEARS.
LONG, LONG AGO THERE WERE TWO ASURAS, BELOVED BROTHERS, WHO WERE LIKE TWO BEINGS WITH ONE SOUL.

THEY LIVED AND RULED OVER THE LAND IN TOTAL HARMONY. AND YET THEY SLEW EACH OTHER FOR THE APSARA, TILOTTAMA.

LAY DOWN SOME RULE BETWEEN YOU BROTHERS LEST YOU QUARREL OVER DRAUPADI, AND SUFFER THEIR FATE.

YUDHISHTHIRA AT ONCE SAW THE WISDOM IN THE SAGE'S WORDS.
WELL THEN, WHEN ANY ONE OF US IS WITH DRAUPADI, IF ANY OF THE OTHER FOUR INTRUDES...

...HE MUST EXILE HIMSELF FOR TWELVE YEARS.

THE DECISION SATISFIED THE SAGE AND HE WENT HIS WAY.

MANY DAYS LATER, A BRAHMANA WHOSE COWS WERE BEING DRIVEN AWAY BY THIEVES, CAME TO THE PALACE CRYING FOR HELP. ARJUNA HEARD HIM BUT -
THE WEAPONS ARE KEPT IN THE ROOM WHERE YUDHISHTHIRA IS WITH DRAUPADI.

I CANNOT GO IN BUT THE WEAPONS ARE ESSENTIAL.

AS HE STRUGGLED FOR A SOLUTION THE BRAHMANA'S CRY GREW LOUDER AND ANGRIER.
THE WORLD REVILES THE KING WHO LEVIES A SIXTH OF THE LAND'S YIELD AND YET FAILS TO PROTECT HIS SUBJECTS. TAKE UP YOUR ARMS, O PANDAVA!

DECIDING THAT NOTHING WAS AS IMPORTANT AS SAVING THE KING FROM INFAMY, ARJUNA ENTERED THE CHAMBER...

...CAME OUT WITH HIS WEAPONS AND HELPING THE BRAHMANA INTO HIS CHARIOT...

...WENT AFTER THE THIEVES...
...AND FORCED THEM TO RETURN THE COWS.

THEN HE CAME BACK TO THE PALACE AND SOUGHT OUT YUDHISHTHIRA.
I HAVE BROKEN THE RULE THAT WHEN ANY ONE OF US IS WITH DRAUPADI, OTHERS SHOULD KEEP AWAY.

YOU HAVE DONE NO WRONG, ARJUNA. I KNOW VERY WELL WHY YOU ENTERED MY CHAMBER.

BUT ARJUNA WAS ADAMANT.
YOU HAVE ALWAYS SAID THAT PREVARICATION HAS NO PLACE IN OBSERVING DHARMA. I WILL NOT WAVER FROM TRUTH.
AND HE LEFT FOR THE FOREST.

ARJUNA AND THE BARDS, MUSICIANS AND ASCETICS WHO ACCOMPANIED HIM TRAVELLED ACROSS THE LAKES AND INTO THE FORESTS...

...TILL THEY REACHED THE SOURCE OF THE GANGA WHERE THE MIGHTY PANDAVA DECIDED TO CAMP.

AND THERE, FOR A FAVOUR CONFERRED ON ULOOPI, A NAGA PRINCESS, ARJUNA RECEIVED A BOON FROM HER.
DENIZENS OF THE DEEP WILL ALWAYS OBEY YOU AND YOU WILL BE INVINCIBLE IN WATER.

AFTER VISITING THE SITES CONSECRATED BY THE SAGES, AGASTYA, VASISHTHA AND BHRIGU...

...ARJUNA WOUND HIS WAY DOWN THE HIMALAYAN SLOPES...
...AND JOURNEYED EASTWARDS TILL HE REACHED THE MAHENDRA MOUNTAINS.

FROM THERE, WALKING ALONG THE COAST...
...HE CAME TO MANIPURA.

WHEN HE CALLED ON THE KING OF MANIPURA, ARJUNA HAPPENED TO SEE THE RULER'S DAUGHTER AND WAS STRUCK BY HER BEAUTY-

I AM ARJUNA - A NOBLE KSHATRIYA, THE SON OF KUNTI AND PANDU.

GIVE ME YOUR DAUGHTER'S HAND IN MARRIAGE, O KING!

THE RULER WAS PLEASED BY ARJUNA'S PROPOSAL, BUT -
SHE IS MY ONLY CHILD. I LOOK UPON HER AS MY SON.

THEREFORE THE CHILD BORN TO HER OF YOU WILL BELONG TO MY LINE.

IF YOU ARE AGREEABLE TO THIS CONDITION, O PANDAVA, YOU MAY WED HER.
SO BE IT.

ARJUNA WED CHITRANGADA AND SPENT THREE YEARS WITH HER AT MANIPURA.
THEN, WHEN A SON WAS BORN TO THEM...

...HE FORMALLY PRESENTED THE BOY TO HER FATHER...

...TOOK LEAVE OF HER...
...AND PROCEEDED TOWARDS GOKARNA ON THE WESTERN COAST.

FROM GOKARNA, ARJUNA WENT NORTH ALONG THE COAST TO PRABHASA.
AND THERE HE STAYED...

...TILL KRISHNA, THE YADAVA, HEARING OF HIS ARRIVAL, CAME TO MEET HIM.
AFTER ARJUNA TOLD KRISHNA ALL THAT HAD HAPPENED DURING HIS TRAVELS...

...THE TWO SET OUT FOR DWARAKA IN KRISHNA'S CHARIOT.

DURING HIS STAY AT DWARAKA, ARJUNA SAW KRISHNA'S SISTER SUBHADRA AT A FESTIVAL ON THE RAIVATAKA MOUNTAIN AND WAS SMITTEN BY KAMADEVA. KRISHNA NOTICED THIS, AND HE APPROVED.

SO WHEN SUBHADRA WAS RETURNING TO DWARAKA AFTER THE FESTIVAL, ACTING ON HIS COUNSEL, ARJUNA RUSHED TOWARDS HER IN KRISHNA'S CHARIOT...

...SWEPT HER INTO IT...
...AND SPED AWAY TOWARDS INDRAPRASTHA.

WHEN THE NEWS OF SUBHADRA'S ABDUCTION REACHED THE YADAVA COURT, THERE WAS A FURORE.
YOKE OUR CHARIOTS!
BRING FORTH OUR BOWS!

WAIT! WHAT ARE YOU WITLESS MEN TALKING ABOUT WHEN WISE KRISHNA SITS SILENT?

AND BALARAMA SOUGHT KRISHNA'S OPINION.
I THINK ARJUNA HAS DONE OUR RACE AN HONOUR. HE IS NOBLE AND SO IS SUBHADRA.

I DO NOT KNOW OF ANY, SAVE SHIVA, WHO CAN VANQUISH ARJUNA! IF YOU ACCOST ARJUNA AND IF HE DEFEATS YOU...

...YOUR REPUTATION WILL BE LOST.

GO AFTER HIM AND BRING HIM BACK HERE WITH HONOUR.

A SECOND KNOT IS BOUND TO LOOSEN THE FIRST HOWEVER CLOSE IT MIGHT HAVE BEEN.

DRAUPADI COULD NOT CONCEAL HER JEALOUSY.

AT LAST ARJUNA CAME OUT...

...TO SUBHADRA WHO WAS CLAD IN RED SILK...

...AND WHISPERED SOMETHING INTO HER EAR.

ACCORDINGLY, WHEN SUBHADRA ENTERED THE WOMEN'S APARTMENTS SHE ENTERED IN THE GARB OF A COWHERDESS...

...AND BOWED TO DRAUPADI.
I AM YOUR MAID.
DRAUPADI WAS AT ONCE MOLLIFIED.

MAY YOUR HUSBAND BE UNRIVALLED.
SO BE IT.

THEN, KRISHNA AND BALARAMA CAME TO INDRAPRASTHA WITH AN ENTOURAGE OF YADAVA MEN BEARING RICH GIFTS FOR THE PANDAVAS AND SUBHADRA.

AFTER SPENDING MANY A PLEASANT DAY WITH THE PANDAVAS...

...BALARAMA AND THE YADAVA ENTOURAGE LEFT FOR DWARAKA...
...BUT KRISHNA STAYED ON.

IT WAS AROUND THEN THAT SUBHADRA GAVE BIRTH TO A STRONG BABY BOY WHO CAME TO BE CALLED **ABHIMANYU.**

ABHIMANYU SOON BECAME THE FAVOURITE OF HIS FATHER, HIS UNCLES AND KRISHNA, WHOM HE TOOK AFTER IN COURAGE, STRENGTH AND FORM.

OVER THE YEARS, DRAUPADI TOO BORE A SON TO EACH OF HER FIVE HUSBANDS. THEY WERE NAMED **PRATIVINDHYA, SUTASOMA, SHRUTAKARMAN, SHATANIKA** AND **SHRUTASENA.**

MEANWHILE, ONE SUMMER'S DAY, WHILE ARJUNA AND KRISHNA WERE RELAXING ON THE BANKS OF THE YAMUNA, A BRAHMANA CAME TO THEM.

I HAVE AN INSATIABLE APPETITE. GIVE ME MY FILL OF FOOD, I BEG OF YOU.

IF YOU NAME THE FOOD THAT WILL GIVE YOU CONTENTMENT, WE WILL STRIVE TO PROCURE IT FOR YOU.
THE KHANDAVA FOREST IS THE MEAL I DESIRE. I AM AGNI.

AGNI WENT ON.
THE FOREST IS GUARDED BY INDRA, THE WIELDER OF THE THUNDERBOLT, BECAUSE HIS NAGA FRIEND, TAKSHAKA, AND HIS CLAN LIVE THERE.

EVERY ATTEMPT OF MINE TO CONSUME THE FOREST IS THWARTED BY HIM WITH TORRENTS OF RAIN.

PRAY STOP THE RAIN, O YOU WHO KNOW ALL ABOUT WEAPONS AND GIVE ME MY FILL OF FOOD THIS ONCE.

O AGNI, IF YOU GIVE US THE TOOLS, WE WILL DO ALL THAT HUMAN VALOUR CAN TO STALL INDRA'S TORRENTS.

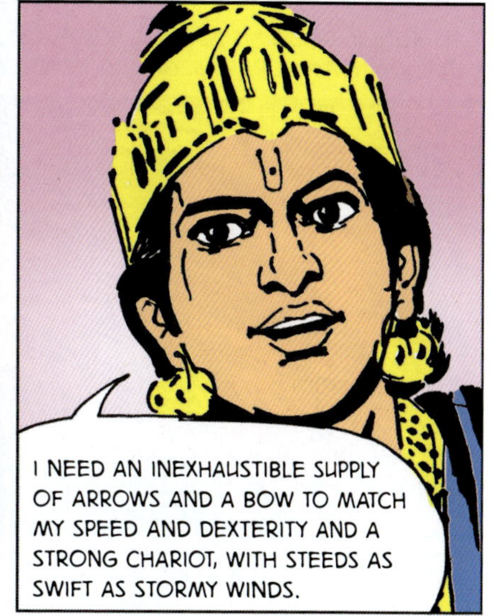
I NEED AN INEXHAUSTIBLE SUPPLY OF ARROWS AND A BOW TO MATCH MY SPEED AND DEXTERITY AND A STRONG CHARIOT, WITH STEEDS AS SWIFT AS STORMY WINDS.

KRISHNA WILL NEED A WEAPON THAT MATCHES HIS PROWESS.

AGNI INVOKED VARUNA WHO PROCURED THE GANDIVA BOW, AN EVER-FULL QUIVER AND A CHARIOT DRAWN BY SPOTLESS WHITE HORSES.

AGNI THEN GAVE KRISHNA THE DISCUS...
THIS WEAPON WHEN HURLED BY YOU WILL DESTROY THE TARGET AND RETURN TO YOU, MAKING YOU SUPERIOR TO MEN AND CELESTIALS.
...AND VARUNA GAVE HIM THE MACE NAMED KAUMODAKI.

DEVOUR THE FOREST, O AGNI. WE SHALL STAND GUARD!

AS AGNI TOOK ON HIS FLAMING FORM AND SURROUNDING THE KHANDAVA FOREST, BEGAN TO CONSUME IT...

...INDRA AMASSED A MULTITUDE OF CLOUDS AND COMMANDED THEM TO RAIN DOWN.

BUT THE COUNTLESS ARROWS THAT ARJUNA LET FLY PREVENTED THE SHOWERS FROM REACHING AGNI...

...AND THE CREATURES BELOW FROM ESCAPING.

THOUGH TAKSHAKA, INDRA'S FRIEND, WAS AWAY WHILE THE FOREST BURNED, HIS SON, ASHWASENA, WAS TRAPPED THERE.

EAGER TO SAVE HIM, INDRA RAISED A VIOLENT STORM...

...WHICH RENDERED ARJUNA UNCONSCIOUS FOR A MOMENT. AND IN THAT MOMENT ASHWASENA MADE HIS ESCAPE.

PIQUED AT BEING TRICKED THUS, ARJUNA CURSED THE SLY SNAKE...
NEVER SHALL YOU BE SPOKEN WELL OF!

...AND AIMED HIS ARROWS STRAIGHT AT INDRA.

INDRA RETALIATED WITH HOWLING GALES AND BILLOWING CLOUDS THAT THUNDERED AND FLASHED.

BUT ARJUNA INVESTED HIS VAYAVA MISSILE WITH THE POWER OF MANTRAS AND LET IT FLY.

THE POWERFUL MISSILE AT ONCE SCATTERED THE CLOUDS...

..AND AGNI MERRILY BLAZED ON AIDED BY COOL BREEZES.

BY THEN YAMA, KUBERA, VARUNA, SKANDA, INDEED ALL THE CELESTIALS OF NOTE CAME FORTH TO ATTACK ARJUNA AND KRISHNA.

AT ONE POINT INDRA UPROOTED A PEAK, THE VERY MANDARA MOUNTAIN...

...AND HURLED IT AT ARJUNA.

BUT EVEN THE MIGHTY MOUNTAIN PEAK WAS NO MATCH FOR ARJUNA'S HARD-HITTING ARROWS. THEY SMASHED IT TO SMITHEREENS!

SUDDENLY, INDRA HEARD A VOICE -
KHANDAVA IS FATED TO BE BURNT. KNOW KRISHNA AND ARJUNA TO BE INVINCIBLE. TURN BACK WITH YOUR RETINUE.

INDRA ACCORDINGLY WITHDREW FOLLOWED BY THE OTHERS, WHILE ARJUNA AND KRISHNA SENT UP A TRIUMPHANT ROAR.

JUST THEN KRISHNA SAW THE ASURA, MAYA ESCAPING FROM TAKSHAKA'S ABODE WITH AGNI HOT ON HIS TRAIL.

AGNI WAS INTENT ON DEVOURING MAYA AND KRISHNA WAS THERE TO HELP HIM. HE RAISED HIS DISCUS WHEN -
ARJUNA! SAVE ME!
FEAR NOT!

AS ARJUNA HAD GRANTED MAYA ASYLUM, NEITHER WOULD KRISHNA HARM HIM NOR COULD AGNI DEVOUR HIM. THE ASURA WAS SAVED...
...AND AGNI CONTINUED TO CONSUME THE FOREST.

WHEN THE KHANDAVA FOREST WAS COMPLETELY BURNT DOWN, INDRA CAME DOWN.
I AM PLEASED WITH YOUR SUPERHUMAN PROWESS. ASK FOR ANY BOON THAT IS RARELY GRANTED TO MORTALS.

WITH AGNI AS WITNESS, ARJUNA ASKED HIM FOR VARIOUS CELESTIAL WEAPONS.
WHEN SHIVA'S GRACE FALLS ON YOU, I SHALL GIVE YOU ALL MY WEAPONS.
AND INDRA LEFT WITH HIS RETINUE.

YOU HAVE SERVED ME WELL, NOW YOU ARE FREE TO GO WHERE YOU CHOOSE.

THEN MAYA WHO WAS SAVED FROM AGNI SPOKE.
I AM THE ARCHITECT OF THE ASURAS. I WISH TO SERVE YOU IN SOME WAY.
IF YOU INSIST, DO SOMETHING FOR KRISHNA.

WHEN MAYA URGED KRISHNA TO SUGGEST WHAT HE COULD DO -
BUILD A HALL FOR YUDHISHTHIRA. LET IT BE ONE THAT MEN WILL MARVEL AT.
SO BE IT.

KRISHNA THEN LED MAYA TO YUDHISHTHIRA. AFTER BEING RECEIVED BY HIM WITH DUE HONOURS...
...MAYA LEFT.

KRISHNA STAYED WITH THE PANDAVAS FOR A FEW MORE DAYS, AND THEN SET OFF TO VISIT HIS FATHER.

WHILE HE WAS AWAY, MAYA RETURNED WITH A PRICELESS MACE FOR BHEEMA...
THIS WILL BE TO YOU WHAT GANDIVA IS TO ARJUNA.

TO ARJUNA HE GAVE A STORE OF RARE, PRECIOUS GEMS...
THE POWERFUL SOUND OF THIS CONCH SENDS SHIVERS DOWN THE WORLD.
...AND METALS AND THE LARGE CONCH-SHELL DEVADATTA.

USING RARE MATERIALS, MAYA BUILT A MANSION WITH A HALL FOR YUDHISHTHIRA IN WHICH WERE SEEN THE BEST DESIGNS KNOWN TO DEVAS, ASURAS AND MANKIND. WHEN THE HALL WAS READY AND THE PANDAVAS WERE HOLDING COURT...

...NARADA, THE WISE SAGE WHOSE KNOWLEDGE SPANNED BYGONE AGES, CAME THERE.
A KING WHO PROTECTS THE SOCIAL ORDERS AND CARRIES OUT HIS ROYAL DUTIES WILL ATTAIN THE REALMS OF INDRA.

WHEN YOUR FATHER KNEW I WAS COMING HERE HE SAID....

TELL YUDHISHTHIRA THAT...
...HE, WITH HIS BROTHERS, MUST CONQUER THE WORLD AND PERFORM THE GRAND RAJASOOYA YAGNA.

DO HIS BIDDING, O PANDAVA.
NARADA THEN SET OFF FOR DWARAKA, KRISHNA'S CITY.

YUDHISHTHIRA WEIGHED HIS STRENGTHS AND HIS WEAKNESSES, HIS RESOURCES AND HIS REQUIREMENTS BUT HE COULD NOT DECIDE WHETHER HE WAS QUALIFIED TO PERFORM THE GRAND YAGNA OR NOT. AT LAST -

KRISHNA CONTINUED -
HE HAS CONQUERED AND IMPRISONED EIGHTY-SIX KINGS WHOM HE WILL SLAUGHTER IN A CRUEL SACRIFICE TO FULFIL A VOW HE HAS TAKEN.

IF YOU KILL HIM AND FREE THOSE KINGS, YOU WILL TRIUMPH OVER HIM AS EMPEROR OF THE KSHATRIYAS...

AND SUCCESSFULLY COMPLETE THE RAJASOOYA YAGNA.

WHEN YUDHISHTHIRA SEEMED RELUCTANT TO TAKE UP THE CHALLENGE, BHEEMA SPOKE UP.
WITH KRISHNA'S STRATEGY, ARJUNA'S WILL TO WIN AND MY STRENGTH, WE COULD SLAY JARASANDHA FOR YOU.

HOW CAN I SEND YOU TO FIGHT JARASANDHA BECAUSE I DESIRE THE STATUS OF EMPEROR?

NO. I THINK THAT THE YAGNA SHOULD NOT BE ATTEMPTED. IT APPEARS BLIGHTED. IT FORBODES DISASTER. IT ROBS ME OF MY PEACE.

KRISHNA LOOKED AT THE GLUM FACES OF ARJUNA AND BHEEMA.
IT IS IMPOSSIBLE TO VANQUISH JARASANDHA IN A BATTLE, I AGREE.

BUT HE COULD BE SLAIN IN SINGLE COMBAT WITH BARE HANDS. IF ARJUNA, BHEEMA AND I GO AND MEET HIM IN PRIVATE...

...HE WILL CERTAINLY AGREE TO ENGAGE IN A DUEL WITH ONE OF US. HIS VANITY WILL PROMPT HIM TO TAKE ON BHEEMA. AND BHEEMA WILL SURELY SEND HIM TO HIS DEATH.

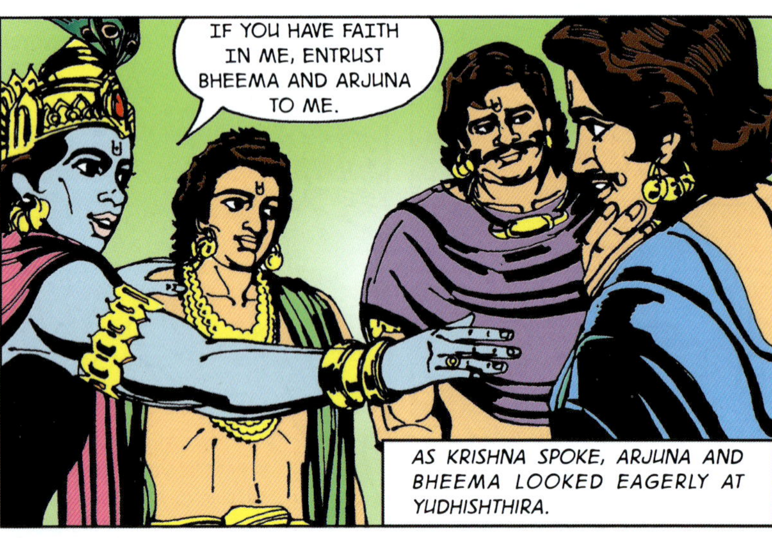
IF YOU HAVE FAITH IN ME, ENTRUST BHEEMA AND ARJUNA TO ME.
AS KRISHNA SPOKE, ARJUNA AND BHEEMA LOOKED EAGERLY AT YUDHISHTHIRA.

YUDHISHTHIRA SAW THEIR FACES AND DECIDED.
O KRISHNA, O BEST OF MEN, YOU ARE THE LORD OF THE PANDAVAS. WE ARE DEPENDENT ON YOU. DO WHAT IS NEEDED, UNDETERRED. LET STRATEGY, THE WILL TO WIN, AND STRENGTH ACCOMPLISH OUR PURPOSE.

DISGUISED AS BRAHMANAS, KRISHNA, ARJUNA AND BHEEMA SET OUT FOR MAGADHA TO OVERCOME JARASANDHA.

AT MAGADHA, THE DISGUISED HEROES ENTERED JARASANDHA'S PALACE AND AT AN OPPORTUNE MOMENT, REVEALED THEIR IDENTITY AND TOLD HIM WHY THEY WERE THERE.
...NOW SET FREE THE IMPRISONED KINGS OR DIE.

I AM A KSHATRIYA. FEAR SHALL NOT DETER ME FROM MY PURPOSE. I AM READY TO FIGHT.

THEN WHICH AMONG THE THREE OF US WOULD YOU TAKE ON?

AS ANTICIPATED BY KRISHNA, JARASANDHA CHOSE BHEEMA, AND THE DUEL BEGAN.

FOR FULL THIRTEEN DAYS THE HEROES FOUGHT WITH NOTHING BUT BARE HANDS.

THEN ON THE FOURTEENTH DAY, PROMPTED AND EGGED ON BY KRISHNA...

...BHEEMA HELD JARASANDHA ALOFT...

...WHIRLED HIM AROUND A HUNDRED TIMES...

...FLUNG HIM TO THE GROUND WITH GREAT FORCE...
...AND THEN KILLED HIM.

THE THREE THEN MOUNTED JARASANDHA'S CHARIOT AND LIBERATED THE HAPLESS KINGS.
O KRISHNA, COMMAND US. WE SHALL DO YOUR BIDDING WHATEVER IT BE.

YUDHISHTHIRA WHO SENT US HERE WISHES TO PERFORM THE RAJASOOYA YAGNA. SUPPORT HIM IN HIS ATTEMPT TO BE THE EMPEROR.
SO BE IT.

THEN, JARASANDHA'S SON SAHADEVA, APPROACHED KRISHNA IN ALL HUMILITY AND OFFERED HIM RICH GIFTS.
KRISHNA ACCEPTED THE GIFTS AND PLACED SAHADEVA ON THE THRONE OF MAGADHA.

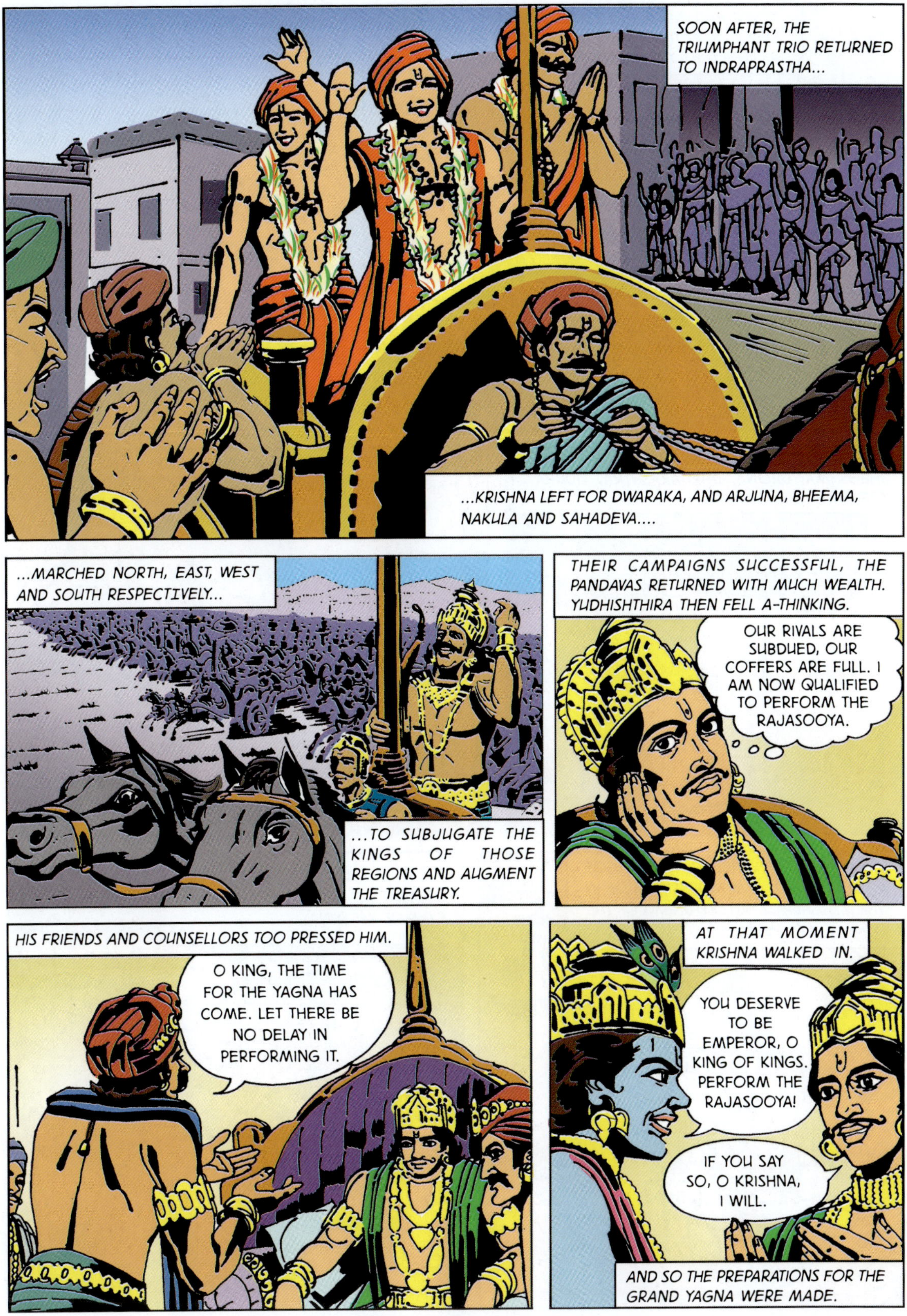

SOON AFTER, THE TRIUMPHANT TRIO RETURNED TO INDRAPRASTHA...

...KRISHNA LEFT FOR DWARAKA, AND ARJUNA, BHEEMA, NAKULA AND SAHADEVA....

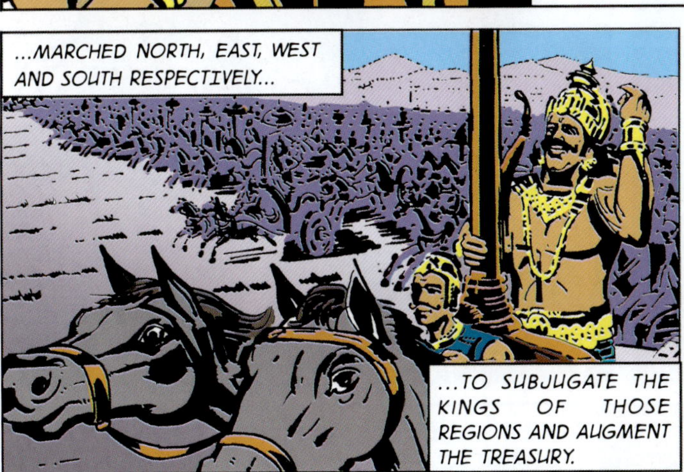

NEVER HAD INDRAPRASTHA SEEN SUCH A FEVER OF ACTIVITY AS VARIOUS DUTIES WERE ASSIGNED BY YUDHISHTHIRA.

SAHADEVA WAS ENTRUSTED WITH THE INVITATIONS.
INVITE ALL! THE LEADING SAGES, SCHOLARS, WARRIORS, LANDLORDS, TRADESMEN, ARTISANS, AND THE TILLERS OF THE SOIL!

NAKULA WAS SENT TO HASTINAPURA TO BRING BHEESHMA, DRONA, DHRITARASHTRA, VIDURA, KRIPA AND THE KAURAVAS.

THE INVITEES FROM HASTINAPURA CAME AND...

...DESPITE THE INEVITABLE CLASH OF EGOS WHICH LED TO A MAJOR SKIRMISH IN WHICH SHISHUPALA, AN OLD ENEMY OF THE YADAVAS, WAS SLAIN...

THE RAJASOOYA WAS SUCCESSFULLY COMPLETED UNDER THE WATCHFUL EYES OF KRISHNA.

AS THE LEADING INVITEES, ESCORTED BY THE OTHER FOUR PANDAVAS, BEGAN LEAVING THE SACRIFICIAL GROUND FOR THEIR RESPECTIVE KINGDOMS...

...KRISHNA TURNED TO YUDHISHTHIRA.
WITH YOUR PERMISSION, I, TOO WILL LEAVE FOR DWARAKA.
KRISHNA. I AM LOATH TO LET YOU GO, BUT I KNOW YOU MUST.

KRISHNA THEN BID KUNTI, DRAUPADI AND SUBHADRA FAREWELL AND SET OFF FOR DWARAKA.
O KING, YOU ARE NOW THE REFUGE OF ALL YOUR SUBJECTS. CHERISH THEM. FARE YOU WELL.

MEANWHILE ON THE WAY BACK TO HASTINAPURA, DURYODHANA WAS PALE AND WITHDRAWN.
WHAT IS THE MATTER, DURYODHANA? WHY DO YOU SIGH SO?
IT WERE BETTER TO DIE THAN LIVE AS I DO!

SHAKUNI LET HIM SPEAK ON.
OH, UNCLE! THAT GRAND YAGNA, HIS IMPERIAL STATUS, THEIR VAST WEALTH! OH, THAT MAGNIFICIENT HALL WITH ITS CELESTIAL DESIGNS!

MIGHTY KINGS PAID HOMAGE TO HIM AND BROUGHT HIM IMMENSE WEALTH LIKE TRIBUTE-PAYING TRADESMEN. WHEN KRISHNA SLEW SHISHUPALA NOT ONE OF THEM QUESTIONED THE ACT.

OH, UNCLE! I BURN WITH ENVY AT THE HAPPINESS, THE POWER AND THE PROSPERITY OF MY FOES.

EVEN IF I WISHED TO CONQUER THE WORLD, WHO IS THERE TO ASSIST ME? I AM ALL ALONE.
THAT IS NOT TRUE, DURYODHANA.

AND SHAKUNI LISTED HIS ALLIES.
YOUR BROTHERS! DRONA! ASHWATTHAMA! KARNA! KRIPA! MY BROTHERS AND I! WE ARE THERE. WE COULD HELP YOU TO CONQUER THE WORLD.
THEN LET US CONQUER THE PANDAVAS!

IF WE CONQUER THEM THE WHOLE WORLD WILL BE MINE! THE KINGS! THAT MAGNIFICENT HALL! ALL THAT WEALTH! ALL WILL BE MINE!

O KING, THE PANDAVAS, KRISHNA, DRUPADA AND HIS SONS CAN NEVER BE VANQUISHED IN BATTLE.

EVEN THE CELESTIALS HAVE NOT BEEN ABLE TO DO IT. BUT I KNOW WHERE AND HOW YUDHISHTHIRA CAN BE DEFEATED. LISTEN!
AND SHAKUNI UNFOLDED HIS WILY PLAN.

BACK AT HASTINAPUR-
HAVING SEEN YUDHISHTHIRA'S PROSPERITY, WHATEVER I HAVE DOES NOT SATISFY ME. HE IS NOT BEFORE ME NOW...

...YET I SEE HIM. MY FOE'S AFFLUENCE CEASELESSLY SHOWS ME HOW DESTITUTE I AM. AND MY HEART BURNS WITH GRIEF AND ENVY.

SHAKUNI AT ONCE TOOK THE CUE.
O DURYODHANA, DO NOT GRIEVE. I KNOW HOW YOU CAN MAKE THAT WEALTH AND PROSPERITY YOURS.

I AM ADEPT AT PLAYING DICE. I KNOW WHEN TO LAY A WAGER AND WHEN NOT TO. YUDHISHTHIRA IS ALSO FOND OF THE GAME. THOUGH HARDLY SKILFUL AT IT.

HE IS SURE TO COME AND PLAY, IF CHALLENGED. BY USING SLEIGHT OF HAND IN THE GAME, I WILL DEFEAT HIM AT EVERY THROW AND WIN ALL HIS WEALTH FOR YOU.

O KING, PERMIT HIM TO WIN THE WEALTH OF THE PANDAVAS AT A GAME OF DICE.

DHRITARASHTRA WAS QUIET FOR A WHILE. THEN -
I AM ALWAYS GUIDED BY VIDURA'S COUNSEL. HE IS JUST AND IMPARTIAL. LET ME CONSULT HIM.

IF YOU CONSULT HIM, HE WILL MAKE YOU REFUSE. IF YOU REFUSE, I WILL KILL MYSELF.

AND WHEN I AM DEAD, O KING, LIVE HAPPILY WITH VIDURA. ENJOY THE EARTH WITH HIM. WHAT USE HAVE YOU FOR ME ANYWAY?

WHEN HIS ELDEST SON SPOKE IN THAT VEIN, THE BLIND KING, THOUGH WELL AWARE OF THE EVILS OF GAMBLING, GAVE IN.
LET WHAT PLEASES YOU BE DONE.

THEN HE SUMMONED HIS MEN.
BUILD THE MOST BEAUTIFUL HALL YOU CAN. LET IT BE CALLED THE CRYSTAL GATE PALACE.

WHEN THE HALL WAS READY, THE ARCHITECTS DESCRIBED IT TO THE BLIND KING.
IT IS STUDDED WITH COUNTLESS JEWELS AND GEMS AND FURNISHED WITH COSTLY COUCHES AND CARPETS INLAID WITH GOLD.

DHRITARASHTRA THEN SUMMONED VIDURA.
GO TO INDRAPRASTHA ON MY BEHALF AND TELL YUDHISHTHIRA THAT THE HALL I HAVE BUILT FOR HIS COUSIN IS AS SPLENDID AS HIS OWN. HE MUST COME AND SEE IT AND...

...ENJOY A BOUT OF DICE THERE WITH HIS COUSINS.
O KING, NOT THAT! I FEAR IT WILL LEAD TO DISCORD BETWEEN THEM!

IF FATE IS NOT AGAINST ME, THAT DISCORD WILL NOT RUIN ME! GO, VIDURA! BRING THE INVINCIBLE YUDHISHTHIRA HERE.
SO, AGAINST HIS WILL, VIDURA SET OUT FOR INDRAPRASTHA.

WHEN HE CAME BEFORE YUDHISHTHIRA–
O VIDURA, YOU LOOK DEJECTED. DO YOU COME IN PEACE? ARE ALL WELL AT HASTINAPURA?

ALL IS WELL WITH HASTINAPURA BUT THE KURU KING COVETS GREATER POWER, MORE WEALTH.
ON HEARING WHAT VIDURA HAD BEEN ORDERED TO SAY...

...YUDHISHTHIRA WAS TAKEN ABACK.
O VIDHURA, GAMBLING COULD END IN STRIFE!
I KNOW THAT. BUT...

YUDHISHTHIRA AT ONCE SAW THROUGH THE ENEMY'S GAME.
O VIDHURA, I AM RELUCTANT TO GAMBLE AT DHRITARASHTRA'S COMMAND. FOR, A FATHER ALWAYS STRIVES TO BENEFIT HIS OWN CHILDREN.
I TRIED TO DISSUADE HIM. BUT...

AGAINST WHOM WILL I HAVE TO PLAY?
THE GANDHARA KING, SHAKUNI. HE IS A DESPERATE GAMBLER...

...WHO ALWAYS RELIES ON SLEIGHT OF HAND IN HIS PLAY! NO. I WILL NOT PLAY. UNLESS, OF COURSE, SHAKUNI CHALLENGES ME. THEN I AM HONOUR BOUND TO ACCEPT.
AND THE VERY NEXT DAY, YUDHISHTHIRA SET OUT WITH HIS ENTOURAGE FOR HASTINAPURA.

THE STAGE WAS SET. THE HALL WAS FULL. DHRITARASHTRA, BHEESHMA, DRONA, KRIPA AND VIDURA, TOO, WERE THERE. AMONG THE KINGS SAT JAYADRATHA, DHRITARASHTRA'S SON-IN-LAW, AND SHALYA, MADRI'S BROTHER.

THEY WERE ALL VALIANT MEN AND THEY WERE ALL LEARNED IN THE VEDAS. AS YUDHISTHIRA AND HIS BROTHERS ENTERED, DURYODHANA AND SHAKUNI STOOD UP.
O KING, ALL AWAIT YOU. LET THE RULES BE FIXED AND THE DICE CAST.
I SHALL PROVIDE THE STAKES AND MY UNCLE HERE WILL PLAY ON MY BEHALF.

AND SO BEGAN THE FATEFUL BOUT. GAME AFTER GAME AND STAKE AFTER STAKE - GOLD, HIS ROYAL CHARIOT, 100,000 SERVING MAIDS, ALL HIS MALE ATTENDANTS, 1000 TUSKERS, 1000 CHARIOTS WITH THEIR HORSES AND CHARIOTEERS, 10,000 WAGONS, 60,000 SOLDIERS - WAS LOST BY YUDHSHTHIRA WITH A TRIUMPHANT CRY FROM SHAKUNI.
LO! I HAVE WON!

LO! I HAVE WON!

LO! I HAVE WON!

AND WITH EACH WIN, WISE VIDURA'S ANXIETY GREW TENFOLD.
O KING, IT IS SUCH SUCCESS THAT BREEDS WAR AMONG MEN AND BRINGS ABOUT THEIR DOOM.

WHAT WILL YOU GAIN BY WINNING THE WEALTH OF THE PANDAVAS? WIN THEM OVER INSTEAD, AND YOU WILL HAVE WON MUCH MORE.

SEND WICKED SHAKUNI BACK TO THE PLACE FROM WHERE HE HAS COME. COMMAND ARJUNA TO SLAY DURYODHANA FOR THE GOOD OF ALL.
BUT DHRITARASHTRA HARDLY HEARD HIM.

DURYODHANA, HOWEVER, DID AND REACTED.
O VIDURA, SAVE YOUR HARSH WORDS AND PROTECT YOUR GOOD REPUTATION. ARE YOU NOT AWARE THAT THERE IS NO GREATER SIN THAN RUNNING DOWN THOSE ON WHOM YOU ARE DEPENDANT?

YOU GO AWAY, INSTEAD. GO WHEREVER YOU WOULD.

A VALIANT, LEARNED MAN WHO LETS ANOTHER'S HEART RULE HIS HEAD, O KING, SINKS LIKE THE VETERAN SAILOR WHO LETS A NOVICE STEER HIS BOAT.

BUT THE GAME WENT ON. ONE AFTER THE OTHER, YUDHIHTHIRA STAKED HIS CATTLE, HIS HORSES, HIS SHEEP, HIS LAND, HIS SUBJECTS WITH THEIR WEALTH, NAKULA, SAHADEVA, ARJUNA, BHEEMA, AND LOST ALL.
I HAVE WON!

AND THEN HE STAKED HIMSELF!
IF WON BY YOU, I SHALL DO WHAT I AM OBLIGED TO DO.

I HAVE WON!

O KING, YOU STILL HAVE SOMETHING DEAR TO YOU - DRAUPADI THE PRINCESS OF PANCHALA.

STAKE HER AND WIN YOURSELF BACK!

YUDHISHTHIRA AGREED -
WITH THE PRINCESS OF PANCHALA AS MY STAKE, I NOW PLAY.

THE ELDERS IN THE ASSEMBLY TREMBLED. BHEESHMA, DRONA AND KRIPA WERE DRENCHED IN SWEAT WHILE VIDURA HELD HIS HEAD BETWEEN HIS HANDS AND SAT LIKE HE WAS DEMENTED.
FOR SHAME!
FOR SHAME!

DHRITARASHTRA, HOWEVER, WAS GLAD AND HE COULD NOT HIDE HIS EXCITEMENT.
IS THE STAKE WON?
IS THE STAKE WON?

THE DIE WAS CAST. THE ASSEMBLY HELD ITS BREATH.
I HAVE WON!

COME VIDURA, BRING THE BELOVED WIFE OF THE PANDAVAS, HERE. ORDER HER TO SWEEP THE CHAMBER. LET HER LIVE AMONG OUR SERVING WOMEN.

DRAUPADI WAS STAKED BY YUDHISHTHIRA AFTER HE HAD STAKED AND LOST HIMSELF, O KING. THEREFORE SHE IS NOT...
FIE ON YOU, VIDURA!

AND DURYODHANA TURNED TO AN ATTENDANT.
VIDURA RAVES IN FEAR. AND HE HAS NEVER WISHED US WELL.

GO PRATIKAMIN, YOU BRING DRAUPADI HERE. YOU HAVE NO FEAR OF THE PANDAVAS.

THE ATTENDANT LEFT AT ONCE FOR THE INNER CHAMBERS.

WHEN PRATIKAMIN ENTERED DRAUPADI'S CHAMBER AND HALTINGLY TOLD HER WHY HE WAS THERE, SHE WAS SHOCKED.
IS THERE A KING WHO WOULD WAGER AWAY HIS WIFE?

WAS HE THAT INTOXICATED BY THE GAME? HAD HE NOTHING ELSE TO STAKE?
HE LOST HIS BROTHERS AND HIMSELF. ONLY THEN DID HE STAKE YOU.

GO BACK TO THAT GATHERING AND ASK THAT GAMBLER, IN THEIR PRESENCE, WHOM HE LOST FIRST, HIMSELF OR ME? THEN COME HERE TO TAKE ME.

THE ATTENDANT DID AS ORDERED.
"WHOSE LORD WERE YOU, O PANDAVA, WHEN YOU STAKED AND LOST ME?" ASKS DRAUPADI.

THE QUESTION STUPEFIED YUDHISHTHIRA. HE DID NOT REPLY.

BUT DURYODHANA DID.
TELL PANCHALI TO COME HERE AND ASK HIM THAT HERSELF. LET US ALL HEAR WHAT THEY HAVE TO SAY TO EACH OTHER.
THOUGH SHAKEN BY THE ORDER, PRATIKAMIN OBEYED.

HE SOON RETURNED, BUT AGAIN WITHOUT DRAUPADI.
PANCHALI SAYS SHE WILL DO AS THE LEARNED KURU ELDERS WHO KNOW THE MORAL CODE TELL HER.

WHEN THE ELDERS, TOO, SAT THERE, SPEECHLESS...

...YUDHISHTHIRA BECKONED TO A TRUSTED ATTENDANT.
TELL PANCHALI TO COME HERE AND WEEP BITTERLY IN FRONT OF HER FATHER-IN-LAW.

DO AS I SAY. BRING HER HERE, PRATIKAMIN. THE KURUS WILL SPEAK IN HER PRESENCE.

THIS TIME, HOWEVER, PRATIKAMIN IGNORED THE COMMAND AND FACED THE ELDERS.
WHAT SHALL I SAY TO DRAUPADI?

THE FOOL IS AFRAID OF BHEEMA.

YOU GO DUSHASANA, AND BRING HER HERE. BY FORCE IF NEED BE.

BUT BRING HER HERE!!!

COME, DRAUPADI. YOU HAVE BEEN WON BY US. ACCEPT US AS YOUR LORDS.

O WRETCH, DO NOT DRAG ME INTO THE SABHA.

O BRUTE, PANDAVAS WILL NEVER FORGIVE YOU. THE KURU ELDERS WILL...

...BUT NOT ONE OF THEM HERE CHASTISES YOU. DRONA, BHEESHMA, VIDURA, THE KING, THEY ALL LOOK SILENTLY ON!

FOR SHAME! THEY HAVE LOST ALL SENSE OF MORALITY. DHARMA IS LOST! KSHATRIYA VALOUR IS DEAD.

AT LAST BHEESHMA SPOKE.
O, DRAUPADI, I AM NOT ABLE TO DECIDE WHAT YOU MUST DO.

THERE ARE OTHER KURUS HERE WHO ARE THE LORDS OF THEIR SONS AND DAUGHTERS-IN-LAW. LET THEM ANSWER MY QUESTION. LET THEM DECIDE.

WHEN NOT ONE OF THEM UTTERED A WORD, DUSHASANA BECAME BOLDER.
YOU ARE OUR SLAVE. YOU WILL DO AS WE TELL YOU. YOU HAVE BEEN LAWFULLY WON BY US.

ONLY THEN DID DRAUPADI LOOK AT HER HUSBANDS. IT WAS A WITHERING LOOK THAT SEARED BHEEMA THE MOST.

O PANCHALI! YOUR ANGER CAUSES ME MORE ANGUISH THAN THE LOSS OF ALL OUR WEALTH, OUR KINGDOM, OURSELVES, EVER COULD.

HA! HA! HA! HA!
SLAVE!
SLAVE!
SLAVE!

BURSTING WITH SUPPRESSED RAGE, BHEEMA TURNED ON YUDHISHTHIRA.
EVEN THE BRAZEN WOMEN WHO SURROUND GAMBLERS ARE NEVER STAKED BY THEM IN A GAME.

HAVING WON THE MIGHTY PANDAVAS FOR HUSBANDS, DOES PANCHALI DESERVE THIS... THIS TORTURE AT THE HANDS OF THESE BASE, DESPICABLE, CRUEL, KURU CURS?

YOU ARE SOLELY TO BLAME. I SHALL BURN YOUR HANDS.

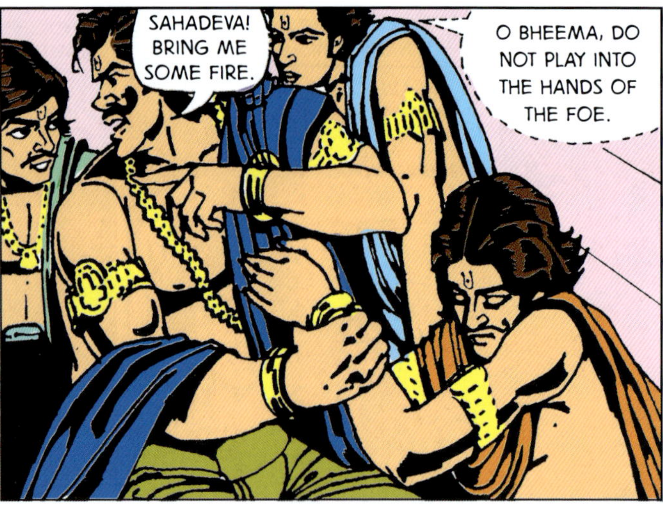
SAHADEVA! BRING ME SOME FIRE.
O BHEEMA, DO NOT PLAY INTO THE HANDS OF THE FOE.

REMEMBER! HE ACTED AGAINST HIS WILL. HE WAS SUMMONED BY THE KURUS AND BOUND BY THE KSHATRIYA CODE.

OH ARJUNA, IF I WERE NOT AWARE OF THAT I WOULD HAVE FORCIBLY HELD HIS HANDS IN A BLAZING FIRE AND BURNT THEM BY NOW!

THE DISTRESS OF THE PANDAVAS AND THEIR QUEEN TOUCHED ONE SOLITARY KAURAVA HEART IN THAT HOSTILE LOT.
O KINGS, IF WE DO NOT RESOLVE A MATTER PUT BEFORE US, HELL WILL BE OUR LOT.

IT WAS VIKARNA ONE OF DHRITARASHTRA'S SONS.
THE DHARMA OF ROYALTY DEMANDS THAT YOU SPEAK OUT. REFLECT IMPARTIALLY ON THE MATTER AND DECLARE WHICH SIDE YOU ARE ON.

WHEN EVEN HIS REPEATED APPEALS BROUGHT NO RESPONSE -
O KINGS. O VENERABLE KURUS, I WILL ANSWER DRAUPADI'S QUESTION.

PEERLESS DRAUPADI IS THE WIFE OF ALL FIVE PANDAVAS. YUDHISHTHIRA FORFEITED HIS AUTHORITY BY PROVING TO BE A VICIOUS GAMBLER. YET, AFTER LOSING HIMSELF, HE STAKED DRAUPADI.

THEN AGAIN, SHAKUNI PREVAILED UPON HIM TO STAKE HER, AND INTOXICATED BY THE GAME, YUDHISHTHIRA CONSENTED.

CONSIDERING THESE CIRCUMSTANCES, I REGARD...
AND VIKARNA RAISED HIS VOICE TO GIVE HIS VERDICT.

...I REGARD DRAUPADI AS NOT WON.

A ROAR OF APPLAUSE FOR VIKARNA AND CENSURE FOR SHAKUNI RENT THE ASSEMBLY.
WISE VIKARNA IS RIGHT!
FIE ON SHAKUNI!
FIE ON VIKARNA!

KARNA WENT MAD WITH RAGE.
O DUSHASANA, THIS VIKARNA WHO SPOUTS WORDS OF WISDOM IS BUT A BOY.

THE SILENCE OF THE OLDER AND WISER SPEAKS THEIR APPROVAL. DRAUPADI HAS BEEN JUSTLY WON.

THERE IS NOTHING WRONG EVEN IN DISROBING THIS UNCHASTE WOMAN WHO HAS TAKEN FIVE HUSBANDS!

DISROBE HER AND THE PANDAVAS, DUSHASANA!
KARNA'S ORDERS WERE AFTER DUSHASANA'S OWN INCLINATIONS.

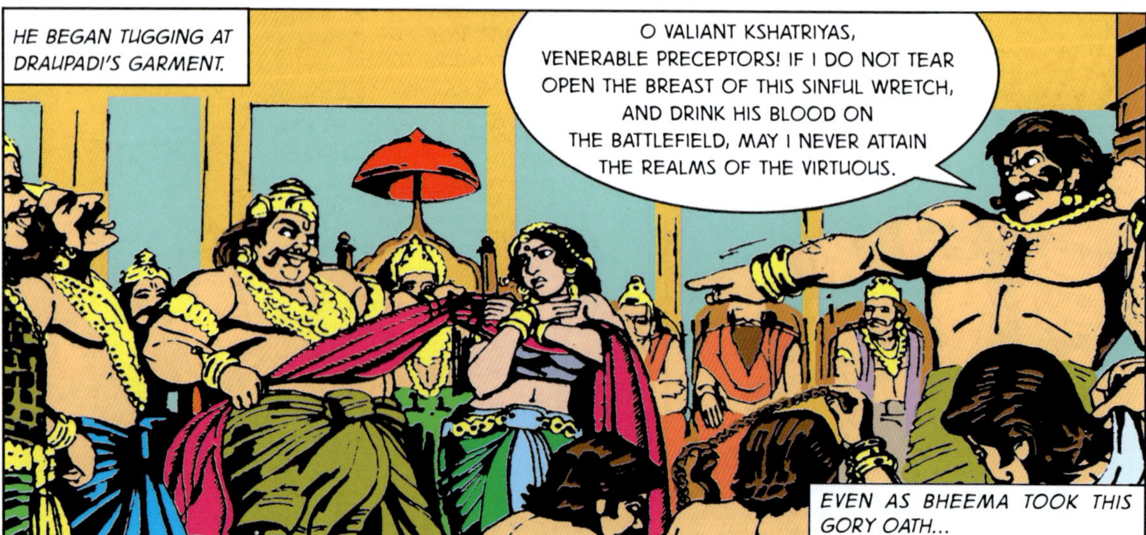
HE BEGAN TUGGING AT DRAUPADI'S GARMENT.
O VALIANT KSHATRIYAS, VENERABLE PRECEPTORS! IF I DO NOT TEAR OPEN THE BREAST OF THIS SINFUL WRETCH, AND DRINK HIS BLOOD ON THE BATTLEFIELD, MAY I NEVER ATTAIN THE REALMS OF THE VIRTUOUS.
EVEN AS BHEEMA TOOK THIS GORY OATH...

...DHARMA TOOK OVER AND PROTECTED DRAUPADI'S MODESTY.

BEFORE DUSHASANA COULD TUG AWAY ONE GARMENT SHE WAS IMMEDIATELY COVERED BY ANOTHER. WHEN A SWELLING HEAP OF SLIPPERY SILKS SWAMPED THE SABHA...

DUSHASANA FINALLY GAVE UP.
DRAUPADI'S QUESTION MUST BE ANSWERED!

THEREUPON, VIDURA SILENCED THE ASSEMBLY.
O KINGS, VIKARNA HAS ANSWERED THE QUESTION AS HE SAW FIT. YOU SHOULD DO THE SAME. DHARMA DEMANDS THAT YOU DO.

WHILE THE KINGS CONTINUED TO SIT TONGUE-TIED...

...KARNA SPOKE.
DUSHASANA, TAKE HER AWAY INTO THE INNER APARTMENTS AND LEAVE HER AMONG THE MENIALS.

NOT YET! O VALIANT KURUS, TELL ME IF I AM A BOND WOMAN OR NOT. I WILL ABIDE ONLY BY YOUR DECISION.

THIS BASE MAN HAS USED HIS MIGHT TO DRAG ME, A PRINCESS BY BIRTH, HERE BEFORE THIS ASSEMBLY AND ITS GAZE.

I WILL NOT GO AWAY NOW TILL MY QUESTION IS ANSWERED. I DEMAND AN ANSWER. AM I WON OR NOT?

BHEESHMA EVEN THEN WAS BAFFLED BUT DURYODHANA SMILED.
LET YOUR HUSBANDS ANSWER THAT QUESTION.

LET THEM DECLARE THAT YUDHISHTHIRA IS NOT THEIR LORD AND BY MAKING A LIAR OF HIM...

...FREE YOU FROM SLAVERY. BETTER STILL LET YUDHSHTHIRA DECLARE WHETHER HE IS OR IS NOT YOUR LORD.

AS USUAL IT WAS BHEEMA WHO REACTED...
IF YUDHISHTHIRA WERE NOT OUR LORD WOULD ANY CREATURE ON EARTH DARE TO TOUCH THE PANCHALA PRINCESS AND ESCAPE WITH HIS LIFE?

WITH MY BARE HANDS I WOULD HAVE SLAUGHTERED THE SONS OF DHRITARASHTRA LIKE SO MANY INSIGNIFICANT ANIMALS.

IF YUDHISHTHIRA SAYS HE IS WON THEN WE ARE ALL WON.

THERE! YOUR HUBANDS ARE SLAVES AND SO ARE YOU.
SELECT A NEW HUSBAND WHO WILL NOT GAMBLE YOU AWAY INTO SLAVERY.
AS KARNA SPOKE...

...DURYODHANA ENCOURAGED HIM IN A MOST CRUDE MANNER.

MAY I NEVER ATTAIN THE REALMS OF MY VALIANT ANCIENTS, IF I DO NOT BREAK THAT THIGH IN BATTLE!

VIDURA KNEW THAT IT WAS NO EMPTY THREAT.
O KURUS, HALT THIS PERSECUTION BEFORE IT IS TOO LATE. BEFORE THE KURU PROSPERITY IS LOST FOREVER.

IF YUDHISHTHIRA HAD STAKED HER BEFORE HE WAS WON, HE WOULD CERTAINLY HAVE BEEN HER MASTER.

LET BHEEMA, ARJUNA AND THE TWINS SAY THAT YUDHISHTHIRA IS NOT THEIR LORD AND DRAUPADI WILL BE FREE.

TAKING THE CUE FROM VIDURA, ARJUNA SPOKE OUT.
THIS SON OF KUNTI, DHARMARAJA, WAS CERTAINLY OUR MASTER BEFORE HE BEGAN TO PLAY...BEFORE HE LOST HIMSELF.

LET THE KAURAVAS DECIDE WHOSE MASTER HE COULD BE NOW.
WHEN THE KAURAVAS WERE ABOUT TO SPEAK...

...THE BRAY OF ASSES, THE HOWLS OF JACKALS AND THE SHRILL CALLS OF CARRION CROWS DROWNED THEIR WORDS.
YEOOOW
EE-AW
EE-AAW
CAAAAW
PEACE!
PEACE!
PEACE!

ALARMED AT THE TURN OF EVENTS, DHRITARASHTRA BLAMED DURYODHANA.
FIE ON YOU, DURYODHANA, FOR INSULTING A WIFE OF THE KURU CHIEFS.

YOU HAVE BROUGHT CERTAIN DOOM UPON YOURSELF BY YOUR WICKED ACTS.
THEN, PROMPTED BY VIDURA, AND ANXIOUS HIMSELF TO SAVE HIS SON AND THEIR KITH AND KIN...

...HE SET ABOUT APPEASING DRAUPADI.
YOU ARE CHASTE AND DEVOTED TO DHARMA, YOU ARE THE MOST EXCELLENT OF ALL MY DAUGHTERS-IN-LAW.

O DRAUPADI, PERMIT ME TO GRANT YOU ANY BOON YOU DESIRE.
GRANT YUDHISHTHIRA HIS LIBERTY, O KING.

LET NOT POSTERITY REGARD PRATIVINDHYA, MY BRILLIANT SON, BORN A PRINCE AND NURTURED BY KINGS, AS THE SON OF A SLAVE.
SO BE IT.

YOU DESERVE ONE MORE BOON, MOST EXCELLENT DAUGHTER.
THEN GRANT BHEEMA AND ARJUNA THEIR LIBERTY AND THEIR WEAPONS AND CHARIOTS.

WHEN DHRITARASHTRA PRESSED A THIRD BOON ON DRAUPADI -
ENOUGH, O LEARNED ONE. I WILL NOT ACCEPT A THIRD BOON.

I DARE NOT. FOR DHARMA, AS WE KNOW, IS DESTROYED BY GREED.

AS FREE MEN, LET MY VIRTUOUS, VALOROUS HUSBANDS ACHIEVE PROSPERITY BY THEIR OWN EFFORTS.

HA! HA! HA! A WOMAN IS THE SAVIOUR OF THE SONS OF MIGHTY PANDU.
KARNA'S TAUNT...

...TURNED BHEEMA INTO A TOWERING INFERNO.
I SHALL KILL ALL THESE CURS RIGHT HERE AND SET YOU UP AS RULER OF THE WHOLE EARTH, YUDHISHTHIRA.
O BHEEMA, THE GREAT DO NOT CARE ABOUT THE HARSH WORDS OF THE INFERIOR.

ARJUNA IS RIGHT. THE GREAT DO NOT REMEMBER THE HOSTILITY OF THEIR FOES BUT ONLY THE GOOD IN THEM.

AFTER SOOTHING BHEEMA, YUDHISHTHIRA STOOD BEFORE DHRITARASHTRA.
WE ARE AT YOUR COMMAND, O KING.
DO NOT REMEMBER THE HOSTILITY OF DURYODHANA IF YOU WOULD REMEMBER ONLY WHAT IS GOOD, THINK OF YOUR MOTHER GANDHARI AND MYSELF.

WITH YOU WHO ARE GUIDED BY WISE VIDURA, THE KURUS ARE EVER SAFE. YOU ARE VIRTUOUS. ARJUNA IS PATIENT AND BHEEMA IS MIGHTY.

KEEP YOUR WEALTH, RETURN TO KHANDAVAPRASTHA WITH YOUR BROTHERS AND RULE YOUR KINGDOM.
AND SO MOUNTING THEIR CHARIOTS, THE PANDAVAS WITH DRAUPADI BEGAN THEIR JOURNEY BACK.

AS SOON AS THEY LEFT, HOWEVER, DUSHASANA, DURYODHANA AND KARNA CAME TO DHRITARASHTRA.
THE PANDAVAS WILL CERTAINLY AVENGE THEMSELVES, FATHER.

AS THEY DROVE OUT, ARJUNA WITH HIS ANGRY MIEN AND RAISED BOW, AND BHEEMA WITH HIS WHIRLING MACE MADE THEIR INTENTIONS CLEAR.

IF THEY NOW SPEED PEACEFULLY TOWARDS THEIR CAPITAL, O KING, IT IS ONLY TO RALLY THEIR FORCES.

ENABLE US TO BANISH THE PANDAVAS TO THE FOREST, FATHER. PERMIT US TO GAMBLE ONCE MORE WITH THEM.

THE LOSERS, SHALL GO INTO THE FOREST FOR TWELVE YEARS, AND REMAIN INCOGNITO IN A CITY FOR A THIRTEENTH. IF RECOGNIZED, THEY SHALL GO BACK INTO THE FOREST FOR ANOTHER TWELVE YEARS.

WITH SHAKUNI THROWING THE DICE, WE ARE BOUND TO WIN.

AND WHILE THE PANDAVAS ARE IN EXILE, WE WILL BE ABLE TO STRENGTHEN OUR POSITION IN THE KINGDOM.

WE WILL ALSO BE ABLE TO ASSEMBLE A VAST, INVINCIBLE ARMY AND TO KEEP IT CONTENT.

THEN, EVEN IF THE PANDAVAS FULFIL THE CONDITIONS AND RETURN, WE COULD EASILY VANQUISH THEM.

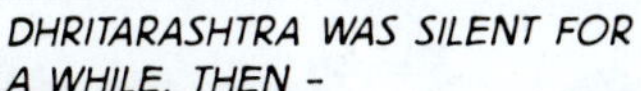
DHRITARASHTRA WAS SILENT FOR A WHILE. THEN -

LET IT BE AS YOU WISH. BRING BACK THE PANDAVAS. LET THEM COME HERE FOR ANOTHER BOUT OF DICE.

BHEESHMA, DRONA, HIS SON ASHWATTHAMA, KRIPA, VIDURA AND VIKARNA PROTESTED.
LET THERE NOT BE ANOTHER BOUT OF DICE.
DO NOT GIVE IN, O KING. LET THERE BE PEACE!

GANDHARI TOO SPOKE OUT.
O GREAT KING, PROSPERITY THAT IS GAINED BY SUCH MEANS IS SHORT-LIVED, WHILE THAT WHICH IS HONESTLY ACHIEVED PASSES ON FROM GENERATION TO GENERATION.

DO NOT REKINDLE A FIRE THAT HAS BEEN PUT OUT. HEED THE COUNSEL OF WISE VIDURA. DO NOT BE LED BY MERE BOYS AND CAUSE THE RUIN OF OUR RACE.

O GANDHARI, IF RUIN IS ORDAINED FOR US, I CANNOT PREVENT IT.

LET IT COME UNHINDERED. LET THE PANDAVAS RETURN. LET MY SONS GAMBLE WITH THEM.
AND PRATIKAMIN WAS SENT AFTER THEM.

THE PANDAVAS HAD TO RETURN. THE NEW STAKE WAS ANNOUNCED, THE DICE WERE THROWN AND -
LO! I HAVE WON.

THE PANDAVAS CAST OFF THEIR FINERY AND COVERED THEM-SELVES WITH DEER-SKINS WHILE THE SNEERING DUSHASANA TAUNTED THEM.
O DRAUPADI, WHAT JOY CAN THESE IMPOTENT HUSBANDS, IN THEIR HIDES AND RAGS BRING YOU?

DRUPADA DID NOT DO WELL TO BESTOW YOU ON THE PANDAVAS. ABANDON THEM. CHOOSE ONE AMONG US FOR A HUSBAND.

I WILL DRINK YOUR BLOOD IN BATTLE, DUSHASANA! I WILL SLAY YOU AND DURYODHANA. SAHADEVA WILL SLAY SHAKUNI AND ARJUNA, KARNA.

O BHEEMA, I VOW TO SLAY KARNA AND ALL HIS FOLLOWERS AND ANY OTHER KING WHO DARES TAKE ME ON IN BATTLE...

...IF ON THE FOURTEENTH YEAR DURYODHANA DOES NOT RETURN OUR KINGDOM TO US WITH DUE HONOUR.

WHILE THE OTHER ELDERS BOWED THEIR HEADS IN SHAME EVEN AS THEY SILENTLY PRAYED FOR THE WELFARE OF THE PANDAVAS, VIDURA SPOKE TO YUDHISHTHIRA.

PRINCESS KUNTI MUST NOT GO TO THE FOREST WITH YOU. SHE SHALL STAY IN MY HOUSE.

MEANWHILE DRAUPADI WENT TO TAKE HER LEAVE OF KUNTI AND THE OTHER LADIES OF THE PALACE.
O FAULTLESS DRAUPADI, THE KURUS ARE FORTUNATE THAT YOUR WRATH DID NOT CONSUME THEM.

PROTECTED AS YOU ARE BY DHARMA, PROSPERITY WILL SOON BE YOURS.

AS DRAUPADI CAME OUT TO JOIN THE PANDAVAS, KUNTI FOLLOWED HER.

WHEN KUNTI SAW HER SONS, SHE CHOKED WITH GRIEF.
HOW COULD THIS HAPPEN TO YOU IN THE PRESENCE OF LEARNED, VALIANT MEN LIKE BHEESHMA, DRONA AND KRIPA?

HAD I KNOWN THAT THIS WOULD BE YOUR LOT, I WOULD NEVER HAVE BROUGHT YOU HERE AFTER YOUR FATHER DIED.

NO. I WILL NOT LET YOU GO WITHOUT ME. I WILL GO WITH YOU.

THE SIGHT OF THE SHATTERED MOTHER WHO HAD ONCE BEEN A TOWER OF STRENGTH, WRUNG THE HEARTS OF THE PANDAVAS AND THEY, TOO, WEPT UNABASHEDLY.

WHILE THEY WIPED HER TEARS AND SHE THEIRS, VIDURA SILENTLY WALKED TOWARDS THEM...

...AND HIDING HIS OWN GRIEF GENTLY LED HER AWAY.

AS THE PANDAVAS AND DRAUPADI, PRECEDED BY DHOUMYA THEIR PRIEST, SET OUT FROM HASTINAPURA, LIGHTNING FLASHED IN A CLEAR SKY, THE EARTH QUAKED...

...RAHU SWALLOWED THE SUN AND METEORS CAME HURTLING DOWN...
YEOW

...WHILE THE FRIGHTENED CITIZENS WAILED IN MISERY ABOVE THE DIN OF RAVENS, JACKALS, AND VULTURES.
FIE ON THE COVETOUS KURU CHIEFS FOR BANISHING OUR LORDS AND MASTERS, THE BLAMELESS SONS OF PANDU!
HOW CAN WE EVER LOVE THOSE WICKED CHIEFS!

FEARLESSLY CENSURING BHEESHMA, DRONA AND KRIPA AND DURYODHANA, THEY FOLLOWED THE PANDAVAS OUT OF THE GATES OF HASTINAPURA.
WHEN A SINFUL MAN WITH THE HELP OF OTHER SINFUL MEN RULES THE KINGDOM...

...OUR VALUES, OUR TRADITIONS, OUR DHARMA, OUR WEALTH WILL BE DOOMED! AND WITHOUT THESE HOW CAN THERE BE HAPPINESS?

DO NOT FORSAKE US, O PANDAVAS. PERMIT US TO FOLLOW YOU.

VIDURA AND OUR MOTHER, KUNTI, ARE STILL AT HASTINAPURA. GO BACK AND COMFORT AND CHERISH THEM. THIS IS WHAT MY BROTHERS AND I WOULD HAVE YOU DO.
THE CITIZENS RELUCTANTLY OBEYED YUDHISHTHIRA.

THE PANDAVAS THEN MOUNTED THEIR CHARIOTS AND...

...DROVE AWAY WITH DRAUPADI AND DHOUMYA.

TOWARDS SUNSET THEY CAME UPON A HUGE BANYAN TREE ON THE BANKS OF THE GANGA. AND THERE THEY HALTED FOR THE NIGHT.

THEY WERE SOON JOINED BY A GROUP OF SEERS...

...WHO WITH THEIR GLOWING FIRES, SOOTHING VEDIC CHANTS AND ERUDITE CONVERSATION...
...TURNED WHAT MIGHT HAVE BEEN A TERRIBLE TWILIGHT HOUR FOR THE PANDAVAS INTO ONE OF SHEER DELIGHT.

AT BREAK OF DAY, WHEN THE PANDAVAS MADE READY TO MOVE ON –
O KING, WE WILL GO WITH YOU.
KING?

YUDHISHTHIRA FELT MISERABLE.
HOW WILL I, A KING DEVOID OF KINGDOM OR WEALTH, FEED YOU?

O KING, WE WILL FEND FOR OURSELVES.
BESIDES, OUR COMPANY WILL CHEER YOU AND THAT WOULD BE SUSTENANCE ENOUGH FOR US.

THEIR GRACIOUS WORDS, HOWEVER, DID NOT ALLAY YUDHISHTHIRA'S FEELINGS OF GUILT AND SHAME.
O FIE ON THE SONS OF DHRITARASHTRA FOR PLACING ME IN SUCH A PREDICAMENT!

THESE SELFLESS SEERS ARE BENT ON FOLLOWING US. OH, DHOUMYA! NEITHER CAN I FORSAKE THEM, NOR DO I HAVE THE POWER TO FEED THEM.

O DHOUMYA, TELL ME WHAT I SHOULD DO.
ARISE AND COME WITH ME.

THE SUN SUSTAINS ALL LIFE. FOR, THE SUN ITSELF ENTERS SPROUTING SEEDS AND TURNS INTO VEGETABLES, FRUITS AND GRAINS - THE FOOD OF ALL BEINGS ON EARTH. SEEK REFUGE IN THE CREATOR AND SUSTAINER OF LIFE.

PROPITIATE SURYA, THE PRESIDING DEITY OF THE SUN.
FOLLOWING DHOUMYA'S INSTRUCTIONS...

...YUDHISHTHIRA INVOKED SURYA BY CHANTING HIS 108 NAMES AND SINGING HYMNS IN HIS PRAISE. THEN -
...O LORD OF ALL FOOD, GRANT ME ENOUGH TO FEED MY REVERED GUESTS.

BEFORE THE CLOSE OF DAY -
FOR TWELVE FULL YEARS WHATEVER IS COOKED FOR A MEAL IN THIS COPPER UTENSIL WILL REMAIN INEXHAUSTIBLE TILL DRAUPADI HAS EATEN.

ON THE FOURTEENTH YEAR FROM NOW YOU WILL REGAIN YOUR KINGDOM.
WITH THIS SURYA VANISHED.

STEPPING OUT OF THE WATER, YUDHISTHIRA FELL AT DHOUMYA'S FEET.

HE COLLECTED SOME ROOTS AND FRUITS, AND EDIBLE GREENS, SHOT DOWN SOME GAME, LIT A FIRE...

...AND ALONG WITH DRAUPADI BEGAN TO COOK.

AND TRUE ENOUGH, THE SMALL QUANTITY THEY COOKED KEPT INCREASING TO FEED THEM ALL - THE SEERS, HIS YOUNGER BROTHERS, HIMSELF AND DRAUPADI.

AFTER DRAUPADI WAS SERVED, HOWEVER...
...THE UTENSIL REMAINED EMPTY.

FEELING CHEERFUL, CONTENT, OPTIMISTIC, THE PANDAVAS FOLLOWED BY THE SEERS SET OUT FOR THE KAMYAKA FOREST.

MEANWHILE AT HASTINAPURA, DHRITARASHTRA WAS SEIZED BY A FIT OF DEPRESSION AND FOREBODING.
SO HE SENT FOR VIDURA.

WHEN THAT WISE ONE CAME -
O VIDURA, NOW THAT EVENTS HAVE TAKEN SUCH A TURN, WHAT SHOULD WE DO?

HOW BEST CAN WE WIN THE CITIZENS OVER? WHAT SHOULD BE DONE FOR OUR GOOD AND THEIRS?

VIDURA'S REPLY WAS SHARP AND SHORT.
RESTORE WHAT WAS THEIRS TO THE PANDAVAS. GRATIFY THEM AND DISGRACE SHAKUNI.

WHEN DHRITARASHTRA REMAINED SILENT, VIDURA WENT ON.
LET SHAKUNI, DURYODHANA, DUSHASANA AND KARNA WAIT UPON THE PANDAVAS.

LET DUSHASANA SEEK DRAUPADI'S PARDON IN A FULL ASSEMBLY. LET YUDHISHTHIRA BE THE SOVEREIGN RULER AND IF DURYODHANA RESISTS...ABANDON HIM!

WHAT ELSE CAN I SAY?
HOW CAN I DENY MY OWN FLESH AND BLOOD FOR THE SAKE OF OTHERS?

VIDURA, ALL YOUR COUNSEL IS FOR THE PANDAVAS AND AGAINST US. THOUGH I ALWAYS HELD YOU IN HIGH ESTEEM, I SEE YOU NOW TO BE A COMMON FOE.

STAY HERE OR GO AWAY. DO AS YOU PLEASE. THIS RACE IS DOOMED.

VIDURA WALKED AWAY...
...AND OUT OF THE PALACE.

BEFORE LONG, AS YUDHISHTHIRA RELAXED WITH HIS BROTHERS, DRAUPADI, DHOUMYA AND THE SEERS, IN A SECLUDED CLEARING IN THE KAMYAKA FOREST...

...THE RUMBLE OF AN APPROACHING CHARIOT CAUGHT HIS ATTENTION.
WHO COULD IT BE?

AS THE CHARIOT NEARED AND HE COULD MAKE OUT WHO IT CARRIED, HE PALED.

IT IS VIDURA!

HAS HE BEEN SENT HERE BY SHAKUNI WITH ANOTHER INVITATION TO PLAY? WITH OUR WEAPONS AS STAKES?

OH, BHEEMA, IF CHALLENGED, I AM BOUND TO ACCEPT. AND IF WE LOSE THE GANDIVA BOW, I DOUBT WE WILL EVER REGAIN OUR KINGDOM.

YUDHISHTHIRA'S FEARS, HOWEVER, WERE SOON DISPELLED.
ABANDONED BY DHRITARASHTRA I HAVE COME TO YOU TO BE YOUR COUNSELLOR.
AFTER HE WAS RESTED, YUDHISHTHIRA TOLD VIDURA ALL THAT HAD PASSED TILL THEN.

LATER, AS VIDURA SPOKE TO YUDHISHTHIRA ON THE ART AND ETHIC OF WINNING AND KEEPING ALLIES, ANOTHER CHARIOT ROLLED UP. IT WAS SANJAYA, ONE OF DHRITARASHTRA'S COUNSELLORS.

WHEN THE PANDAVAS HAD FORMALLY WELCOMED HIM-
THE KING IS REPENTANT AND REMEMBERS YOU. RETURN TO HIM, O WISE VIDURA.
SO WITH YUDHISHTHIRA'S CONSENT...

...VIDURA RETURNED TO HIS BROTHER AT HASTINAPURA.

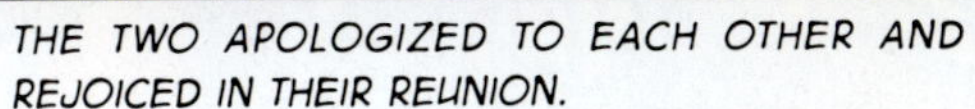
THE TWO APOLOGIZED TO EACH OTHER AND REJOICED IN THEIR REUNION.

VIDURA HAS COME BACK. IF HE SUCCEEDS IN REINSTATING THE PANDAVAS, I WILL SLAY MYSELF.
WHILE DURYODHANA FRETTED...

...SHAKUNI WAS UNPERTURBED.
YOUR FEARS ARE UNFOUNDED. THEY WILL NEVER BREAK THEIR WORD.

HE IS RIGHT AND EVEN IF THEY DO, WE COULD DEFEAT THEM AT DICE ONCE AGAIN.
KARNA, TOO, WAS NOT UNDULY PERTURBED.

BUT WHEN DURYODHANA CONTINUED TO SIT WITH A GLUM FACE, KARNA OFFERED A SUGGESTION.
IF YOU WISH, WE WILL MOUNT OUR CHARIOTS AND ATTACK THEM IN THE FOREST.

DEMORALIZED AS THEY ARE, WE COULD EASILY VANQUISH THEM. IF WE ATTACK THEM **NOW.**

SO BE IT!
LET US ATTACK!
GO FOR YOUR CHARIOTS!
AND THE FOUR CHARGED OUT IN THEIR CHARIOTS.

BUT, DIVINING THEIR INTENTIONS, VYASA, THEIR GRANDFATHER, APPEARED AT THE PALACE GATE...

...IN TIME TO BAR THEIR WAY...

...AND MAKE THEM TURN BACK.

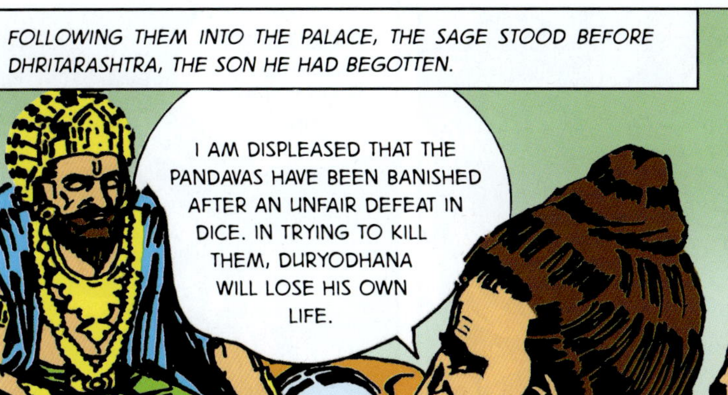
FOLLOWING THEM INTO THE PALACE, THE SAGE STOOD BEFORE DHRITARASHTRA, THE SON HE HAD BEGOTTEN.
I AM DISPLEASED THAT THE PANDAVAS HAVE BEEN BANISHED AFTER AN UNFAIR DEFEAT IN DICE. IN TRYING TO KILL THEM, DURYODHANA WILL LOSE HIS OWN LIFE.

CHECK THE FOOL! IF YOU DO NOT INTERFERE NOW...
...THE CONSEQUENCES WILL BE DISASTROUS FOR ALL.

WHAT DO BHEESHMA, DRONA AND VIDURA THINK? WHAT DO YOU THINK?
NONE OF THEM APPROVED OF HOLDING THE GAME. NEITHER DID GANDHARI NOR EVEN I.

BUT, DELUDED BY ATTACHMENT FOR MY SON, I GAVE IN. I COULD NOT DENY HIM.
I AGREE THAT ONE'S OFFSPRING ARE MORE DEAR TO ONE THAN ANYTHING IN THIS WORLD.

AND SO IT IS WITH ME. AS YOU ARE MY SON, SO WAS PANDU AND SO IS VIDURA.

BUT YOU HAVE A HUNDRED AND ONE SONS. PANDU HAS LEFT BEHIND ONLY FIVE, AND THEY ARE IN DISTRESS.

MEANWHILE, AT THE KAMYAKA FOREST, THE EXILES HAD VISITORS; KRISHNA, SUBHADRA, ABHIMANYU, AND DRAUPADI'S BROTHER DHRISHTADYUMNA, WITH HER FIVE SONS.

AND THE EVER-CALM KRISHNA SEEMED DETERMINED TO CONSUME ALL CREATION.

ALARMED TO SEE HIS ALTER-EGO IN THAT STATE, ARJUNA BEGAN TO SOOTHE HIM. BUT -
O KRISHNA, HOW DID THOSE BASE, INFERIOR, INSIGNFICANT MEN DARE HUMILIATE ME! ME, THE SISTER OF DHRISHTADYUMNA, THE WIFE OF THE PANDAVAS, A FRIEND OF YOURS!

BUT I BLAME THE PANDAVAS. THEY WHO NEVER DENY THEIR PROTECTION TO ANY, FORSOOK ME, THEIR OWN WIFE!

BHEESHMA AND DHRITARASHTRA, MY FATHERS-IN-LAW, WANTED TO MAKE ME THEIR SLAVE! O KRISHNA, FIE ON BHEEMA'S MIGHT AND FIE ON ARJUNA'S GANDIVA, WHICH ONLY YOU THREE CAN WIELD!

FIE ON THE GANDIVA, THAT DURYODHANA STILL LIVES AFTER WHAT HE DID TO ME!

NOW CHOKING WITH ANGER, NOW SIGHING WITH SORROW, DRAUPADI POURED OUT HER WOES.
I AM THE MOTHER OF THESE FIVE MIGHTY SONS - ALL GREAT ARCHERS AND INVINCIBLE WARRIORS. WHY DO THEY, TOO, APPEAR UNAFFECTED BY MY PLIGHT?

O KRISHNA, I HAVE NO ONE. NEITHER SONS...NOR HUSBANDS...NOR BROTHERS...NOR FATHER...NOR FRIENDS...NOR EVEN YOU...

ELSE, WOULD ALL OF YOU TOLERATE THE CRUEL TREATMENT METED OUT TO ME BY INFERIOR FOES?
DO NOT GRIEVE, FAIR ONE.

YOU SHALL YET BE THE QUEEN OF KINGS. AND MY WORDS ARE NEVER IN VAIN.
WHAT KRISHNA PROMISES, ALWAYS COMES TRUE. SO DO NOT WEEP, DEAR DRAUPADI.

DHRISHTADYUMNA, TOO, CONSOLED HIS SISTER WITH A PROMISE.
WHEN THE TIME COMES, I WILL KILL DRONA AND SHIKHANDIN WILL KILL BHEESHMA. SO DO NOT WEEP, SWEET SISTER.

HAD I NOT BEEN AWAY FROM DWARAKA AT THAT TIME THERE WOULD HAVE BEEN NO GAMBLING.

I WOULD HAVE COME TO HASTINAPURA AND PREVENTED IT. I WOULD EVEN HAVE USED FORCE IF IT WERE CALLED FOR.

NOW EVEN I AM HELPLESS. WE WILL HAVE TO WAIT AND SEE WHAT HAPPENS IN THE FOURTEENTH YEAR.
AND MOUNTING THEIR CHARIOTS, THE VISITORS LEFT.

WHEN THEY HAD GONE, YUDHISHTHIRA TURNED TO ARJUNA.
WE HAVE TO PASS TWELVE YEARS IN THIS VAST LONELY FOREST. FIND A CHARMING SPOT WHERE THOSE YEARS COULD BE PLEASANTLY SPENT.

DWAITAVANA HAS A LAKE, AND ABOUNDS IN A VARIETY OF FLORA AND FAUNA. IT IS FAVOURED BY SAGES AND SEERS. IF YOU APPROVE...

...THAT IS WHERE WE WOULD LIKE TO LIVE.
THEN WE SHALL GO THERE FORTHWITH.
AND SO THE PANDAVAS, ALONG WITH THE SEERS WHO HAD JOINED THEM, SET OUT FOR DWAITAVANA.

AT DWAITAVANA, YUDHISHTHIRA AND THE REST SPENT MANY AN EVENING HOUR DISCUSSING THEIR EXILE.
ONLY FOUR VICIOUS, WRETCHES DID NOT SHED TEARS THAT DAY - DURYODHANA, KARNA, SHAKUNI AND DUSHASANA.

AND NOW HAVING BROUGHT US TO THIS PLIGHT, THAT WRETCHED SON OF DHRITARASHTRA MAKES MERRY WITH HIS FRIENDS.

WHAT WAS OUR FORMER GLORY AND WHAT OUR PRESENT STATE! DOES IT NOT PAIN YOU? DOES IT NOT ANGER YOU?

YUDHISHTHIRA'S EQUANIMITY BEWILDERED DRAUPADI.
YOU DO NOT FLARE UP... YOU SEEM TO BE DEVOID OF ANGER... SOMETHING STRANGE IN A KING...

O KING, IT IS WELL KNOWN THAT THERE IS A TIME FOR FORGIVENESS AND A TIME FOR ANGER. EACH SHOULD BE EXPRESSED AS THE HOUR DEMANDS.

THE HOUR NOW DEMANDS, NOT YOUR FORGIVENESS BUT A DISPLAY OF YOUR MIGHT BORN OF ANGER.

WHEN I KNOW THAT ANGER HAS BEEN GIVEN TO MAN FOR HIS DESTRUCTION, THE DESTRUCTION OF THE WORLD ITSELF, THAT NO GOOD IS EVER BORN OF ANGER, HOW CAN I INDULGE IN IT? DIM-WITTED PERSONS MAY LET ANGER OVERPOWER THEM.

BUT I KNOW THAT THIS WORLD AND THE OTHER BELONG TO HIM WHO FORGIVES.

YOUR PIOUS ACTS HAVE NOT WON FOR YOU EVEN THIS WORLD.

DRAUPADI THEN BECAME PENSIVE.
WHEN I SEE YOU IN THIS MISERABLE STATE AND THE VICIOUS SONS OF DHRITARASHTRA PROSPERING, I DO WONDER.

I AM INCLINED TO BLAME THE CREATOR. O BEST OF MEN, HOW ELSE COULD A MIND LIKE YOURS BE LURED TO THE VICE OF GAMBLING?

HOW ELSE COULD A MIND LIKE YOURS PLACE ROYAL ETHICS BEFORE UNIVERSAL MORALITY?

O KING, YOU LOST EVERYTHING BECAUSE YOUR MIND WAS CLOUDED BY THE CREATOR.

WE CANNOT ESCAPE ACTION BECAUSE IT IS PREORDAINED.

THAT MAKES THE CREATOR ACCOUNTABLE FOR ALL OUR THOUGHTS AND DEEDS.

IF THE SINS OF IMPIOUS DEEDS ACCRUE TO THE PRIME MOVER, THEN THE CREATOR IS SINFUL.

IF NOT, THE WORLD BELONGS TO THE MIGHTY, AND...

...I PITY THE FEEBLE.
THOUGH HE SMILINGLY HEARD HER OUT...

...YUDHISHTHIRA CHIDED DRAUPADI FOR HER IMPIOUS SKEPTICISM.
ONE SHOULD NEVER QUESTION OR CRITICIZE RELIGION OR THE CREATOR.
AND HE REFUTED HER ARGUMENTS AT LENGTH.

I NEITHER DISRESPECT THE CREATOR NOR QUESTION THE VALIDITY OF RELIGION. ALL I SOUGHT TO SAY IS...

...WHILE THE CREATOR IS THE GIVER OF FRUITS, GOOD AND BAD, THE CHOICE IS GUIDED BY ONE'S INTELLIGENCE AND EFFORT.

YUDHISHTHIRA PROMPTLY DEFENDED HIS STAND.
I ACT VIRTUOUSLY NOT FOR THE FRUITS BUT BECAUSE I SEE THE PIOUS AND THE GOOD DO SO. AND...

...I AM BENT THAT WAY. I ADHERE TO VIRTUE FOR ITS OWN SAKE.
BHEEMA WHO WAS SILENT ALL THIS WHILE...

...SIGHED WITH ANGER.
WHAT VIRTUE IS THERE, O KING, IN LIVING AMONG ASCETICS IN THIS FOREST, DEPRIVED OF YOUR DHARMA, ARTHA AND KAMA?

O KING, MIGHT AND POWER ARE THE PRIME VIRTUES OF A KSHATRIYA AND SWERVING FROM THE DHARMA OF ONE'S ORDER IS NEVER LAUDED. OUR KINGDOM, WON BY VIRTUE AND PROWESS WAS ROBBED IN OUR VERY PRESENCE...

...THROUGH YOUR NEGLECT.

IT WAS AN ACT OF FOLLY THAT WE OBEYED YOU AND DID NOT KILL THE SONS OF DHRITARASHTRA THEN AND THERE.

WHILE YUDHISHTHIRA REMAINED TRANQUIL, BHEEMA RAVED ON.
O KING, WE SUFFER THIS MISERY FOR THE PETTY VIRTUE OF KEEPING A PLEDGE MADE TO DESPERATE GAMBLERS!

A PRISONER OF YOUR PLEDGE, YOU CRY, "VIRTUE! VIRTUE!" HAS DESPAIR DRAINED YOU OF ALL MANLINESS?

VANQUISH THE KAURAVAS, AND WASH OFF THE SIN BY GIVING AWAY A PART OF YOUR WEALTH AS KINGS ARE WONT TO DO. ONLY COWARDS, INCAPABLE OF FIGHT, NURTURE NUMBING DESPAIR.

IT IS ONLY YOUR WEAK CHARACTER, O KING, THAT MAKES YOU SHY AWAY FROM VIOLATING YOUR PLEDGE.

WHAT YOU SAY IS TRUE. I CANNOT BLAME YOU FOR LOSING PATIENCE WITH ME.

MY FOLLY ALONE HAS BROUGHT THIS CALAMITY UPON YOU, BHEEMA, BUT...

...WHAT IS THE USE OF SPEAKING HARSH WORDS TO ME NOW?

CONSCIOUS AS YOU ARE OF YOUR STRENGTH, WHY DID YOU NOT STOP ME BEFORE I AGREED ON THE STAKES?

WHY DID YOU NOT BURN MY HANDS DURING THE PLAY AS YOU WANTED TO? WHY DID YOU PERMIT ARJUNA TO HOLD YOU BACK, BHEEMA?

HAVING AGREED TO THE STAKES IN THE PRESENCE OF ALL THE KURU ELDERS, I CANNOT BREAK MY WORD NOW. WE WILL HAVE TO WAIT FOR THE FOURTEENTH YEAR.

O KING, ONLY HE WHO IS IMMORTAL OR HE WHO KNOWS THE EXACT SPAN OF HIS LIFE CAN WAIT FOR A PARTICULAR MOMENT.

IF WE WAIT, OUR LIVES WILL BE SHORTER BY THAT MANY YEARS BRINGING US NEARER TO DEATH. FOR...

THEN BHEEMA SMILED.

NOT IN THE LEAST RUFFLED BY HIS YOUNGER BROTHER'S LONG TIRADE...

...YUDHISHTHIRA REFLECTED.
I AM FULLY AWARE OF THE DUTIES OF SCHOLARS, KINGS AND COMMONERS.

AND I ALSO KNOW THAT HE WHO TRULY SEES IS GUIDED IN HIS CONDUCT BY THE PRESENT AND THE FUTURE.

AS I REALIZE THE COMPLEX NATURE OF DHARMA, HOW CAN I FORCIBLY SUPPRESS IT? IT WOULD BE AS FOOLISH AS ATTEMPTING TO CRUSH MT. MERU.
AND HE PONDERED FOR A WHILE.

THEN -
O MIGHTY BHEEMA, NOW YOU LISTEN TO WHAT I HAVE TO SAY.
AND YUDHISHTHIRA GAVE BHEEMA THE REAL REASONS FOR THE COURSE HE HAD CHOSEN.

THE KINGS WE HAVE HUMILIATED IN BATTLE WILL NATURALLY SUPPORT DURYODHANA WITH THEIR WEALTH AND THEIR ARMIES, TO SEE US DEFEATED.

DURYODHANA HAS HONOURED THE OFFICERS OF THE KURU ARMY WITH MUCH WEALTH. I AM CERTAIN THEY WILL WILLINGLY SACRIFICE THEIR LIVES FIGHTING FOR HIM.

BHEESHMA, DRONA AND KRIPA, WHOM THE VERY DEVAS CANNOT DEFEAT, HAVE THE SAME AFFECTION FOR THE KAURAVAS AND US. BUT THEY ARE INDEBTED TO OUR FOES FOR THE ROYAL FAVOURS THEY ENJOY.

THEY WOULD, I AM CERTAIN, LAY DOWN THEIR LIVES IN BATTLE FOR DURYODHANA, TO DISCHARGE THAT DEBT.

UNAIDED YOU CANNOT DEFEAT THEM. AND WITHOUT DEFEATING THOSE VETERANS IN CELESTIAL WEAPONS, YOU CANNOT SLAY DURYODHANA.

I WILL TELL YOU HOW THEY CAN ALL BE SLAIN, YUDHISHTHIRA.
IT WAS VYASA.

DIVINING YOUR AGONY, I SPED HERE TO DISPEL IT. COME WITH ME.
AND THE SAGE LED YUDHISHTHIRA AWAY FROM THE OTHERS...

...TO A FAR CORNER OF THE FOREST.

THERE THE SAGE GRACED HIM WITH THE SECRET LORE OF PRATISMRITI. THEN -
THIS LORE WILL ENABLE VIRTUOUS AND PATIENT ARJUNA TO ATTAIN WHAT IS DESIRED.

LET HIM GO TO THE REALMS OF THE DEVAS AND ACQUIRE WONDROUS MISSILES FROM INDRA AND SHIVA. YOU SHOULD LEAVE THIS FOREST AND GO TO ANOTHER.

YOUR PROLONGED STAY HERE WITH THE NUMEROUS BRAHMANAS YOU SUPPORT, WOULD SOON DEPLETE IT OF ITS DEER AND DESTROY ITS RARE HERBS AND CREEPERS.
AND VYASA WENT HIS WAY.

YUDHISHTHIRA CHOSE TO RETURN TO THE KAMYAKA FOREST.

THERE, ONE DAY, HE TOLD ARJUNA IN PRIVATE ABOUT VYASA'S GREAT GIFT.
O BROTHER, RECEIVE THAT LORE FROM ME AND ATTAIN THE GRACE OF THE CELESTIALS. AND...

...ARMED AND ARMOURED GO NORTH SUBMITTING TO NONE. GO TO INDRA. HE IS BOUND TO GIVE YOU ALL HIS MYSTERIOUS MISSILES.
THEN HE IMPARTED THE PRATISMRITI TO ARJUNA.

WHEN AT LAST ARJUNA WAS READY TO SET OUT -
MAY YOU OBTAIN YOUR DESIRE.
O ARJUNA, MAY WE NEVER AGAIN BE BORN IN THE ORDER OF KINGS!

THE PAIN INFLICTED BY DURYODHANA WAS DEEP. BUT THIS IS WORSE.

THOUGH LIFE WILL BE UNBEARABLE HERE WITHOUT YOU, GO. COME BACK VICTORIOUS. MAY THE CELESTIALS PROTECT YOU.

ARMED WITH HIS EVER-FULL QUIVER, HIS GANDIVA BOW AND A SWORD, ARJUNA PROCEEDED TOWARDS THE NORTH ON HIS SUPER-HUMAN MISSION.

THE FALL OF HIS FOOT AND THE SPAN OF HIS STRIDE WARNED CREATURES BIG AND SMALL TO STAY CLEAR OF HIS PATH.

HE WALKED NIGHT AND DAY ACROSS HILL AND DALE TILL AT LAST HE REACHED THE HIMALAYAS.
CROSSING THIS MIGHTY RANGE...

...HE CAME TO THE FORMIDABLE GANDHAMADANA.
THIS MOUNTAIN, TOO, HE CROSSED....

...AND CAME TO INDRAKILA IN THE DOMAIN OF THE DEVAS. THERE -
HALT!

THIS PEAK IS THE ABODE OF PEACEFUL SEERS IN THE LOFTIEST STATE OF LIFE. THEY KNOW NEITHER HUNGER NOR THIRST.

HAVING ATTAINED THESE REGIONS, YOU TOO HAVE OBTAINED THAT STATE.

SO CAST OFF YOUR ARMOUR AND LAY DOWN YOUR WEAPONS. YOU HAVE NO USE FOR THEM NOW.
IN RESPONSE, ARJUNA'S GRIP ON HIS BOW TIGHTENED.

THE ASCETIC OBSERVED THAT AND SMILED.
I AM INDRA. ASK FOR THE BOON YOU SEEK.

O GREAT ONE, I SEEK YOUR MISSILES WITH THE MYSTERIES OF THEIR USE.

HAVING OBTAINED THIS STATE, YOU DO NOT NEED MY MISSILES.

SEEK DIVINE BLISS OR IMMORTALITY ITSELF INSTEAD, O SON OF KUNTI.

BUT ARJUNA STUCK TO HIS GOAL.
I DESIRE NONE OF THESE. NOR ALL THE PROSPERITY OF THE CELESTIALS. ALL I WANT ARE YOUR MISSILES TO AVENGE OUR INSULT.

THEN ASPIRE FOR A VISION OF SHIVA, THE THREE-EYED DEITY, MY CHILD. WHEN YOU SEE HIM, YOUR DESIRE WILL BE FULFILLED.
AND INDRA VANISHED.

ARJUNA STAYED THERE AND BEGAN THE SEVEREST OF AUSTERITIES TO ACHIEVE THAT END.

MEANWHILE, THE ABSENCE OF ARJUNA IN THOSE DAYS OF DEPRIVATION MADE BHEEMA RESTIVE.
O KING, WHILE WE SIT HERE AND WAIT FOR THE FOURTEENTH YEAR, THE SONS OF DHRITARASHTRA STEADILY GROW IN MIGHT.

YOU HAVE SENT ARJUNA AWAY. WITHOUT HIM I CANNOT SLAY THEM.

THIS IS THE OUTCOME OF YOUR LOVE FOR GAMBLING... YOUR ADDICTION TO DICE!

BESIDES, YOUR PLEDGE TO LIVE ONE YEAR INCOGNITO SEALS OUR FATE. THERE IS NOT A SINGLE CITY THAT DURYODHANA'S SPIES CANNOT REACH.

EVEN IF THEY DO FAIL, HE WILL SUMMON YOU TO DICE, DEFEAT YOU, AND SEND US BACK TO THIS FOREST!

FOR, NOT ONLY ARE YOU UNSKILLED AT THE GAME, BUT YOU BECOME INTOXICATED BY IT AS WELL!

WHILE THE TWO BROTHERS STOOD THUS, SAGE BRIHADASHWA CAME BY.

YUDHISHTHIRA FORMALLY RECEIVED HIM AND THEN BROKE DOWN.
O SAGE, SUMMONED TO A GAME OF DICE, I WHO AM NO EXPERT AT IT, LOST MY ALL, SAW MY DEAR WIFE HUMILIATED, AND NOW LIVE AS AN EXILE IN THIS FOREST.

I AM DEPRIVED OF EVEN MY ONE GREAT CONSOLATION IN THIS MISERY - ARJUNA'S REASSURING PRESENCE.

IS THERE A KING MORE WRETCHED THAN I? HAVE YOU HEARD OF OR MET ONE, O GREAT SAGE?

THE NISHADHA KING, NALA, WAS AS FOND OF DICE AS YOU AND AS UNSKILLED.

LIKE YOU HE WAS DEFEATED BY HIS BROTHER, PUSHKARA, AND HAD TO LIVE IN THE FOREST WITH DAMAYANTI, HIS WIFE. BUT...

...WHILE YOU HAVE YOUR WEAPONS, YOUR CHARIOTS AND COOKS, AND YOUR BROTHERS AND YOUR RETINUE, HE HAD NONE. SO DO NOT LAMENT.
AND THE SAGE NARRATED THE STORY OF NALA AND DAMAYANTI.

NALA PAID HEAVILY FOR THE PLEASURES OF GAMBLING. BUT HE REGAINED HIS LOST GLORY. SO WILL YOU.

AS FOR YOUR CONSTANT FEAR THAT YOU MIGHT AGAIN BE SUMMONED TO PLAY, AND LOSE, I WILL RID YOU OF IT.

I AM AN EXPERT AT DICE. I WILL TEACH YOU ALL THE PLOYS OF THE GAME.
THE SAGE DID SO, AND WENT HIS WAY.

A FEW DAYS LATER, WANDERING ASCETICS BROUGHT NEWS OF ARJUNA.
HE IS NOW DEEP IN MEDITATION ON THE HIGHEST PEAK. HE BEGAN HIS ASCETIC PENANCES NEARLY FOUR MONTHS AGO.

NONE BEFORE HIM HAS ATTEMPTED WHAT HE PRACTISES.
HE NOW LIVES ON AIR ALONE.

THE THOUGHT OF ARJUNA, HIS BELOVED BROTHER, BATTLING WITH THE VERY ELEMENTS FILLED YUDHISHTHIRA'S EYES WITH TEARS.

TOWARDS THE END OF THE FOURTH MONTH, ARJUNA'S PENANCES WERE INDEED SO POTENT THAT THE SEERS IN THE VICINITY APPROACHED SHIVA IN ALARM.
STOP HIM, O SHIVA! THE VERY EARTH SMOULDERS WITH THE FIRE OF HIS AUSTERITY. HE MUST BE STOPPED FOR THE GOOD OF ALL!

DO NOT BE ANXIOUS. I WILL GIVE HIM WHAT HE SEEKS TODAY.
REASSURED, THE SEERS RETURNED TO THEIR ASHRAMAS.

SHIVA, DISGUISED AS A KIRAATA, APPEARED, ALONG WITH UMA HIS CONSORT AND HIS WEIRD ENTOURAGE, AT THE SPOT WHERE ARJUNA STOOD.

JUST THEN -
IT WAS AN ASURA, IN DISGUISE WHO IRKED BY ARJUNA'S GROWING SPIRITUAL POWER...

...HAD COME THERE TO KILL HIM.
SINCE YOU WISH TO KILL ME WHEN I HAVE DONE YOU NO HARM, YOU SHALL DIE.

BOTH ARJUNA AND THE KIRAATA LET FLY THEIR ARROWS.

SURPRISED TO SEE TWO ARROWS...

...ARJUNA TURNED ROUND AND FACED THE ARCHER EVEN AS THE BOAR FELL DEAD.

I WAS THE FIRST TO TAKE AIM. WHY DID YOU KILL THE BOAR? IT IS AGAINST THE RULES OF HUNTING. I SHOULD SLAY YOU FOR IT.

THE KIRAATA SMILED.
WE ARE FOREST-DWELLERS. THIS IS OUR HOME. WHY ARE YOU HERE? YOU LOOK TOO SOFT TO BE IN THESE DANGEROUS FORESTS.

I DID SLAY THE BOAR.
IT WAS MY ARROW THAT SLEW IT.

YOU VAIN, WICKED WRETCH, I WILL SLAY YOU TOO. DEFEND YOURSELF.
AND IN THIS MANNER, SHIVA DELIBERATELY PROVOKED ARJUNA TO A FIGHT.

THE TWO FOUGHT LONG AND HARD. BUT TO ARJUNA'S AMAZEMENT NEITHER ARROWS...

...NOR THE GANDIVA...
...NOR HIS SWORD....

...NOR ROCKS...
...SEEMED TO BE OF ANY USE.

I WILL CRUSH YOU TO DEATH!

BUT IT WAS ARJUNA WHO FELL LIKE ONE DEAD.
WHEN HE CAME TO...

...HE FASHIONED AN IMAGE OF SHIVA FROM CLAY, PLACED A FLOWER GARLAND AROUND IT AND CLOSED HIS EYES IN WORSHIP.

WHEN ARJUNA OPENED HIS EYES -
THE KIRAATA! SHIVA!

O ARJUNA, YOUR COURAGE AND PATIENCE ARE MATCHLESS. YOUR SKILL AND STRENGTH ALMOST EQUAL MINE.

O EXALTED ONE, FORGIVE ME FOR WHAT I HAVE DONE.
I AM PLEASED WITH YOU.

I SHALL GIVE YOU MY FAVOURITE MISSILE, THE PASHUPATA, WHICH WHEN DISPATCHED WITH MANTRAS PRODUCES THOUSANDS OF DARTS, MACES AND POISONOUS SERPENTINE ARROWS.

SHIVA GAVE ARJUNA THE MISSILE AND TOLD HIM THE SECRETS OF ITS USE.
NOW GO TO SWARGA!
WITH THAT COMMAND...

...SHIVA ASCENDED TO THE REGIONS ABOVE.

AS ARJUNA SAT MARVELLING OVER ALL THAT HAD JUST PASSED...

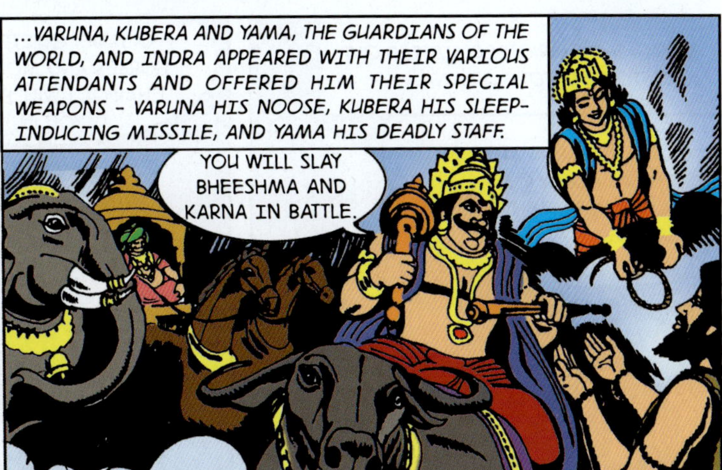
...VARUNA, KUBERA AND YAMA, THE GUARDIANS OF THE WORLD, AND INDRA APPEARED WITH THEIR VARIOUS ATTENDANTS AND OFFERED HIM THEIR SPECIAL WEAPONS - VARUNA HIS NOOSE, KUBERA HIS SLEEP-INDUCING MISSILE, AND YAMA HIS DEADLY STAFF.
YOU WILL SLAY BHEESHMA AND KARNA IN BATTLE.

MATALI MY CHARIOTEER SHALL COME DOWN AND TAKE YOU TO SWARGA. THERE WILL I GRANT YOU ALL MY WEAPONS.

INDRA AND THE LOKAPAALAS THEN BLESSED ARJUNA...
...AND RETURNED TO THEIR VARIOUS REALMS...

...WHILE HE AWAITED THE GREAT CELESTIAL CHARIOT ON THAT FORMIDIBLE MOUNTAIN PEAK.

DISPELLING ALL DARKNESS, AS IT BLAZED THROUGH THE SKIES, THE SPHERICAL CHARIOT ZOOMED DOWN TOWARDS HIM.

MATALI, THE CHARIOTEER, STEPPED OUT AND STOOD BEFORE ARJUNA.
O SON OF KUNTI, AT YOUR FATHER'S COMMAND ASCEND WITH ME TO HIS REALMS.

O SAGE, QUIETEN THE HORSES AND MOUNT THE CHARIOT. I WILL FOLLOW YOU IN.
WHILE MATALI STEADIED THE STOMPING STEEDS AND MOUNTED THE CHARIOT....

...ARJUNA BOWED IN GRATITUDE TO THE MOUNTAIN.
FAREWELL, O KING OF MOUNTAINS WHO CONTAINS SEERS AND SHRINES. I HAVE HAPPILY EATEN THE FRUITS OF YOUR TREES, DRUNK THE WATER OF YOUR SPRINGS AND RESTED ON YOUR LAP. TODAY I MOVE ON.

THEN HE STEPPED INTO THE CHARIOT....

...WHICH SOARED INTO THE SKY UNDER MATALI'S EXPERT CONTROL.

AS THEY COURSED THROUGH SWARGALOKA, ARJUNA SAW THOUSANDS OF HUGE CHARIOTS LIKE THEIR OWN, EACH RADIATING ITS OWN LIGHT.

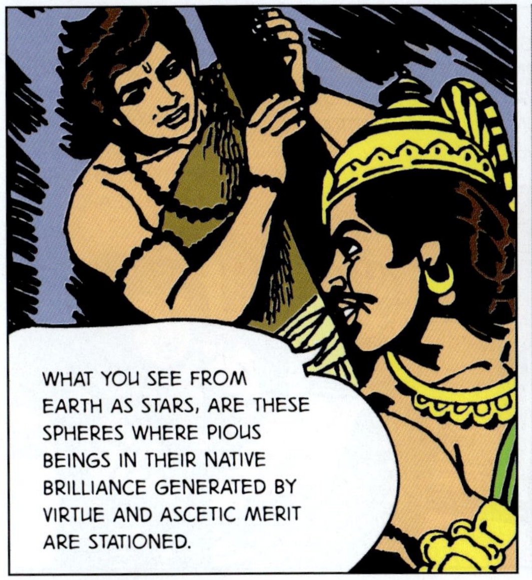
WHAT YOU SEE FROM EARTH AS STARS, ARE THESE SPHERES WHERE PIOUS BEINGS IN THEIR NATIVE BRILLIANCE GENERATED BY VIRTUE AND ASCETIC MERIT ARE STATIONED.

AND THEN THEY SAW AIRAVATA AT THE GATES OF AMARAVATI, INDRA'S CITY.

AS THEY ENTERED THE CITY -
YOUR FATHER COMMANDED ME TO BRING YOU TO HIM THROUGH THE STARRY WAY.

SO THEY COURSED THROUGH THAT ROUTE LIT BY REALIZED BEINGS...

...AND ENTERED INDRA'S COURT.
THE KING OF THE DEVAS ROSE AND LED ARJUNA TO HIS OWN SACRED SEAT.

THERE HE SEATED HIS SON BESIDE HIM WHILE CONCHES BLEW, APSARAS DANCED FOR JOY...
...AND ATTENDANTS WASHED HIS FEET.

THEN INDRA LED ARJUNA INTO HIS PALACE...

...AND GAVE HIM HIS FAVOURITE WEAPON, THE THUNDERBOLT, AND VARIOUS BEAMS OF LIGHTNING WITH THE MANTRAS FOR THEIR USE.
HOW ANXIOUSLY MY BROTHERS MUST BE WAITING FOR THESE WEAPONS!

LATER WHEN SAGE LOMASHA CAME TO MEET INDRA -
O SAGE, GO TO EARTH AND SEEK OUT YUDHISHTHIRA IN THE KAMYAKA FOREST.

TELL HIM THAT ARJUNA IS SAFE AND WILL RETURN BEFORE LONG WITH ALL THE WEAPONS HE CAME HERE FOR.

HE HIMSELF SHOULD VISIT ALL THE TIRTHAS AND SHRINES.
SO BE IT.
O SAGE, LET HIM BE ACCOMPANIED BY YOU.
AND LOMASHA LEFT FOR EARTH.

MEANWHILE AT THE KAMYAKA FOREST -
THIS FOREST IS VOID WITH ARJUNA'S ABSENCE. I FIND IT DESOLATE, UNBEARABLE.

WITHOUT HIM, EVERY SPOT IS DARK AND DISMAL. I, TOO, FIND NO PEACE OF MIND HERE.
I DO NOT WISH TO LIVE HERE ANY LONGER.

AT NIGHT, WHEN I SEE HIS EMPTY BED OF GRASS IN OUR ASHRAMA, I LONG TO GO FAR, FAR AWAY FROM HERE.

O DHOUMYA, WITHOUT ARJUNA NO ONE HAS ANY PEACE OF MIND IN THIS FOREST. WE SHALL MOVE ON.

CAN YOU TELL US OF SOME OTHER FOREST WHICH IS SACRED, ABOUNDS IN FOOD, AND IS INHABITED BY SEERS?
AS DHOUMYA BEGAN LISTING SUCH SACRED SPOTS AND THEIR MERITS...

...LOMASHA CAME THERE.
O SON OF KUNTI, I COME TO YOU FROM THE REALMS OF INDRA, AT HIS BEHEST. I SAW YOUR BROTHER THERE, SHARING THE SEAT OF THE LORD OF THE DEVAS.

LOMASHA THEN TOLD THEM IN GREAT DETAIL ABOUT ARJUNA'S DEEDS AND ACHIEVEMENTS.
HE WILL RETURN SOON WITH THE CELESTIAL WEAPONS...

MEANWHILE ARJUNA WOULD LIKE YOU TO VISIT ALL THE TIRTHAS ESCORTED BY ME.

THE PANDAVAS SET OUT ON THE PILGRIMAGE. ON THE WAY-
O LOMASHA, WHY DO WE WHO ALWAYS ADHERE TO THE PATH OF VIRTUE SUFFER UNTOLD MISERIES WHILE THE WICKED PROSPER?

THEY ONLY APPEAR TO BE PROSPERING, O PANDAVA. THAT VERY ILL-GOTTEN WEALTH AND PROSPERITY SPELLS THEIR DOOM.

AND YOU WHO TREAD THE HARD PATH OF VIRTUE WILL GAIN RENOWN AND PROSPERITY.

WHEN THEY REACHED THE EAST COAST, YUDHISHTHIRA WENT TO THE SUMMIT OF THE MAHENDRA MOUNTAIN WHERE PARASHURAMA WAS ENGAGED IN THE MOST AUSTERE OF PENANCES.

FROM THERE THEY TURNED THEIR CHARIOTS SOUTH TOWARDS THE BANKS OF THE GODAVARI AND DOWN THE SHORES OF THE SOUTHERN OCEAN...

...AND THEN ACROSS TO SHURPARAKHA ON THE WEST COAST.

FROM SHURPARAKHA THEY WENT NORTH TO PRABHASA, WHERE BALARAMA, KRISHNA AND A FEW YADAVA NOBLES CAME TO SEE THEM. THESE VALIANT MEN...

...WEPT TO SEE THEIR ROYAL KINSMEN IN MATTED LOCKS, TRAVEL-WORN AND EMACIATED.
WHEN THEY SEE VIRTUOUS YUDHISHTHIRA SO MISERABLE WHILE VICIOUS DURYODHANA RULES THE EARTH...

...THE IGNORANT MIGHT CONCLUDE THAT A VICIOUS LIFE IS PREFERABLE TO A VIRTUOUS ONE.

AND ONE CANNOT BLAME THEM.

YUDHISHTHIRA, THE SON OF DHARMA, CONSTANT, TRUTHFUL, GENEROUS... YUDHISHTHIRA WHO WOULD GIVE UP A KINGDOM BUT NEVER THE PATH OF VIRTUE WANDERS IN THE FORESTS...

...WHILE DURYODHANA PROSPERS!

HOW CAN THE KURU ELDERS SLEEP IN PEACE AFTER BANISHING THE SONS OF KUNTI! FIE ON THOSE WICKED LEADERS OF THE BHARATAS.

LOOK AT DRAUPADI, A PRINCESS BORN, COMPELLED TO BRAVE THE HARDSHIPS OF LIFE IN A FOREST.

WHY DID THE EARTH NOT SINK FOR SHAME THAT FATEFUL DAY WHEN THE SON OF DHARMA WAS DRIVEN AWAY TO THE FOREST AND DURYODHANA BEGAN TO FLOURISH?

YUYUTSU, ALSO KNOWN AS SATYAKI, PUT UP WITH BALARAMA'S LAMENT FOR A WHILE. THEN -
ENOUGH! THIS IS NOT THE TIME FOR TEARS, BALARAMA! IT IS A TIME FOR ACTION.

WE MUST ACT ACCORDING TO OUR STATUS AND THE CIRCUMSTANCES.

DO NOT LOOK AT YUDHISHTHIRA FOR HIS CONSENT. THOSE WHO HAVE THEIR OWN TO CARE FOR THEM, NEED NOT TROUBLE TO DO ANYTHING THEMSELVES.

WHY SHOULD THE SONS OF KUNTI SUFFER SUCH MISERY WHEN THEY HAVE YOU AND KRISHNA AND ME?

WITH OUR COMBINED ARMIES WE SHOULD ATTACK AND SLAY THE SONS OF DHRITARASHTRA IN BATTLE.

AND ABHIMANYU SHOULD RULE THE EARTH WHILE YUDHISHTHIRA HONOURS HIS PLEDGE.

AND WHEN YUDHISHTHIRA IS READY TO RULE THE EARTH, THERE WILL BE NO DURYODHANA OR SHAKUNI OR KARNA TO CONTEND WITH.
TRUE, SATYAKI, BUT...

...YUDHISHTHIRA WILL NEVER STRAY FROM THE CODE OF KINGS. HE WILL NEVER ACCEPT A SOVEREIGNTY NOT WON BY HIS VALOUR. NOR WILL HIS BROTHERS. NOR WILL DRAUPADI.

O SATYAKI, KRISHNA AND I KNOW EACH OTHER WELL. LET HIM DECIDE WHEN WE SHOULD ACT. THEN TOGETHER WE WILL DEFEAT DURYODHANA.

YOU TOO, MY FRIENDS, MUST NEVER STRAY FROM THE PATH OF VIRTUE.

GO BACK TODAY. WE SHALL MEET AGAIN IN JOY.

THE YADAVAS RETURNED HOME...
...AND THE PANDAVAS MOVED ON.

THEY CONTINUED NORTHWARDS TILL THEY CAME TO THE NARMADA WHERE LOMASHA TOLD THEM ABOUT SAGE CHYAVANA...

...ABOUT KING USHINARA...

...AND ABOUT ASHTAVAKRA.

AND THEY JOURNEYED ON TILL THEY CAME TO THE FOOT OF THE MOUNTAINS IN THE DOMAIN OF KUBERA, THE KING OF THE YAKSHAS.
WE WILL NOW ASCEND THE PEAKS OF SHVETA, KAILASA AND MANDARA.

THOSE REGIONS, PROTECTED BY TERRIBLE RAKSHASAS AND YAKSHAS HAVE BECOME INACCESSIBLE.

MAY ALL THE CELESTIALS - VARUNA, YAMA, THE MARUTS, MOTHER GANGA - ALL PROTECT YOU, IN YOUR SOJOURN IN THOSE REGIONS. O RULER OF THE EARTH, BE CAREFUL.

THE SAGE'S WARNING TROUBLED YUDHISHTHIRA -
THE JOURNEY AHEAD IS FRAUGHT WITH DANGER, BHEEMA...

PERHAPS YOU SHOULD TAKE DRAUPADI TO A PLACE OF SAFETY. TAKE SAHADEVA AND DHOUMYA WITH YOU AND GO IN OUR CHARIOTS.

NAKULA AND I WILL PROCEED WITH LOMASHA ON FOOT.

BUT BHEEMA VEHEMENTLY TURNED DOWN THE PLAN–
I WILL NEVER LEAVE YOU HERE ALONE IN THESE DANGEROUS, RUGGED REGIONS. WE WILL ALL GO TOGETHER.

IF WE CANNOT GO IN OUR CHARIOTS, I WILL CARRY DRAUPADI.

O KING, DO NOT WORRY ABOUT ME. I CAN WALK.

THEY LEFT THEIR CHARIOTS, COOKS AND SERVANTS BEHIND WITH THE CHIEF OF THE PULINDAS, A MOUNTAIN TRIBE, AND PROCEEDED ON FOOT.
O BHEEMA, I YEARN FOR A SIGHT OF ARJUNA.

I HAVE WANDERED THESE FIVE LONG YEARS HOPING THAT WE WOULD SEE HIM AT ONE OF THE SACRED SPOTS.

WITH THIS DESIRE WE HAVE SURMOUNTED ALL THE OBSTACLES WE HAVE ENCOUNTERED SO FAR. HOPEFULLY WE WILL BE RE-UNITED ON GANDHAMADNA MOUNTAIN.

AFTER A LONG TREK THROUGH RUGGED, CRAGGY TERRAIN...

...THEY WERE ALMOST THERE, WHEN A VIOLENT STORM BROKE OUT. BLINDED BY CLOUDS OF DUST AND REELING UNDER A GUSTY GALE...

...THEY DROPPED DOWN ON ALL FOURS AND BEGAN FEELING THEIR WAY ABOUT FOR SHELTER.

BHEEMA AND DRAUPADI CREPT UNDER A TREE.

SO DID LOMASHA AND NAKULA, WHILE SAHADEVA SLID UNDER A ROCK.

YUDHISHTHIRA AND DHAUMYA ENTERED A DENSE WOOD.

THEN CAME THE RAIN THUNDERING AGAINST THE MOUNTAIN, IN TORRENTS, SWELLING, SURGING AND SWEEPING PAST ALL THINGS IN ITS PATH.

THE STORM, HOWEVER, SOON ABATED. THE WATER SUBSIDED AND ALL WAS QUIET.

HEAVING SIGHS OF RELIEF...

...THE PANDAVAS TRUDGED ON.

BUT BARELY HAD THEY COVERED A SHORT DISTANCE WHEN –
O KING, DRAUPADI HAS FALLEN, UNCONSCIOUS.

YUDHISHTHIRA FELT WRETCHED.
HER FATHER WAS CONFIDENT THAT WITH THE SONS OF PANDU FOR HUSBANDS SHE WOULD KNOW ONLY HAPPINESS.

SEE WHAT MY ADDICTION TO DICE HAS DONE! FORLORN IN THE FORESTS SHE LIES HERE ON THE COARSE GROUND, A VICTIM OF MY WRETCHED GAMBLING.
WHILE YUDHISHTHIRA BLAMED HIMSELF FOR THEIR MISERY...

...DRAUPADI SLOWLY OPENED HER EYES.

HOW WILL SHE CROSS THE MANY MOUNTAINS ON OUR ROUTE?

AND LO! GHATOTKACHA, BHEEMA'S SON BORN OF RAKSHASI HIDIMBAA, STOOD BEFORE THEM.
I AM HERE TO DO YOUR BIDDING. COMMAND ME.

BHEEMA EMBRACED HIM.
BHEEMA, LET THIS POWERFUL RAKSHASA CHIEF CARRY DRAUPADI SO SHE CAN GO WITH ME TO GANDHAMADANA.

MY HEROIC RAKSHASA HORDES WILL CARRY ALL OF YOU TO GANDHAMADANA.

WHILE THE REST FLEW ON THE SHOULDERS OF THE RAKSHASAS...

...LOMASHA COURSED THROUGH THE SKIES ON HIS OWN SPIRITUAL ENERGY.
FLYING OVER THE LONG, TEDIOUS, RUGGED, TERRESTRIAL ROUTE TO GANDHAMADANA IN NO TIME...

...THE GROUP NEARED BADARI, THE SPRAWLING BANYAN TREE IN THE ASHRAMA OF THE IMMORTAL SAGES OF KAILASA.

LIFE IN THAT REGION KNEW NEITHER THE VAGARIES OF THE ELEMENTS NOR THE MISERIES BORN OF THAT KNOWLEDGE.

THE PANDAVAS SPENT SIX GLORIOUS DAYS THERE ABSORBING ITS SANCTITY. ON THE MORNING OF THE SEVENTH DAY...

...A STRONG WIND FROM THE NORTH-EAST WAFTED IN A CELESTIAL LOTUS OF GOLDEN HUE.
A SAUGANDHIKA FLOWER!

DRAUPADI PICKED UP THE FLOWER.
WHAT HEAVENLY FRAGRANCE! O BHEEMA, FOR MY SAKE WON'T YOU GO, BRING ME HUNDREDS OF THESE TO TAKE BACK TO KAMYAKA!

THIS ONE I WILL GIVE TO YUDHISHTHIRA. GO BHEEMA.
WHILE DRAUPADI RAN OFF WITH IT TOWARDS YUDHISHTIRA...

...BHEEMA SCANNED THE DIRECTION FROM WHICH THE FABULOUS FLOWER HAD COME AND SET OUT AT ONCE TO GRATIFY HIS BELOVED.

IT WAS ON THIS ERRAND OF LOVE THAT THE RENOWNED ENCOUNTER BETWEEN BHEEMA AND HANUMAN, WHOM HE TOOK TO BE AN ORDINARY OLD MONKEY, OCCURRED.

AFTER TEASING HIS STEP-BROTHER FOR A WHILE, HANUMAN, THE SON OF VAYU REVEALED HIS IDENTITY. THEN -
THIS IS THE PATH TO HEAVEN. NO MORTAL MAY PASS THIS WAY.

THE SAUGANDHIKA FOREST THAT YOU SEEK LIES IN THAT DIRECTION. YOU WILL FIND THE FLOWERS IN A LAKE IN THE GARDENS OF KUBERA GUARDED BY RAKSHASAS AND YAKSHAS.

TREAD CAUTIOUSLY AND DO NOT TELL ANYONE THAT I LIVE HERE. BUT DO REMEMBER ME IN YOUR TALK.
AS HANUMAN EMBRACED HIM....

...BHEEMA FELT A NEW STRENGTH COURSE THROUGH HIS LIMBS.
OUT OF BROTHERLY LOVE FOR YOU, I SHALL PERCH ON ARJUNA'S FLAG STAFF WHEN YOU FIGHT THE KAURAVAS...

...ADD MY BLOOD-CURDLING ROARS TO YOURS AND CHILL THE VERY HEARTS OF YOUR FOES. YOU WILL THEN DEFEAT THEM WITH EASE.
AND HANUMAN VANISHED.

BHEEMA TOOK THE PATH HE WAS TOLD.
FOR MY SAKE BRING ME HUNDREDS OF THEM.
SPURRED ON BY DRAUPADI'S DESIRE...

...HE REACHED THE FOREST AT NOON. AND THERE HE SAW THEM, BY THE HUNDREDS, GLISTENING IN THE SUN.

HE SAW HIMSELF GIVING HIS EXILE-WORN BELOVED THE CELESTIAL FLOWERS.

OBLIVIOUS OF THE CURIOUS EYES WATCHING HIS EVERY MOVE, BHEEMA FIRST QUENCHED HIS THIRST...

...AND THEN WADED FURTHER IN TO GATHER THE LOTUSES WHEN -
HALT THERE! GO NO FURTHER!

CLAD AS AN ASCETIC BUT ARMED WITH WEAPONS! WHO ARE YOU?
WHAT BRINGS YOU HERE?

WHEN BHEEMA TOLD THEM WHO HE WAS AND WHY HE WAS THERE -
O PANDAVA BHEEMA, THIS IS KUBERA'S FAVOURITE PLAYGROUND.

NOT EVEN THE CELESTIALS DARE DRINK OF THIS LAKE OR SPORT HERE WITHOUT HIS PERMISSION.

AND YOU INTEND TO CARRY AWAY THE LOTUSES!
GO, SEEK HIS PERMISSION, FIRST.

UNDAUNTED, BHEEMA STOOD WHERE HE WAS.
O RAKSHASAS, I DO NOT SEE HIM HERE. EVEN IF I DID, I WOULD NOT BEG HIM FOR THE FLOWERS.

I BELONG TO THE ORDER OF KINGS AND THESE LOTUSES WERE NOT CREATED IN KUBERA'S ABODE BUT SPRANG FROM THE BREAST OF THE MOUNTAIN.

SO THEY BELONG TO ALL, TO ME AS MUCH AS TO KUBERA! WHERE THEN DOES THE QUESTION OF SEEKING HIS PERMISSION ARISE?

AND BHEEMA BEGAN TO WADE FARTHER OUT INTO THE LAKE.
STOP!
DESIST!

SEIZE HIM!
BIND HIM!

HACK HIM DOWN!
EAT HIM UP!

WHEN OVER A HUNDRED OF THEM WERE SLAIN...

...THE RAKSHASAS AND THE YAKSHAS FLED...

...TO KUBERA WITH THEIR TALE. THAT LORD OF WEALTH, JUST SMILED.
LET HIM TAKE AS MANY LOTUSES AS HE WANTS FOR HIS BELOVED.
THE GUARDS TOOK HIS LEAVE AND RETURNED TO THEIR POSTS.

MEANWHILE, AS BHEEMA GATHERED THE FLOWERS, THE SUN PALED...

...AND METEORS CAME HURTLING DOWN,...

...WHILE VIOLENT WINDS LIFTED PEBBLES AND GRAVEL FROM THE GROUND AND ROCKETED THEM TO THE SKIES. BUT BHEEMA DID NOT FLINCH.

YUDHISHTHIRA, HOWEVER, WAS ALARMED.
SUCH OMENS PORTEND A FIERCE BATTLE OR DISASTER OF SOME SORT!

WHERE IS BHEEMA? IS HE OUT TO ACHIEVE SOME GREAT FEAT? HAS HE ALREADY ACHIEVED IT?

I WANTED MORE LOTUSES OF THE KIND I GAVE YOU. PERHAPS HE HAS GONE TO THE NORTH-EAST TO BRING THEM FOR ME.

WE MUST FIND HIM AT ONCE.

GHATOTKACHA, YOU CARRY DRAUPADI. LET THE RAKSHASAS CARRY THE REST OF US.

BHEEMA HAS EVIDENTLY ENTERED THE FORBIDDEN SAUGANDHIKA FOREST, AND YOU KNOW WHERE IT IS TO BE FOUND.

SOON -

WHEN YUDHISHTHIRA SAW THE MUTILATED CORPSES -
OH, BHEEMA! WHAT HAVE YOU DONE?

IF YOU WISH ME WELL, YOU MUST NEVER AGAIN ACT SO RASHLY! NEVER AGAIN OFFEND THE CELESTIALS.

THE PANDAVAS STAYED ON FOR A WHILE IN THAT REGION ON THE GANDHMADANA SLOPES, TAKING IN ITS SACRED SPLENDOUR.

THEN ONE DAY -
WE HAVE SEEN MANY REMOTE TIRTHAS INCLUDING THE ASHRAMA AT BADARI.

WE HAVE SEEN THE CELESTIAL LAKE WHERE MORTALS FEAR TO TREAD.

WE SHALL NOW TAKE THAT PATH THERE AND ENTER KUBERA'S ABODE.
THE MOMENT YUDHISHTHIRA SAID THAT.

...A VOICE FLASHED A WARNING FROM THE REALMS ABOVE.
O PANDAVA, MORTALS MAY NOT USE THAT PATH. GO BACK TO BADARI!

FROM THERE PROCEED TO VRISHAPARVA'S ASHRAMA AND ON TO THAT OF ARSHTISHENA. AND FROM THERE, YOU SHALL SEE KUBERA'S ABODE.

YUDHISHTHIRA AND THE REST OBEDIENTLY FLEW BACK...

...TO BADARI.

PERMIT ME TO GO AWAY NOW. I SHALL BE WITH YOU WHEN NEEDED.
AND GHATOTKACHA WITH HIS HORDES WENT HIS WAY.

WHILE AT BADARI, BHEEMA SLEW JATASURA, A RAKSHASA WHO WINNING YUDHISHTHIRA'S CONFIDENCE IN THE GUISE OF A BRAHMANA, TRIED TO STEAL THEIR WEAPONS AND ABDUCT DRAUPADI.

AND LATER, WHILE THEY WERE AT ARSHTISHENA'S ASHRAMA, HE SLEW RAKSHASA MANIMAT, A FRIEND OF KUBERA'S...

...AND THEREBY BROUGHT THAT DEITY BEFORE THEM. TO THEIR SURPRISE, KUBERA WAS PLEASED.
MAY YOU ANIHILATE YOUR FOES AND GRATIFY YOUR FRIENDS.
BY SLAYING MANIMAT, BHEEMA HAD UNWITTINGLY ABSOLVED KUBERA OF A CRIME!

ALL IS WELL WITH ARJUNA. HE WILL SOON JOIN YOU HERE.

MEANWHILE MY ATTENDANTS SHALL WAIT UPON YOU TO FULFIL ALL YOUR WISHES.

THE PANDAVAS HOWEVER HAD BUT ONE PRESSING WISH - TO SEE ARJUNA.

AND THEN ONE DAY, A FIERY OBJECT SUDDENLY APPEARED IN THE SKY AND CAME ZOOMING DOWN TOWARDS THEM.

IT WAS INDRA'S CHARIOT BRINGING THE HERO HOME.

MATALI, INDRA'S CHARIOTEER, GREETED THE OTHER PANDAVAS, SPOKE AFFECTIONATELY TO THEM...

...ASCENDED THE CHARIOT AND SOARED UP INTO THE SKY.

ARJUNA REMOVED THE CROWN AND ORNAMENTS INDRA HAD GIVEN HIM...

...AND HANDED THEM TO DRAUPADI.

AND THAT NIGHT, LYING WITH NAKULA AND SAHADEVA ON EITHER SIDE OF HIM, ARJUNA SPOKE OF HIS ADVENTURES.
...AND THERE I SAW A BRAHMANA. HE TRIED TO DISSUADE ME. BUT...

AND HE TOLD THEM EVERYTHING THAT HAD HAPPENED IN THE FIVE YEARS HE WAS WITH INDRA.
EVEN AS I WORKED TOWARDS MY REAL GOAL, THAT OF MASTERING THE SCIENCE OF CELESTIAL WEAPONRY...

...I DID MASTER THE ARTS OF DANCE AND MUSIC AS INDRA WISHED.

WHEN I HAD LEARNT ALL THAT CHITRASENA - THE GANDHARVA WHO WAS MY MENTOR AND FRIEND - COULD TEACH ME...

...INDRA PLACED HIS HANDS ON MY HEAD AND SAID:
YOU HAVE ACQUIRED FIFTEEN CELESTIAL WEAPONS WITH THE FIVE MODES OF USING THEM.

LEAVE ALONE MEN WITH THEIR IMPERFECTIONS, EVEN THE CELESTIALS CANNOT VANQUISH YOU NOW, ARJUNA!

THE TIME HAS COME TO PAY YOUR PRECEPTOR'S DUES.

THE FEE INDRA DEMANDED WAS THE ANNIHILATION OF THE NIVAATAKAVACHAS, THE INVINCIBLE ASURA FOES OF THE DEVAS.

THEY ARE THIRTY THOUSAND IN NUMBER AND LIVE IN THE OCEAN.

HE GAVE ME HIS CHARIOT WITH MATALI TO STEER IT, ORNAMENTS LIKE HIS OWN AND THIS IMPENETRABLE COAT OF MAIL. THEN HE HIMSELF FASTENED A DURABLE STRING TO MY GANDIVA.

AND THUS I SET OUT. WHEN WE NEARED THE OCEAN, WE SAW THEIR CITY IN THE DISTANCE.

MATALI CHARGED...

...BUT THE NIVAATAKAVACHAS SLAMMED SHUT THE GATES.

I RAISED MY CELESTIAL CONCH AND BLEW IT LOUD AND HARD.

THE ASURAS ACCEPTED THE CHALLENGE AND CAME OUT IN THEIR THOUSANDS WITH JAVELINS, SPEARS, MACES, CLUBS, AXES AND SWORDS.

AFTER A DREADFUL BATTLE IN WHICH I SLEW HUNDREDS AND THOUSANDS OF THEM...

...WE ENTERED THE CITY WHICH WAS EVEN MORE SPLENDID THAN INDRA'S AMARAVATI, AND CAPTURED IT FOR HIM.

THE CITY, MATALI SAID, HAD BELONGED TO INDRA, BUT EMPOWERED BY A BOON FROM BRAHMA, THE NIVAATAKAVACHAS HAD DRIVEN AWAY THE DEVAS AND OCCUPIED IT.

ON OUR WAY BACK TO INDRALOK THROUGH THE SKIES WE PASSED A SHIMMERING AERIAL CITY WHICH MOVED BY WILL ALONE.

"WHILE I MARVELLED AT THE SIGHT MATALI EXPLAINED."
THAT IS HIRANYAPURA, THE CITY BUILT BY BRAHMA HIMSELF FOR THE KAALAKEYAS AND THE PAULOMAS.

PULOMAA AND KAALAKAA, TWO ASURA WOMEN OF YORE, HAD PERFORMED AUSTERITIES FOR THOUSANDS OF CELESTIAL YEARS AND OBTAINED IT AS A BOON FROM HIM.

AND THEN HE ORDERED ME TO ATTACK THE CITY.
DESTROY IT, ARJUNA. USE THE THUNDERBOLT MISSILE.

AS WE ATTACKED...

THOSE ASURAS RESORTED TO THE SORCEROUS AND THE SPECTRAL, SPECIAL TO THEM.

THEN AT TIMES THEY PLUNGED DOWN TO THE OCEAN BED AND INTO THE EARTH...

...AT TIMES INTO THE SKIES, SOMETIMES MOVING STRAIGHT...

...SOMETIMES VEERING IN HUGE CURVES.

AT LAST, MEDITATING ON SHIVA, I RAISED MY GANDIVA, PICKED UP THE RUDRA MISSILE...

...SHOT DOWN THE CITY.

...AND VANQUISHED THOSE ENEMIES OF INDRA. MATALI WAS PLEASED.
YOU HAVE ACHIEVED IN BATTLE WHAT EVEN INDRA COULD NOT! O ARJUNA, PRAISE BE TO YOU.

HAVING SLAIN THE MIGHTY NIVAATAKAVACHAS AND DESTROYED HIRANYAPURA, WE RETURNED TO INDRA...

...WHO AFTER LISTENING TO MATALI'S DETAILED ACCOUNT OF BOTH ENCOUNTERS, CRIED OUT:
WELL DONE, WELL DONE!!!

YOU HAVE SURPASSED THE CELESTIALS IN BATTLE! WITH YOUR MIGHT WILL YUDHISHTHIRA CONQUER THE WORLD AND RULE IT, ARJUNA.

AND THEN HE SAID TO ME:
ALL THE CELESTIAL WEAPONS ARE WITH YOU. NO CREATED BEING SHALL BY ANY MEANS BE CAPABLE OF CONQUERING YOU.

THE MIGHT OF BHEESHMA, DRONA, KRIPA, KARNA, SHAKUNI AND ALL THE OTHER KINGS TOGETHER WILL NOT ADD UP TO EVEN A SIXTEENTH PART OF YOURS, ARJUNA.

HE THEN GAVE ME BEAUTIFUL GARMENTS AND PLACED THE CROWN ON MY HEAD.
YOU MAY NOW GO TO YOUR BROTHERS.

THUS AM I HERE, O YUDHISHTHIRA, AFTER PASSING FIVE LONG YEARS, NEVER FORGETTING THE SHAME OF THAT GAMBLING.

TOMORROW I WILL SHOW YOU THE CELESTIAL WEAPONS WITH WHICH I KILLED THE NIVAATAKAVACHAS.

AND WITH THAT PROMISE ARJUNA FELL ASLEEP SURROUNDED BY HIS BROTHERS.

ON THE MORROW, WHEN ARJUNA SENT THE FIRST MISSILE OUT INTO THE SKIES FOR HIS BROTHERS TO SEE...

...THE EARTH QUAKED, THE WIND STOPPED AND THE OCEANS FROZE, THE SUN TURNED SOMBRE AND FIRES DIED OUT.

JUST THEN-
ARJUNA! FORBEAR! WITHDRAW THAT MISSILE BEFORE IT ANNIHILATES THE THREE WORLDS!
IT WAS THE CELESTIAL SAGE, NARADA.

INDISCRIMINATE USE OF THESE POTENT MISSILES WILL LEAD TO A HOLOCAUST!

NEVER SHOW SUCH IMPRUDENCE AGAIN, ARJUNA!

YOUR BROTHERS SHALL SEE THE MISSILES AT WORK WHEN YOU AIM THEM AT HUMAN FOES IN BATTLE.
NARADA FADED OUT AND...

...NATURE TO THE RELIEF OF ALL BEINGS, CRAWLED BACK TO NORMALCY.

BASKING IN KUBERA'S HOSPITALITY AND ARJUNA'S ROUSING PRESENCE, THE PANDAVAS AND DRAUPADI HARDLY NOTICED THAT FOUR FULL YEARS HAD SPED BY. SO IDYLLIC WAS THAT PERIOD THAT THEY SEEMED TO BE ENJOYING A BOON RATHER THAN SUFFERING AN EXILE!

BHEEMA WAS THE FIRST TO REALIZE THE EFFECTS OF SUCH SURROUNDINGS. ONE DAY-
O KING, THOUGH DURYODHANA SOUGHT TO DEPRIVE US OF ALL HAPPINESS, WE HAVE BEEN MORE THAN HAPPY HERE.

BUT IN THIS LUXURY HERE WE WILL FORGET ALL THAT WE HAVE SUFFERED.

I'M NOT SAYING WE SHOULD ATTACK AND SLAY DURYODHANA NOW. WE HAVE TO HONOUR YOUR PLEDGE...

BELIEVING US TO BE IN SOME FOREST NEAR HASTINAPURA, OUR FOES WILL NEVER SEEK US HERE. WE COULD THUS PASS EVEN THE THIRTEENTH YEAR OF DISGUISE HERE.

BUT WHAT GLORY IS THERE IN HIDING FROM FOES? IT WOULD BE MORE CREDITABLE TO FACE THEM BRAVELY!

SO BESTIR YOURSELF, O KING! PLAN THE STRATEGY TO PUNISH AND DESTROY YOUR FOES AND WIN ACCLAIM FOR YOURSELF!
THE POINT WENT HOME. YUDHISHTHIRA AT ONCE DECIDED TO MOVE ON.

SO THE ELEVENTH YEAR OF THEIR EXILE SAW THE PANDAVAS IN THE HIMALAYAS, NEAR THE YAMUNA, ON THEIR WAY BACK TO DWAITAVANA.

THERE AS BHEEMA WENT HUNTING FOR GAME IN THE FOREST ONE DAY -
A GIANT SERPENT!

AS HE NEARED THE SERPENT, IT COILED ITSELF AROUND HIM — TIGHTER AND TIGHTER SQUEEZING AWAY HIS VERY MIGHT.

BHEEMA STRUGGLED TO FREE HIMSELF BUT SOON GAVE UP.
I AM BHEEMA, THE PANDAVA WITH THE STRENGTH OF TEN THOUSAND ELEPHANTS. HOW IS IT THAT YOU HAVE OVERPOWERED ME?

DO YOU POSSESS SOME ESOTERIC KNOWLEDGE? ARE YOU EMPOWERED BY A BOON?

WHO ARE YOU? WHAT WOULD YOU DO WITH ME?
I AM VERY HUNGRY. I PLAN TO EAT YOU.

I WAS THE ROYAL SAGE NAHUSHA. PROSPERITY MADE ME ARROGANT AND SO I WAS REDUCED TO THIS STATE BY THE CURSE OF A MAHARISHI. WHEN, AS I HURTLED EARTHWARDS, I BEGGED TO BE FREED.

"...I WAS TOLD:
IF SOME ONE WHO HAS REALIZED THE RELATION BETWEEN ATMAN AND BRAHMAN IS ABLE TO ANSWER YOUR QUESTIONS YOU WILL BE FREED.

"AND HE ADDED:
TILL THEN, EVEN BEINGS STRONGER THAN YOU IF SEIZED BY YOU WILL LOSE ALL THEIR STRENGTH.

IT IS MY GOOD LUCK THAT YOU ARE FATED TO BE MY FOOD TODAY.

NEITHER AM I ANGRY, NOR DO I BLAME MYSELF. FOR MAN IS NOT ALWAYS THE MASTER OF HIS HAPPINESS OR SORROW. MAN HAS TO SUBMIT TO DESTINY.

I HAVE BEEN DRAINED OF MY MIGHT BY YOU FOR NO EVIDENT REASON BUT IT IS DESTINY'S WILL SO I AM NOT DISTRESSED FOR MYSELF. BUT...

...HEARING OF MY DEATH, MY BROTHERS WILL GIVE UP ALL EFFORTS TO REGAIN THEIR KINGDOM.

IT WAS I WHO, EAGER FOR VICTORY, INCITED THOSE VIRTUOUS ONES TO...

O BROTHER! THIS SERPENT IS NAHUSHA, THE ROYAL SAGE, LIVING OUT A CURSE. HE PLANS TO EAT ME.
LOOKING FOR BHEEMA YUDHISHTHIRA HAD REACHED THE SPOT.

O SERPENT, RELEASE MY MIGHTY BROTHER.
RELEASE THIS ROYAL REPAST THAT FATE HAS BROUGHT MY WAY? NEVER!

YUDHISHTHIRA, HOWEVER PERSISTED.
WE WILL GIVE YOU SOME OTHER FOOD TO SATE YOUR HUNGER.
I DO NOT WANT ANY OTHER FOOD. BUT...

...IF YOU CAN ANSWER THE QUESTIONS I ASK YOU, I WILL LET HIM GO.
ASK, O SERPENT. I WILL ANSWER THEM IF I CAN.

THE SERPENT POSED HIS FIRST QUESTION.
O KING, WHOM WOULD YOU CALL A BRAHMANA?
ONE WHO IS TRUTHFUL, GENEROUS, MERCIFUL, BENEVOLENT, AND AN ASCETIC.

BUT THESE QUALITIES ARE OFTEN FOUND IN SHUDRAS, TOO.
ONE IN WHOM THEY ARE FOUND IS NO SHUDRA.

HE IS A BRAHMANA. AND THE BRAHMANA WHO LACKS THEM IS A SHUDRA!

THE SERPENT WAS NOT SATISFIED.
IF A BRAHMANA IN WHOM THESE QUALITIES ARE ABSENT IS NO BRAHMANA, THEN THE DISTINCTION OF CASTES SERVES NO PURPOSE.

SO THE WISE AVER. THAT IS WHY, TODAY, CHARACTER AND NOT CASTE DETERMINES ONE'S RANK IN THE FOUR SOCIAL ORDERS.

THEREFORE DO I CALL HIM A BRAHMANA WHO OBSERVES THE PRINCIPLES OF GOOD CONDUCT.
CONTENT WITH THIS ANSWER...

...THE SERPENT SHOT HIS SECOND QUESTION.
WHAT IS IT THAT OUGHT TO BE KNOWN?
THE SUPREME BRAHMAN - A STATE DEVOID OF PAIN AND PLEASURE.

IMPOSSIBLE! THERE CAN BE NO STATE IN WHICH BOTH ARE ABSENT!
WHY NOT? IF THE STATE OF PLEASURE IS CHARACTERIZED BY THE ABSENCE OF PAIN...

...CAN THERE NOT BE A STATE CHARACTERIZED BY THE ABSENCE OF THE TWO?
THE SERPENT WAS SATED BY THE ANSWER.

HE LOOKED PLEASED AND BEGAN TO UNCOIL HIMSELF.
O YUDHISHTHIRA, HOW CAN I DEVOUR THE BROTHER OF ONE WHO KNOWS WHAT OUGHT TO BE KNOWN?

THEN AFTER A LONG DISCOURSE WITH YUDHISHTHIRA ON ETHICS, MORALITY AND PHILOSOPHY -
TRUTHFULNESS AND SELF-CONTROL, NOT BIRTH INTO A CASTE, FAMILY OR RACE ARE THE MEANS BY WHICH ONE ATTAINS BRAHMAN.

MAY ALL BLISS BE YOURS!
NAHUSHA THEN SHED HIS SERPENTINE FORM AND IN HIS DIVINE FRAME ASCENDED TO SWARGA.

IN THE AUTUMN OF THE ELEVENTH YEAR, THE PANDAVAS ENTERED THE KAMYAKA FOREST WHERE KRISHNA AND SATYABHAMA CAME TO SEE THEM.
YOUR SONS ARE IN DWARAKA WITH ABHIMANYU AND SUBHADRA, DRAUPADI.

THEY ARE ADORED BY ALL AND THOUGH YOUR FATHER AND BROTHER TEMPT THEM WITH TERRITORIES AND KINGDOMS THEY REFUSE TO RETURN.

KEEN AS THEY ARE ON ACQUIRING EXCELLENCE IN ARMS, EVEN A PROMISE OF CELESTIAL BLISS CANNOT LURE THEM AWAY NOW.

KRISHNA THEN TURNED TO YUDHISHTHIRA.
KEEP YOUR PLEDGE IF YOU MUST. STAY IN THE FORESTS IF YOU WILL. BUT PERMIT US TO...

...SLAY THAT VILEST OF SINNERS AND HIS MEN RIGHTAWAY. THEN WHEN YOU ENTER HASTINAPURA IN THE FOURTEENTH YEAR IT WILL BE WITH A FREE HEART.

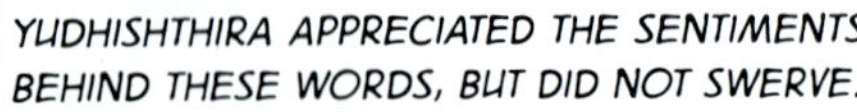
YUDHISHTHIRA APPRECIATED THE SENTIMENTS BEHIND THESE WORDS, BUT DID NOT SWERVE.

LET THE THIRTEENTH YEAR BE OVER AND WE SHALL, AS EVER BE GUIDED BY YOU, KRISHNA.

WHILE YUDHISHTHIRA AND KRISHNA TALKED ON, THE IMMORTAL SAGE MARKANDEYA APPEARED ON THE SCENE...

...AND AFTER LISTENING FOR A WHILE TO THE WISE TALES OF YORE THAT HE TOLD TO ILLUSTRATE A POINT IN PHILOSOPHY OR A QUESTION IN ETHICS...

...KRISHNA AND SATYABHAMA GOT READY TO LEAVE.
O DRAUPADI, YOU WILL CERTAINLY SEE YOUR ENEMIES SLAIN AND YUDHISHTHIRA RULING THE EARTH ONCE AGAIN.
AFTER THEY LEFT...

...MARKANDEYA MOVED ON WITH THE PANDAVAS TO DWAITAVANA THE RETREAT OF SAGES AND SEERS.

IN THE TWELFTH YEAR, A WANDERING BRAHMANA CAME TO DHRITARASHTRA WITH NEWS OF THE PANDAVAS.
THE MIGHTY PANDAVAS ARE EMACIATED AND WORN OUT. POOR DRAUPADI LOOKS FORSAKEN DESPITE SUCH HEROES FOR HUSBANDS.

DHRITARASHTRA SIGHED AND QUIVERED WITH TRUE REMORSE.
ALAS! MY FOLLY ALONE IS RESPONSIBLE FOR THIS!

THAT DESPERATE GAMBLER SHAKUNI PLAYED FOUL AND DRIVEN BY ATTACHMENT TO MY WICKED SONS, I COLLUDED.

ALAS! THE HOUR OF DOOM IS NIGH! WHY ELSE WOULD ARJUNA WHO ATTAINED HEAVEN IN HIS MORTAL FRAME RETURN TO EARTH?

MYSTERIOUS WEAPONS... A FATAL BOW... ARJUNA WIELDING BOTH... IS THERE A BEING WHO CAN WITHSTAND THIS COMBINATION?

WHEN SHAKUNI WENT TO DURYODHANA WHO WAS WITH KARNA AND REPEATED ALL THAT HE HAD HEARD, THE PRINCE'S FACE FELL.
DO NOT GRIEVE, O KING.

GO TO DWAITAVANA IN ALL YOUR GLORY AND EXULT OVER YOUR FOES IN THEIR MISERY.

WHAT GREATER HAPPINESS COULD THERE BE THAN THAT?
LET THE BARK-CLAD DRAUPADI SEE YOUR BEDECKED, ORNAMENTED WIFE AND GRIEVE OVER HER OWN FATE.

AFTER MUCH SCHEMING AND PLOTTING, THE THREE WENT TO DHRITARASHTRA.
O KING, OUR CATTLE ARE NOW STATIONED IN A CHARMING PLACE. AND IT'S TIME FOR BRANDING THE CALVES.

SHAKUNI TOOK THE CUE FROM KARNA.
THIS IS ALSO AN EXCELLENT SEASON FOR DURYODHANA TO GO ON A HUNT. THEREFORE YOU SHOULD GRANT YOUR SON PERMISSION TO GO THERE.

DHRITARASHTRA, HOWEVER, ADDRESSED DURYODHANA.
HUNTING AND SUPERVISING THE CATTLE ARE FINE. BUT...

...I HAVE HEARD THAT THE PANDAVAS ARE SOMEWHERE NEAR THAT PLACE. SO I THINK YOU SHOULD NOT GO THERE, MY SON.

BUT SHAKUNI PROMPTLY ALLAYED THAT FEAR WITH A FALSE PROMISE.
WE WILL NOT GO WHERE THEY LIVE.

THERE IS NO CHANCE, THEREFORE FOR ANY MISCONDUCT ON OUR PART.
WHEN HE HEARD THIS, ONCE AGAIN DHRITARASHTRA ACTED AGAINST HIS BETTER JUDGEMENT AND GAVE IN.

AT DWAITAVANA, MEANWHILE, YUDHISHTHIRA AND DRAUPADI WERE ALL SET TO PERFORM A YAGNA THAT ONLY CELESTIALS AND ASCETICS COULD.

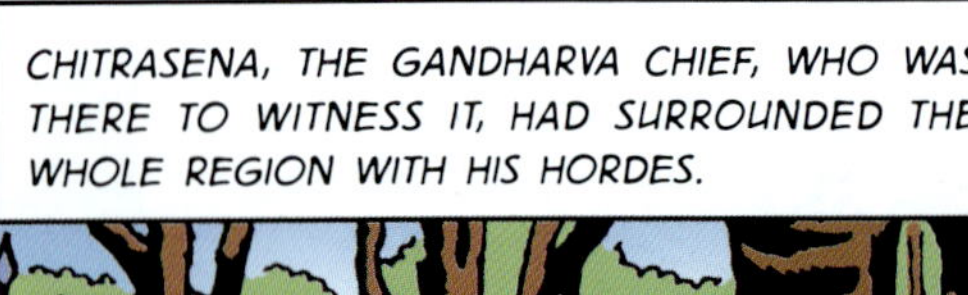
CHITRASENA, THE GANDHARVA CHIEF, WHO WAS THERE TO WITNESS IT, HAD SURROUNDED THE WHOLE REGION WITH HIS HORDES.

SO WHEN DURYODHANA'S VANGUARD REACHED THE LAKE AND WAS ABOUT TO ENTER THE FOREST –
HALT! DO NOT ENTER THESE WOODS!

DURYODHANA'S WARRIORS BARKED A COUNTER ORDER.
MIGHTY DURYODHANA HAS COME HERE TO SPORT. LEAVE THIS PLACE AT ONCE!
HA! HA! HA! HA!

SO, EVIL DURYODHANA IS A FOOL AS WELL! COMMANDING US THE DENIZENS OF HEAVEN ITSELF AS IF WE WERE HIS SERVANTS!
HA! HA! HA! HA

AND YOU KNAVES BRING SUCH A COMMAND TO US!
GO BACK TO THAT KURU KING! OR ELSE.
THE WARRIORS FLED WITHOUT MUCH ADO.

WHEN DURYODHANA HEARD THEIR TALE, HE TURNED LIVID WITH ANGER.
BE IT INDRA HIMSELF WHO THWARTS MY WISHES, I WILL ATTACK HIM AND DECIMATE HIS MEN!
AND THE KAURAVAS GOT READY FOR BATTLE.

WHEN THE GANDHARVAS SAW THEM COME...

...THEY RUSHED TO CHITRASENA FOR ORDERS.
ATTACK THEM! ANNIHILATE THE IMPUDENT WRETCHES!
LED BY THEIR CHIEF...

...THE GANDHARVAS RETALIATED WITH A VENGEANCE. UNNERVED BY THE FURY OF THEIR ATTACK...
...THE KAURAVAS AND THEIR MEN RAN HELTER-SKELTER.

KARNA ALONE STOOD HIS GROUND AND FOUGHT BACK.
HACK DOWN HIS CHARIOT!
KILL HIS CHARIOTEER!
HIS HORSES! SLAY THEM.

THE KAURAVAS, IT SEEMED, WERE ABOUT TO LOSE THEIR BEST WARRIOR WHEN...

...A KAURAVA CHARIOT RUMBLED TOWARDS HIM. KARNA DUCKED AND WITH ONE GREAT BOUND...

...LEAPT INTO IT...
...AND SPURRED THE HORSES ON...

...AWAY FROM THE SCENE TO SAFETY.
IT WAS VIKARNA'S CHARIOT! KARNA'S UNDAUNTED VALOUR HAD BROUGHT DURYODHANA, DUSHASANA, SHAKUNI AND VIKARNA BACK TO THE CHARGE.

LETTING KARNA GO, THE GANDHARVAS TURNED THEIR FURY ON DURYODHANA...

...AND IN NO TIME VANQUISHED HIM.

DUSHASANA AND THE LADIES OF THE ROYAL HOUSEHOLD, TOO, WERE TAKEN CAPTIVE.
HIS TERRIFIED MEN FLED THE FIELD.

AND THEY RAN TO YUDHISHTHIRA.
THE GANDHARVAS HAVE CAPTURED DURYODHANA, HIS BROTHERS AND THE ROYAL LADIES. RESCUE THEM, O PANDAVA.
PROTECT US.

BHEEMA LAUGHED.
COUNSELLED BY A GAMBLER, THE WICKED WRETCH CAME HERE TO HUMILIATE US. NOW HE REAPS THE DISGRACE HE DESERVES AND...
BHEEMA!

THIS IS NOT THE TIME FOR TAUNTS. THE GANDHARVAS, OUTSIDERS, HAVE DARED TO SULLY THE HONOUR OF OUR CLAN IN OUR PRESENCE.

BESIDES, DURYODHANA IN TROUBLE NEEDS YOUR HELP, HIS MEN YOUR PROTECTION! WHAT GREATER JOY COULD THERE BE FOR YOU?

GO WITH YOUR BROTHERS. GO, RESCUE HIM, HIS BROTHERS AND THE LADIES OF OUR CLAN. IF POSSIBLE BY CONCILIATION, IF NOT...

ARJUNA SPOKE UP.
BY FEEDING THE EARTH WITH GANDHARVA BLOOD. WE WILL RESCUE THE KURUS.
THIS VOW COMING FROM ARJUNA BROUGHT SIGHS OF RELIEF FROM THE KURUS. THEIR KING WOULD BE SAVED.

THE FOUR MAIL-CLAD PANDAVAS RODE UP TO THE GANDHARVAS.
SET MY BROTHER, DURYODHANA FREE!
O CHILD, WE OBEY THE COMMANDS OF NONE BUT OUR KING.
HA! HA!
HA!

THIS QUARREL WITH MORTALS AND HIS CONDUCT WITH THEIR LADIES DO NOT BEFIT YOUR KING. SET THEM FREE.
HA! HA!

IF YOU WILL NOT DO IT IN PEACE, I WILL HAVE TO RESCUE THEM BY FORCE!
ARJUNA RAISED HIS GANDIVA...

...AND SENT A SHOWER OF SHARP SURE ARROWS INTO THEIR MIDST.
A FEARFUL BATTLE WAS FOUGHT BETWEEN THE AGILE GANDHARVAS AND THE VALOROUS PANDAVAS.

IT WAS AN EXTRAORDINARY BATTLE. THE FOUR PANDAVAS PITTED AGAINST THE GANDHARVA HORDES LED BY CHITRASENA!

AND IN THAT BATTLE, ARJUNA SENT HUNDREDS AND THOUSANDS OF THEM INTO A COMA WHILE THE REST FLED IN FEAR.

IT WAS ONLY THEN THAT CHITRASENA ATTACKED -

BUT THE ATTACK WAS ABORTED WITH A SINGLE ARROW FROM ARJUNA'S BOW.

CHITRASENA RESORTED TO THE TRICKS OF HIS TRIBE — ILLUSION.

BUT THE GANDHARVA HIMSELF HAD BEEN ARJUNA'S MENTOR IN INDRALOKA! SO ARJUNA KNEW HOW TO HANDLE EVEN SUCH MANOEUVRES.

RELENTLESSLY CHASED BY ARJUNA'S UNERRING AIM...
...OUT OF SHEER FATIGUE...

...THE GANDHARVA CHIEF DISCLOSED HIMSELF.
LOOK! IT IS I, CHITRASENA YOUR FRIEND, WHO FIGHTS YOU.

AND THAT WAS THE END OF THE BATTLE.
O VALIANT ONE, WHY DO YOU PERSECUTE DURYODHANA AND HIS WIVES?
THEY CAME TO MOCK YOU AND DRAUPADI.

"AWARE OF THIS INDRA SENT FOR ME.
GO AND BRING DURYODHANA AND HIS MEN HERE TO ME IN CHAINS.

THE WRETCH IS ALREADY IN CHAINS. I SHALL NOW TAKE HIM TO INDRA'S REALMS.

ARJUNA SMILED.
YUDHISHTHIRA HAS ORDERED ME TO RESCUE HIM. HE IS OUR BROTHER, SO SET HIM FREE.

THE VAIN WRETCH DOES NOT DESERVE TO BE LET OFF. HE HAS DECEIVED AND WRONGED YUDHISHTHIRA AND DRAUPADI.

YUDHISHTHIRA DOES NOT KNOW WHY HE CAME HERE. LET HIM DECIDE AFTER HE KNOWS ALL THE DETAILS.
AND THEY WENT TO YUDHISHTHIRA.

YUDHISHTHIRA'S DECISION, HOWEVER STOOD UNCHANGED.
YOU HAVE DONE US A GREAT FAVOUR BY SPARING DURYODHANA'S LIFE.

NOW THE GLORY OF RESCUING HIM IS OURS. THE HONOUR OF OUR CLAN STANDS REDEEMED.

I AM PLEASED. SET THEM FREE AND GO YOUR WAYS.
THE GANDHARVAS ACCORDINGLY SET THE CAPTIVES FREE AND LED BY CHITRASENA LEFT THE SCENE.

O COUSIN, NEVER AGAIN ACT SO IMPETUOUSLY. IT WILL ONLY BRING YOU MISERY.

MAY YOU AND YOUR BROTHERS PROSPER. GO BACK HOME WITH A CHEERFUL HEART.
YUDHISHTHIRA'S AFFECTIONATE WORDS SHAMED DURYODHANA TO THE CORE.

HE SET OUT FOR HASTINAPURA LIKE A CORPSE PROPELLED BY AN UNSEEN HAND.

AS HE APPROACHED HASTINAPURA, HIS HEART SANK. SO HE SET UP CAMP OUTSIDE THE CITY AND THERE KARNA FOUND HIM.
YOU ARE BACK AND YOU HAVE DEFEATED THE GANDHARVAS! WHAT A GREAT FEAT!

AND DUSHASANA TOO WEPT.

TO HAVE MY SECRET MOTIVE EXPOSED... TO BE MADE OVER IN CHAINS TO YUDHISHTHIRA IN FULL VIEW OF OUR WOMEN...

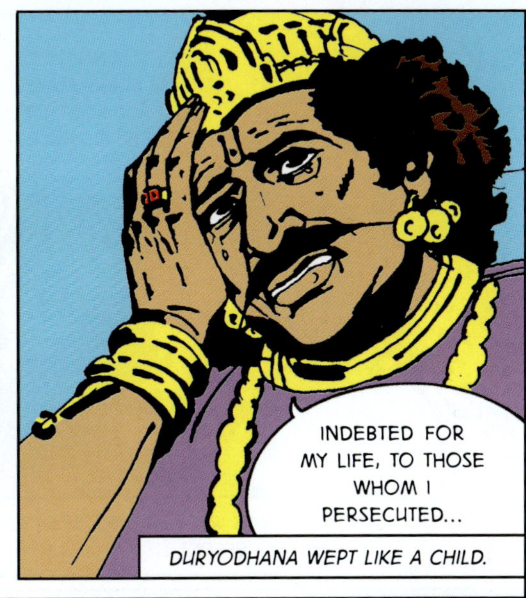
INDEBTED FOR MY LIFE, TO THOSE WHOM I PERSECUTED...
DURYODHANA WEPT LIKE A CHILD.

DO NOT ASK ME TO RULE IN YOUR STEAD, DURYODHANA! YOU ALONE SHALL BE OUR KING.

THIS MAUDLIN SCENE IRKED KARNA.
O KURUS! STOP WEEPING LIKE COMMONERS! NOTHING IS LOST. THE PANDAVAS, YOUR SLAVES HAVE MERELY DONE THEIR DUTY.

FOR THE PROTECTION THEY ENJOY, IT IS THE DUTY OF SLAVES TO HELP THEIR KING.

WHAT THEN IS THERE TO GRIEVE SO MUCH ABOUT? DID THE PANDAVAS RESORT TO DEATH BY FASTING WHEN **THEIR** PROSPERITY BECAME **YOURS**?

WHEN KARNA'S REPROACHES SEEMED TO HAVE NO EFFECT...
ARISE, O KING, LEST OTHER KINGS MAKE YOU A TARGET OF THEIR RIDICULE!

...SHAKUNI TOOK OVER.
O KING, WOULD YOU SEEK DEATH AND THROW AWAY ALL THAT I HAVE WON FOR YOU?

YOU ARE ALIVE AND FREE. ACT AS A KING BORN TO RULE. REWARD THE PANDAVAS FOR THEIR PROMPT LOYALTY.

GIVE THEM BACK THEIR KINGDOM. SEEK THEIR FRIENDSHIP. SUCH VIRTUOUS ACTION WOULD WIN YOU ADDITIONAL FAME.

SHAKUNI'S COUNSEL ONLY GALLED DURYODHANA FURTHER.
GO AWAY. I NO LONGER HAVE ANY USE FOR VIRTUE, WEALTH, PLEASURE, KINGSHIP OR EVEN FRIENDSHIP. GO AWAY.

HE WAS DETERMINED TO GIVE UP HIS LIFE.
LEAVE ME AND GO BACK TO HASTINAPURA. LET ME PAY FOR MY FOLLY AND MY ARROGANCE.

SHAKUNI AND KARNA GAVE UP.
WE WILL NOT GO BACK WITHOUT YOU. HOW CAN WE?
THE COURSE YOU HAVE CHOSEN SHALL BE OURS, TOO.
AND THEY SAT DOWN BESIDE HIM.

AND THERE THEY SLEPT THAT NIGHT. BEFORE LONG -

THE VISITANT SPIRITED DURYODHANA AWAY TO THE SCENE OF A YAGNA.
DESIST FROM THE IGNOBLE ACT OF SUICIDE. YOU ARE OF CELESTIAL ORIGIN. YOU NEED HAVE NO FEAR.

NO WEAPON, NOT EVEN THE MYSTERIOUS, CAN DESTROY THE UPPER HALF OF YOUR BODY FOR IT IS MADE WHOLLY OF VAJRAS.

THE LOWER HALF, MADE OF FLOWERS, WILL KEEP YOU EVER ATTRACTIVE TO WOMEN.
DURYODHANA KEPT THIS VISION TO HIMSELF.

WHEN DAY BROKE, KARNA HUGGED HIM AND SIGHED.
MY FRIEND, WHY DO YOU WANT TO DIE?

I PROMISE YOU THAT WHEN THE THIRTEENTH YEAR ENDS I WILL SLAY ARJUNA IN BATTLE AND...

THIS TIME, DURYODHANA STOOD UP AND...

...TO KARNA'S DELIGHT BEGAN TO RANT AND RAVE –
I WILL DEFEAT THE PANDAVAS.

BEFORE LONG, HASTINAPURA SAW THE RETURN OF THEIR KING FROM HIS EVENTFUL EXCURSION TO THE CATTLE-STATION AT DWAITAVANA.

WHEN HE ENTERED BHEESHMA'S PRESENCE WITH KARNA, SHAKUNI AND DUSHASANA –
O KING, AT LEAST NOW MAKE PEACE WITH THE PANDAVAS. YOU SAW HOW THEY CAME TO YOUR RESCUE...

...WHILE THIS DASTARD, NO MATCH FOR ANY ONE OF THEM, FLED FOR HIS LIFE LEAVING YOU TO FACE THE FIGHT ALONE.
HA HA!
AND WITH THAT RUDE LAUGH...

...DURYODHANA WALKED AWAY FOLLOWED BY THE OTHERS, LEAVING THE OLD VETERAN BENT WITH SHAME.

BHEESHMA'S ILL WILL FOR YOU SURFACES WHEN HE INSULTS ME IN YOUR PRESENCE AND PRAISES THE PANDAVAS.

FOUR OF THEM TOGETHER CONQUERED THE EARTH FOR YUDHISHTHIRA. I SHALL DO IT FOR YOU ALL ALONE. THEN WILL BHEESHMA SEE MY VALOUR AND REPROACH HIMSELF.

O KING, COMMAND ME TO VICTORY! I SWEAR BY MY WEAPONS IT SHALL BE YOURS.
GO KARNA.
DURYODHANA WAS TOUCHED AND ELATED.

KARNA MARCHED OUT WITH A VAST ARMY.

THE DAY HE RETURNED HOME, VICTORIOUS AND WEALTHY....

...WAS A DAY OF JUBILATION FOR DURYODHANA. HE WAS DELIGHTED.
O KARNA, TODAY I HAVE RECEIVED FROM YOU WHAT I NEVER DID FROM EITHER BHEESHMA, DRONA OR KRIPA, MY PROTECTOR!

NOT LONG AFTER THAT, A MESSENGER FROM HASTINAPURA CAME ONE DAY TO THE PANDAVAS.
THE KURU KING, DURYODHANA THE LORD OF ALL MEN, IS PERFORMING A GREAT YAGNA. I HAVE BEEN SENT HERE BY HIM TO INVITE YOU TO IT.

IT WOULD PLEASE US TO COME, BUT OUR PLEDGE TO LIVE IN THE FOREST FOR THIRTEEN YEARS FORBIDS US.
WHILE YUDHISHTHIRA'S REPLY WAS POLITE...

...BHEEMA'S WAS VIOLENT.
TELL DURYODHANA, THE GREAT PANDAVA WILL COME WHEN IT IS TIME TO POUR THE FAT OF HIS FURY ON THE SONS OF DHRITARASHTRA IN THE YAGNA OF BATTLE.
THE MESSENGER LEFT AND FAITHFULLY REPEATED THEIR WORDS TO DURYODHANA.

DURYODHANA'S YAGNA WAS SUCH A SUCCESS THAT WHEN IT WAS OVER HE BEGAN TO DREAM OF THE RAJASOOYA.
WHEN WILL I PERFORM THAT PRIME YAGNA?
AFTER WE SLAY THE PANDAVAS IN BATTLE.

AND THEN KARNA TOOK AN OATH.
TILL I SLAY ARJUNA, I SHALL NOT WASH MY FEET. NOR SHALL I EAT FLESH NOR DRINK ANY INTOXICATING BREW. AND...

...WHATEVER IS ASKED OF ME, I SHALL NEVER REFUSE.

SLEEP ELUDED THE ELDEST PANDAVA. ONE NIGHT AS HE TOSSED RESTLESSLY ABOUT -
WE ARE THE DEER OF DWAITAVANA... THE FEW WHO HAVE ESCAPED YOUR BROTHERS' ARROWS.

HELP US PRESERVE OUR SPECIES. GO TO SOME OTHER FOREST LEST WE BECOME EXTINCT.
SO BE IT.

SO BE IT. I SHALL DO AS YOU SAY.

WHEN NEWS OF DURYODHANA'S DESIGNS AND KARNA'S DIRE OATH WERE BROUGHT TO YUDHISHTHIRA BY HIS SPIES...

...HE BECAME DISTRAUGHT WITH ANXIETY.

KARNA'S EARRINGS FASHIONED OUT OF THE VERY ELIXIR OF IMMORTALITY, BLOTTED OUT ALL OTHER POSITIVE IMAGES.
SHOULD I MOVE AWAY FROM DWAITAVANA?

THE NEXT MORNING, YUDHISHTHIRA TOLD HIS BROTHERS ABOUT IT.
...THEY ARE THE SEEDS, AS IT WERE, OF THEIR SPECIES AND SEEK OUR COMPASSION.

WE HAVE FED FREELY ON THEIR KIN FOR A FULL YEAR AND EIGHT MONTHS.

WE SHOULD NOW MOVE ON. LET US RETURN TO THE KAMYAKA FOREST.
AND SO THEY DID.

BUT THE MOVE DID NOT BRING YUDHISHTHIRA THE PEACE HE SOUGHT, FOR, HIS SPIES CAME THERE BEFORE LONG WITH FRESH NEWS.
THE SON OF DHRITARASHTRA IS CONVINCED THAT...

...DONATING AND ENJOYING IT ARE THE BEST WAY TO USE WEALTH.
YUDHISHTHIRA PALED.

HE KNEW WHAT SUCH VIRTUES IN THEIR FOE COULD DO FOR THEM!

O YUDHISHTHIRA, FOR ONE WHO HAS SUBDUED HIS SENSES, ANOTHER'S PROSPERITY HOLDS NO FEAR.
IT WAS VYASA, THE SEER, COME WITH HIS TIMELY INSIGHT...

...TO RESOLVE HIS GRANDSON'S DOUBTS.
SEEK TO ENJOY HAPPINESS AND ENDURE MISERY, LIKE A SOWER BIDING HIS SEASON.

A MAN WHO GIVES EVERYONE HIS DUE, AND GRANTS BOONS AS WELL, IS HAPPY AND ENJOYS EVERY OBJECT OF PLEASURE. BUT...

THE SAGE CONTINUED -
...HE WHO PRACTISES ASCETICISM IS FREE FROM ENVY AND ACHIEVES THE GREATEST HAPPINESSS - PEACE OF MIND.

O SAGE, WHICH IS MORE DIFFICULT TO PRACTISE - CHARITY OR ASCETICISM?
CHARITY, MY CHILD.

AND HE ELABORATED ON HIS ANSWER.
MAN THIRSTS FOR WEALTH AND SECURES IT WITH ENORMOUS EFFORT.

RISKING HIS VERY LIFE MAN DARES DEEP SEAS AND DENSE FORESTS IN SEARCH OF WEALTH. LOVE OF WEALTH GOADS HIM TO RAISE CROPS, TEND CATTLE OR SERVE OTHERS.

TO PART WITH THE WEALTH THUS EARNED IS VERY HARD INDEED.

THAT IS WHY THERE IS NOTHING MORE HARD TO PRACTISE THAN CHARITY. BUT...

THE SEER CLARIFIED HIS STATEMENT.
...THE DONATION OF ILL-GOTTEN WEALTH IS STERILE.
FOR HE KNEW WHAT TROUBLED THE ELDEST PANDAVA.

YOUR ASCETICISM, WILL RESTORE YOUR LOST KINGDOM TO YOU. BECAUSE...

...THERE IS NOTHING ASCETICISM CANNOT ACHIEVE IN ITS SUPREME WISDOM. AFTER THE THIRTEENTH YEAR, THE KINGDOM OF YOUR FATHER AND GRANDFATHER WILL BE YOURS AGAIN.
AND VYASA WENT HIS WAY.

SOME DAYS LATER IN AN UNGUARDED MOMENT, DRAUPADI WAS ABDUCTED BY THE SINDHU KING, JAYADRATHA.
YOUR VIOLENCE LEAVES ME COLD. MY WORTHY HUSBANDS WILL SOON MAKE YOU REPENT FOR YOUR FOLLY.

AND THEY DID. TRACKING HIM DOWN...

...THEY FIRST MADE SHORT WORK OF HIS ARMY.

HIS MEN DECIMATED, THE TERRIFIED KING PUSHED DRAUPADI OUT OF HIS CHARIOT...

...AND SPED AWAY. BUT, THE INTREPID BHEEMA, WAS NOT GOING TO LET HIM ESCAPE.
O KING, TAKE DRAUPADI AND RETURN HOME. CONSOLE HER.

I SHALL NOT SPARE THAT STUPID KING OF SINDHU EVEN IF INDRA HIMSELF WERE TO SUPPORT HIM.
WAIT, BHEEMA.

FOR THE SAKE OF OUR COUSIN, HIS WIFE DUSHALA, YOU MUST NOT SLAY HIM BHEEMA.

YUDHISHTHIRA'S WORDS ANGERED DRAUPADI ALL THE MORE.
FOR MY SAKE YOU MUST! YOU MUST SLAY THAT EVIL, DESPICABLE, INFAMOUS WRETCH OF A MAN!!

NEVER FORGIVE HIM AND SHOW HIM NO MERCY.
THUS GOADED BY DRAUPADI, ARJUNA AND BHEEMA WENT AFTER JAYADRATHA-

THE TWO PANDAVAS SPURRED THEIR CHARIOTS ON AND SOON CLOSED IN UPON THEIR FOE.

ABDUCTING A WOMAN BY FORCE! YOU DASTARD!

WAIT! DO NOT RUN AWAY! NO KING WOULD LEAVE HIS MEN TO THE MERCY OF THE FOE AND FLEE.

BHEEMA LEAPED OUT OF HIS OWN CHARIOT...

...AND CHASED THE FLEEING KING -

CATCHING UP WITH HIM, HE PULLED THE MAN OFF THE GROUND BY HIS HAIR...

...AND THEN THREW HIM DOWN -
YOU FOOL! YOU DARED HURT DRAUPADI!

S-SPARE MY LIFE. I... I W-WANT TO LIVE.
YOU DO NOT DESERVE TO LIVE! YOU WRETCH!

AS JAYADRATHA CRINGED BEFORE BHEEMA'S NAKED FURY -
DESIST, BHEEMA! REMEMBER OUR KING'S ORDERS.

BHEEMA WAS DISGUSTED.
HM-M! OUR KING IS OVER MERCIFUL AND YOU SUPPORT HIM. WHAT SHALL I DO?

I KNOW!
HE SHAVED OFF JAYADRATHA'S FINE CROP OF HAIR LEAVING FIVE UGLY TUFTS ON HIS HEAD.

O FOOL, I WILL SPARE YOUR LIFE IF YOU AGREE TO DECLARE IN OPEN COURT THAT YOU ARE OUR SLAVE.
I DO. I WILL. SO BE IT.

WHEN THEY BROUGHT THE CAPTIVE KING HOME -
O KING, TELL DRAUPADI THAT THIS VILE MAN HAS BECOME THE SLAVE OF THE PANDAVAS.

RELEASE THAT PITIFUL, DISFIGURED SLAVE OF THE PANDAVAS, O BHEEMA.
IF YOU HAVE ANY REGARD FOR ME, SET HIM FREE BHEEMA.
ARJUNA HELPED JAYADRATHA TO RISE...

...AND LED HIM TO YUDHISHTHIRA.
WEAK AND TIMID YOURSELF, YOU WOULD ABDUCT A WOMAN! FIE ON YOU. HOWEVER...

...THAT YOUR PERCEPTION OF RIGHT AND WRONG MAY IMPROVE AND TURN YOU AWAY FROM SUCH HEINOUS CRIMES...

...I SET YOU FREE. YOU MAY GO BACK TO YOUR KINGDOM WITH YOUR CHARIOTS AND WARRIORS.
HUMBLED BEYOND MEASURE...

...JAYADRATHA WALKED AWAY WITH HEAD AND HEART HEAVY WITH SHAME.

THE SINDHU KING WENT STRAIGHT TO GANGOTRI AND PERFORMED PENANCES TO WIN SHIVA'S FAVOUR. THAT DEITY WAS PLEASED AND OFFERED HIM A BOON.
O LORD, EMPOWER ME TO SLAY ALL THE FIVE SONS OF PANDU IN BATTLE.
THAT CANNOT BE.

WHEN EVEN THE CELESTIALS CANNOT VANQUISH ARJUNA, HOW CAN MERE MAN SLAY HIM?

YOU SHALL, HOWEVER, DEFEAT THE OTHER FOUR AND YUDHISHTHIRA'S ARMY FOR ONE DAY.
SHIVA VANISHED AND JAYADRATHA WENT BACK TO HIS KINGDOM.

MEANWHILE, THOUGH DRAUPADI WAS RESCUED, THE INCIDENT LEFT YUDHISHTHIRA SHAKEN AND GUILT-RIDDEN.
IT WAS OUR CARELESSNESS THAT BROUGHT ABOUT THIS MISFORTUNE ON OUR PIOUS, VIRTUOUS WIFE.

HOW ELSE COULD SHE WHO HAD DELIVERED US FROM THE KAURAVAS, BE ABDUCTED BY THAT FOOLISH KING?

TO CONSOLE AND COMFORT HIM, SAGE MARKANDEYA TOLD HIM THE ANCIENT TALES OF SITA AND RAMA AND SAVITRI AND SATYAVAN.

TOWARDS THE CLOSE OF THE TWELFTH YEAR THE PANDAVAS RETURNED TO DWAITAVANA, WHERE THEY SUBSISTED ON A VEGETARIAN DIET. THERE ONE DAY -
O KING! O PANDAVAS!

...MY FIRE-STICKS AND CHURNING-ROD GOT ENTANGLED IN THE HORNS OF THAT DEER!

PLEASE PURSUE IT AND RETRIEVE THEM FOR ME!
THE PANDAVAS RAN AFTER THE DEER.

AS THEY NEARED IT -

BUT THEY COULD NOT PIERCE IT.
AND AS THEY STRUGGLED TO SLAY IT...

...THE DEER SUDDENLY BECAME INVISIBLE.

BAFFLED, DEMORALISED AND THIRSTY, THE PANDAVAS SANK TO THE GROUND.
GO NAKULA!

SEE IF YOU CAN FIND SOME WATER.
NAKULA WENT. WHEN HE DID NOT RETURN...

...SAHADEVA, ARJUNA AND BHEEMA WERE SENT ONE AFTER THE OTHER, EACH IN SEARCH OF THE LAST. WHEN EVEN BHEEMA DID NOT RETURN –
I HAD BETTER GO AND LOOK FOR THEM.
AND YUDHISHTHIRA SET OUT.

BEFORE LONG HE CAME UPON A LAKE. AND WHAT HE SAW THERE ALL BUT SENT HIM INTO A SWOON.

O BHEEMA, YOU PROMISED TO BREAK DURYODHANA'S THIGH IN BATTLE! YOU ARJUNA WERE DECLARED INVINCIBLE BY THE CELESTIALS THEMSELVES.

O NAKULA! O SAHADEVA!
WHY DO YOU ALL LIE DEAD DESTROYING ALL MY HOPES!
AFTER LAMENTING THUS FOR A WHILE...

...YUDHISHTHIRA'S GRIEF SOON GAVE WAY TO REASON.
THEIR BODIES BEAR NO WOUNDS... THEIR WEAPONS LIE UNTOUCHED... NO FOOTPRINTS AROUND THEM... I WILL QUENCH MY THIRST AND...

IT IS I WHO KILLED THEM. IF YOU LOVE YOUR LIFE DO NOT DRINK THAT WATER. IT IS POSSESSED BY ME.

AND IF YOU, TOO, REFUSE TO ANSWER MY QUESTIONS BEFORE YOU DRINK, YOU WILL BE MY FIFTH VICTIM.

IT WAS A YAKSHA.
I DO NOT COVET WHAT IS POSSESSED BY YOU. ASK YOUR QUESTIONS, O YAKSHA. I WLLL TRY AND ANSWER THEM.

OVER THIRTY QUESTIONS WERE SHOT RAPIDLY AND WERE ANSWERED PROMPTLY AND CORRECTLY. AT LAST -
WHO IS TRULY HAPPY?
ONE WHO IS FREE FROM DEBT, LIVES A SIMPLE LIFE AND IS HOME-LOVING.

WHAT EVOKES CONSTANT WONDER?
THE BELIEF OF THE LIVING IN THEIR IMMORTALITY THOUGH THEY WITNESS DEATH CLAIMING THEIR FELLOW-MEN DAILY.

WHO POSSESSES THE GREATEST WEALTH?
ONE WHO IS UNMOVED BY THE PLEASANT OR THE UNPLEASANT, PROSPERITY OR ADVERSITY.

WELL ANSWERED! LET ONE OF YOUR BROTHERS BE REVIVED.

WHICH ONE DO YOU CHOOSE?
NAKULA, THE SON OF MADRI.

NAKULA? BUT BHEEMA IS DEAR TO YOU AND ARJUNA IS THE ONE YOU RELY ON.

WHY CHOOSE NAKULA WHO IS ONLY A STEP-BROTHER?
I WISH TO BE FAIR TO BOTH MY MOTHERS. I, A SON OF KUNTI AM ALIVE. LET A SON OF MADRI, TOO, LIVE.

THE YAKSHA WAS PLEASED.
O PANDAVA, SINCE JUSTICE IS DEARER TO YOU THAN SELF-INTEREST, LET ALL YOUR BROTHERS COME ALIVE.

AND LO!

WHO ARE YOU? ARE YOU A FRIEND? ARE YOU OUR PATRIARCH?

I AM YOUR FATHER, DHARMA. I CAME HERE TO SEE YOU AND TEST YOU. AND I AM PLEASED.

GIVE THAT BRAHMANA THESE FIRE-STICKS AND CHURNING-ROD. IT WAS I WHO, IN THE FORM OF A DEER, BORE THEM AWAY, TO DRAW YOU HERE.

THE THIRTEENTH YEAR OF YOUR EXILE HAS DAWNED. YOU WILL PASS IT, UNRECOGNIZED, IN THE KINGDOM OF VIRATA.

YOU WILL BE ABLE TO ASSUME, AT WILL, WHATEVER GUISE YOU CHOOSE.
AND DHARMA BECAME INVISIBLE.

THEN, IGNORING ALL CODES, THE GODS TURNED BLATANTLY PARTISAN. INDRA RESOLVED TO EXPLOIT KARNA'S OATH OF GENEROSITY.
I WILL RID YUDHISHTHIRA OF HIS ONE GREAT FEAR.

SURYA WAS DETERMINED TO SAVE KARNA, HIS SON.
TO FAVOUR THE PANDAVAS, INDRA WILL COME TO YOU IN THE GUISE OF AN OLD BRAHMANA AND BEG FOR YOUR EARRINGS AND COAT OF MAIL.

IF YOU LOVE YOUR LIFE, IF YOU WISH TO DEFEAT ARJUNA, ON NO ACCOUNT SHOULD YOU PART WITH THEM.

THOUGH SURYA REVEALED HIMSELF AS THE PRESIDING DEITY OF THE SUN, KARNA WOULD NOT BREAK HIS OATH.
IF AT ALL I AM DEAR TO YOU, O SUSTAINER OF ALL LIFE, DO NOT ASK ME TO DEVIATE FROM MY VOW.

O CHILD, INDRA SEEKS YOUR DEATH AT ARJUNA'S HANDS!
PARDON ME, O GRACIOUS LORD, BUT I PREFER DEATH TO FALSEHOOD AND INFAMY.

BESIDES IF INDRA SEEKS MY DEATH BY SUCH DECEPTION, THE DEED WILL BRING HIM DISGRACE AND ME, THE RENOWN I CRAVE.
OF WHAT USE IS RENOWN WITHOUT LIFE? LISTEN TO ME...

AT LAST, WHEN SURYA FOUND THAT KARNA WOULD NOT SWERVE-
WHY I SEEK YOUR VICTORY IS A SECRET THAT WILL BE REVEALED TO YOU IN DUE TIME.

MEANWHILE, TRUST ME AND DO AS I SAY.
AND HE TOLD KARNA WHAT HE MUST DO.

REMEMBER. YOU WILL PART WITH YOUR NATIVE GIFTS - THE GIFTS THAT ENSURE YOUR INDESTRUCTIBILITY - ONLY ON THIS CONDITION.
SO BE IT.
AND SURYA FADED AWAY.

AT NOON THE NEXT DAY -
GIVE ME ALMS. PARE OFF YOUR COAT-OF-MAIL. CUT OFF YOUR EARRINGS AND GIVE THEM TO ME.

KARNA LOOKED UP AND SMILED.
O INDRA, AS LORD OF THE CELESTIALS YOU SHOULD BE CONFERRING BOONS. BESIDES...
SURYA WAS AWARE OF MY... HE HAS TOLD YOU...

IF I GIVE YOU MY NATIVE ARMOUR, I COULD BE SLAIN AND YOU, O GREAT DEVA, WOULD BE RIDICULED. SO...

...TAKE THEM BY ALL MEANS. BUT IN EXCHANGE I WANT...
EXCEPT FOR MY VAJRA MISSILE, SEEK WHAT YOU DESIRE FROM ME.

GIVE ME AN INFALLIBLE MISSILE WITH WHICH I CAN SLAY IN BATTLE THE ONE FOE WHO MIGHT STRIKE TERROR IN ME.
INDRA DELIBERATED FOR BUT AN INSTANT.

THEN -
ACCEPT THIS MISSILE. IT WILL SLAY ONE MIGHTY FOE OF YOURS AND RETURN TO ME. BUT...

...THAT FOE WILL NOT BE THE ONE YOU SEEK TO SLAY FOR HE IS PROTECTED BY KRISHNA.

THOUGH OUTWITTED, KARNA CHEERFULLY KEPT HIS WORD. INDRA WAS DELIGHTED.
O KARNA, FOR KEEPING YOUR PLEDGE, MAY YOUR WOUNDS HEAL AND YOUR SCARS VANISH AT ONCE!

PLEASED WITH HIMSELF, INDRA THEN SOARED UPTO HIS REALMS, WHILE KARNA MADE HIS WAY TOWARDS THE PALACE.

WHILE NEWS OF KARNA'S GREAT LOSS FOR A LIMITED GAIN PLUNGED THE KAURAVAS DEEP INTO GLOOM AND INACTION...

...IT GAVE THE PANDAVAS THE LIFT THEY NEEDED FOR THE MOST DIFFICULT LAP OF THEIR LONG EXILE.

TAKING LEAVE OF THE SEERS AND SAGES IN THE FOREST...
THE THIRTEENTH YEAR HAS BEGUN. PERMIT US TO DEPART INTO OBLIVION.
...THE PANDAVAS, DHOUMYA AND DRAUPADI WALKED AWAY.

YUDHISHTHIRA THEN TOOK HIS BROTHERS AND DRAUPADI ASIDE AND –
WE SHALL SPEND THIS YEAR SERVING VIRATA, THE AGED KING OF THE MATSYAS. HE IS LOVED BY ALL AND HE LOVES THE PANDAVAS.

WHAT WORK WOULD EACH ONE OF YOU TAKE UP AT HIS COURT?

ARJUNA'S HEART BLED FOR HIS KING.
WHAT WILL YOU WHO WERE NEVER BORN TO SERVE DO, O KING?

YUDHISHTHIRA SMILED.
I SHALL PRESENT MYSELF AS KANKA, A BRAHMANA SKILLED IN DICE AND FOND OF THE GAME. I SHALL BECOME HIS COURTIER AND...

...CASTING DICE OF BLACK AND WHITE AND MOVING IVORY PAWNS OF YELLOW AND WHITE AND RED AND BLUE ON EXQUISITE BOARDS I SHALL ENTERTAIN HIM WITH MY PLAY.

IF ASKED ABOUT MY ANTECEDENTS I WILL SAY I WAS A CLOSE FRIEND OF YUDHISHTHIRA'S. AND AS LONG AS I HUMOUR THE KING NOBODY WILL FIND ME OUT.

AND WHAT OFFICE WILL YOU SEEK, YOU MIGHTY BHEEMA?
THAT OF A COOK AND WRESTLER. I WILL CALL MYSELF VALLAVA.

BY MY CULINARY SKILLS AND GREAT MIGHT I WILL GAIN ABSOLUTE CONTROL OVER ALL THE FOOD AND DRINK AND SERVANTS IN THE PALACE KITCHENS.

AND IF THE KING IS CURIOUS, I WILL SAY: I WAS YUDHISHTHIRA'S COOK AND WRESTLER EARLIER, O KING.

AND WHAT DISGUISE FOR YOU, O WIELDER OF THE GANDEEVA, WHO DWELT FIVE YEARS IN THE REALMS OF INDRA ACQUIRING THE MYSTERIES OF SUPERHUMAN WEAPONS?

AND ARJUNA FELL SILENT.

NAKULA CHOSE TO BECOME A GROOM AND CALL HIM SELF GRANTHIKA.
IF ASKED ABOUT MY CREDENTIALS I WILL SAY I WAS ONCE THE HEAD GROOM IN YUDHISHTHIRA'S STABLES.

AND YOU, SAHADEVA? WHAT DISGUISE WOULD YOU CHOOSE?
I WILL GO AS TANTIPALA, A COWHERD AND HEAD THE CATTLE-KEEPERS AT VIRATA'S PALACE. NO ONE WILL FIND ME OUT.

THEN CAME DRAUPADI'S TURN.
UNACCUSTOMED TO HARD WORK AS OUR BELOVED, DELICATE WIFE, BORN TO A LIFE OF LUXURY, WHAT WILL SHE DO?

THERE IS A CLASS OF WOMEN CALLED SAIRANDHRIS, WHO SERVE IN OTHERS' HOMES FOR A LIVING.

I WILL DECLARE MYSELF A SAIRANDHRI WHO IS SKILLED IN HAIR-DRESSING AND WAIT UPON VIRATA'S QUEEN. IF ASKED I WILL SAY I WAS ONCE DRAUPADI'S ATTENDANT.

DO NOT LOOK SO PAINED, O KING. ONCE IN SUDESHNA'S SERVICE, I WILL BE LOOKED AFTER BY HER.

AND NO ONE WILL SUSPECT WHO I REALLY AM.
O DRAUPADI, YOU ARE HIGHBORN AND INNOCENT.

EFFACE YOURSELF SO THAT YOU ARE SPARED THE VULGAR GAZE OF MEN.
THEIR ROLES THUS DETERMINED...

...YUDHISHTHIRA TURNED HIS MIND TO OTHER MATTERS.
LET DHOUMYA, ALONG WITH OUR CHARIOTEERS AND DRAUPADI'S MAIDS, GO TO DRUPADA'S PALACE, AND KEEP OUR SACRED FIRES ALIVE THERE.

LET INDRASENA AND OUR ATTENDANTS PROCEED TO DWARAKA WITH THE EMPTY CHARIOTS.

TO ALL WHO ENQUIRE LET THEM SAY: THE PANDAVAS LEFT US AT DWAITAVANA. WE DO NOT KNOW WHERE THEY HAVE GONE.
THE INSTRUCTIONS CARRIED OUT...

...THE PANDAVAS AND DRAUPADI LEAVING THEIR FOREST LIFE BEHIND, HEADED FOR THE MATSYA KINGDOM.

WHEN THEY NEARED THE CAPITAL CITY, YUDHISHTHIRA SUDDENLY STOPPED.
IF WE ENTER THE CITY ARMED, WE WOULD ATTRACT UNDUE ATTENTION. BESIDES, YOUR MIGHTY GANDEEVA WOULD GIVE US AWAY. AND...

...IF EVEN ONE OF US IS RECOGNIZED WE WILL HAVE TO GO BACK INTO EXILE FOR ANOTHER TWELVE YEARS. LET US HIDE OUR WEAPONS SOMEWHERE.

ARJUNA HAD A SUGGESTION.
NEAR THAT DREARY CEMETERY, THERE IS A THICK, DARK SNAKE-INFESTED FOREST, IN THE MIDST OF WHICH STANDS A HUGE, SPRAWLING SHAMI TREE THAT FEW CAN CLIMB.

IF WE STOW OUR WEAPONS AWAY IN THAT TREE, NO ONE WOULD SEE US DO IT AND...

...WE COULD ENTER THE CITY WITH CONFIDENCE AND LIVE THERE WITHOUT ANXIETY.

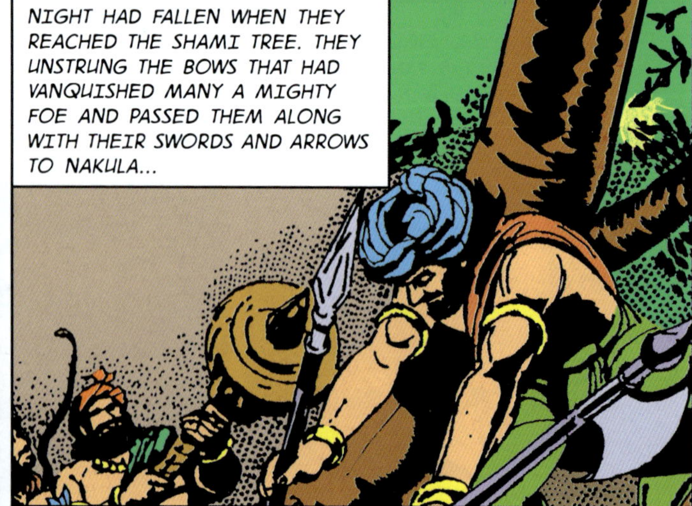
NIGHT HAD FALLEN WHEN THEY REACHED THE SHAMI TREE. THEY UNSTRUNG THE BOWS THAT HAD VANQUISHED MANY A MIGHTY FOE AND PASSED THEM ALONG WITH THEIR SWORDS AND ARROWS TO NAKULA...

...WHO TIED THEM TO STRONG BRANCHES SAFE FROM THE EYES OF MEN AND THE FURY OF THE ELEMENTS.
THERE! THEY SHOULD REMAIN SAFE AND DRY HERE.

TO MAKE THE WEAPONS DOUBLY SAFE THEY BROUGHT A CORPSE FROM THE CEMETERY AND HUNG IT CONSPICUOUSLY ON THE TREE.
THE STENCH SHOULD KEEP PEOPLE FROM CLIMBING THE TREE.
AND THEY SPENT THE NIGHT THERE TO SEE IF ANYONE CAME BY.

IT WAS DAWN WHEN A FEW SHEPHERDS AND COWHERDS, DRAWN BY THE STENCH, CAME THERE TO INVESTIGATE.
HEY! WHO ARE YOU?
HOW DID THAT CORPSE GET UP THERE?

THAT IS THE DEAD BODY OF OUR 180-YEAR-OLD MOTHER. WE HAVE HUNG IT UP THERE IN KEEPING WITH A TRADITION OF OUR TRIBE.

WHO ARE YOU?
WE ARE ...JAYA, JAYANTA, VIJAYA, JAYATSENA AND JAYADBALA.

AS THE COWHERDS WALKED AWAY STILL HOLDING THEIR NOSES -
LET US KEEP THOSE NAMES TO ALERT THE OTHERS IN CASE THE NEED ARISES.

AND THEN, AS THE YEAR WAS ABOUT TO END, THE FORMIDABLE KEECHAKA, QUEEN SUDESHNA'S BROTHER AND THE COMMANDER OF VIRATA'S ARMIES CHANCED TO SEE DRAUPADI.

HE WAS CAPTIVATED BY HER FACE AND FORM!

WHO IS THIS ENCHANTING GODDESS? SHE SHOULD NOT BE SERVING YOU. SHE SHOULD GRACE MY PALACE AND RULE OVER ME, SUDESHNA!

YOU DESIRE ONE WHO DOES NOT MERIT THAT HONOUR. I AM BUT A HUMBLE SAIRANDHRI, A HAIR DRESSER.

BESIDES, I AM MARRIED. SO YOUR CONDUCT IS NOT PROPER. DO NOT INVITE INFAMY OR SOME DEADLY DISASTER UPON YOURSELF BY DESIRING ME.

DRAUPADI'S GENTLE REBUKE ONLY MADE HER ALL THE MORE DESIRABLE.
IF YOU REJECT ME WHO SPEAKS TO YOU SO SWEETLY, O TIMID ONE, YOU WILL REPENT.

IN LOOKS, MIGHT, VIRILITY AND PROSPERITY, I STAND UNMATCHED. I, KEECHAKA, AM THE REAL LORD, THE PROTECTOR OF THIS KINGDOM.

WHEN YOU COULD BE ITS MISTRESS BASKING IN LUXURY WHY DO YOU PREFER SERVITUDE?
O KEECHAKA, WHY DO YOU DESIRE ME?

YOU CAN NEVER HAVE ME. I HAVE FIVE GANDHARVAS FOR HUSBANDS WHO WILL SLAY YOU FOR SOLICITING THEIR BELOVED WIFE.

DO NOT THROW AWAY YOUR LIFE, KEECHAKA.

BE SENSIBLE. SEEK YOUR GOOD AND PRESERVE YOUR LIFE.
AND DRAUPADI LEFT THE CHAMBER.

REJECTED BY DRAUPADI, KEECHAKA APPEALED TO HIS SISTER.
O DAUGHTER OF KEKAYA, O SUDESHNA, PROMPT YOUR SAIRANDHRI TO COME INTO MY ARMS OR I SHALL DIE OF DESIRE.

THE INTELLIGENT SUDESHNA WAS MOVED BY HER BROTHER'S PLIGHT.
HE WISHES TO MAKE HER HIS QUEEN. AND SHE IS RELUCTANT. PERHAPS SHE FEARS HER GANDHARVA HUSBANDS. PERHAPS MY PRESENCE INHIBITS HER... HM.M...

AND SO -
I SHALL SEND HER TO YOU ON THE PRETEXT OF FETCHING ME SOME FOOD AND DRINK. WHEN SHE COMES, WOO HER IN PRIVATE AND SHE MIGHT RESPOND.

ACCORDINGLY, THE NEXT DAY -
SAIRANDHRI, GO TO KEECHAKA AND BRING ME SOME WINE. I AM VERY THIRSTY.

O QUEEN, I CANNOT GO THERE. YOU KNOW HOW SHAMELESS HE IS. I WILL NOT SWERVE. AND...

...AND HE WILL INSULT ME. YOU HAVE MANY OTHER MAIDS. PLEASE SEND ONE OF THEM.
WHEN I HAVE SENT YOU, HE WILL NOT HARM YOU. GO.

DRAUPADI HAD NO CHOICE BUT TO OBEY SUDESHNA, HER MISTRESS.
LET KEECHAKA NOT OVERPOWER ME.

AND LIKE A FRIGHTENED DOE SHE ENTERED HIS HOUSE.
WELCOME! WELCOME! IT IS INDEED AN AUSPICIOUS DAY FOR ME THAT I HAVE GOT YOU HERE AS THE MISTRESS OF MY HOUSE.

EXOTIC NECKLACES AND EARRINGS OF GOLD, RUBIES AND GEMS AND SILKS AND DEER-SKINS SHALL BE YOURS.

COME, SIT ON THIS EXQUISITE BED I HAVE MADE FOR YOU AND DRINK THIS SPECIAL WINE WITH ME.

YOUR SISTER HAS SENT ME TO YOU FOR SOME WINE. BE QUICK, FOR SHE TOLD ME SHE WAS VERY THIRSTY.

O GENTEEL LADY, LET OTHERS FETCH AND CARRY FOR HER. YOU FULFIL MY DESIRE.
WRETCH! I SHALL SEE YOU DRAGGED IN THE DUST FOR THIS!

DRAUPADI TURNED AND FLED. BUT -

THE THREAT OF VIOLATION DRAWING FORTH ALL THE LATENT POWERS OF A WOMAN, SHE DASHED THE VILE KEECHAKA TO THE GROUND...

...AND RAN TOWARDS YUDHISHTHIRA.

KEECHAKA HOWEVER, CAUGHT UP WITH HER...

...AND KICKED HER IN THE VERY PRESENCE OF THE KING!

BUT HE LOST HIS BALANCE, REELED...
...AND FELL.

BHEEMA WAS ON THE POINT OF GETTING UP WHEN -
O COOK, IF YOU NEED WOOD GO OUT AND FELL TREES.

SUPPRESSING HIS RAGE, BHEEMA MEEKLY WALKED OUT.

DRAUPADI WAS SHOCKED.
THEY WOULD STILL RESPECT THAT PLEDGE. THEY WOULD EVEN NOW REMAIN INCOGNITO!

SHE LET HER FURY LOOSE ON THE KING.
THAT I SHOULD BE WRONGED IN YOUR VERY PRESENCE, O KING, IS A BLOT ON YOU!

IF KEECHAKA IS BRUTAL, IGNORANT AND IMMORAL, YOU ARE EQUALLY SO.

AND SO ARE THESE COURTIERS WHO WAIT UPON A KING SUCH AS YOU!
SAIRANDHRI!

DO NOT DISTURB THE PLAY IN VIRATA'S COURT. IN YOUR IGNORANCE, YOU WEEP LIKE AN ACTRESS. GO, NOW, TO SUDESHNA.

YOUR GANDHARVA HUSBANDS ARE SURE TO DO WHAT YOU DESIRE. THEY WILL SLAY THE ONE WHO HAS WRONGED YOU.

THEY TO WHOM I AM THE WIFE, ARE VERY KIND. BESIDES WITH THE ELDEST ADDICTED TO GAMBLING, IT IS THEY WHO SEEM TO BE ALL TOO VULNERABLE.
WITH THIS PARTING BARB, DRAUPADI LEFT THE COURT AND...

...SOBBING ALL THE WAY RAN TO SUDESHNA.
WHY DO YOU WEEP, GENTLE ONE? HAS ANYONE HURT YOU?
W-WHEN I WENT FOR THE WINE K... KEECHAKA...

BUT DRAUPADI WAS NOT AS CONFIDENT AS SHE SOUNDED.

RETURNING TO HER QUARTERS, SHE WASHED HER BODY AND HER CLOTHES. THEN -

THAT NIGHT WHEN ALL THE PALACE WAS ASLEEP, SHE ENTERED THE ROYAL KITCHENS.

ARISE! ARISE! O BHEEMA, YOU LIE LIKE ONE DEAD? IF YOU ARE ALIVE, HOW IS IT THAT THE WRETCH WHO HAS INSULTED YOUR WIFE IS NOT DEAD?

BHEEMA AWOKE AND SAT UP WITH A START.
WHY HAVE YOU COME HERE?
WHAT ELSE CAN SHE WHO HAS YUDHISHTHIRA FOR A HUSBAND DO?

ALAS! BECAUSE OF THAT DESPERATE GAMBLER, I AM NOW SUDESHNA'S BONDMAID.
YOU LOOK PALE!

TELL ME QUICKLY WHAT YOU WANT OF ME AND RETURN TO YOUR BED BEFORE OTHERS WAKE UP.

YOU TOO, BHEEMA? OF WHAT USE IS LIFE TO ME WHEN EVEN YOU DO NOT UNDERSTAND WHAT I SUFFER?

AND DRAUPADI WEPT HER WOES. THEN –
SHE WHO SERVED ONLY KUNTI, WHO NEITHER FEARED HER, NOR YOU, NOR YOUR BROTHERS, NOW AS VIRATA'S SLAVE, POUNDS SANDALWOOD INTO PASTE FOR HIM, EVER AFRAID OF HIS DISPLEASURE.

LOOK AT THESE HANDS. UNFORTUNATE THAT I AM, I STILL LIVE, O PANDAVA, WHEN I SHOULD BE DEAD!

AT THIS, THAT VERITABLE GIANT BROKE DOWN AND WEPT LIKE A CHILD.
FIE ON THE MIGHT OF MY ARMS AND FIE ON THE GANDEEVA!

THE THOUGHT THAT DURYODHANA, KARNA, SHAKUNI AND DUSHASANA ARE NOT YET SLAIN BURNS ME.

I WOULD HAVE CRUSHED KEECHAKA'S SKULL WHEN I SAW HIM KICK YOU. BUT THE SON OF DHARMA RESTRAINED ME IN TIME.

SUBDUE YOUR RAGE, DRAUPADI. YUDHISHTHIRA WILL END HIS LIFE IF HE HEARS YOU CENSURE HIM SO. BE PATIENT.

A FEW DAYS FROM NOW THE THIRTEENTH YEAR WILL COME TO AN END AND YOU SHALL BE THE REIGNING QUEEN.
BUT THE WORK OF THE HOUR MUST BE SPEEDILY DONE. IT CANNOT WAIT.

WHAT IS IT? CONFIDE IN ME.
IT IS THAT VILE KEECHAKA.

AND DRAUPADI TOLD BHEEMA ABOUT ALL THAT HAD HAPPENED AFTER HE HAD LEFT THE COURT.
...THEN, WHEN YOU LEFT, I REBUKED KANKA AND THE KING. BUT...

...THAT SOVEREIGN LET KEECHAKA OFF WITHOUT EVEN CHASTISING HIM! MIGHTY KEECHAKA IS OBVIOUSLY A FEARED FAVOURITE. SO HE IS SURE TO STALK ME AND VIOLATE MY PERSON. AND...

...IF THAT HAPPENS, I WILL TAKE MY LIFE.

O BHEEMA, YOU MUST SLAY THE VILE WRETCH.
I WILL. I WILL SLAY HIM AND ALL HIS FRIENDS.
AND BHEEMA TOLD HER WHAT SHE MUST DO.

THE NEXT MORNING, AS DRAUPADI HAD FORESEEN, KEECHAKA ACCOSTED HER IN THE PALACE.
I KICKED YOU IN THE VERY PRESENCE OF THE KING, YET NO ONE STIRRED, NOT EVEN HE, FOR I AM THE TRUE LORD OF THE KINGDOM.

ACCEPT ME AND I SHALL BE YOUR SLAVE.

TIMID GIRL, PERMIT OUR UNION.
I WOULD, O MIGHTY KEECHAKA, WERE I NOT TERRIFIED OF MY GANDHARVA HUSBANDS. HOWEVER...

...IF YOU PROMISE TO KEEP OUR TRYST A SECRET FROM EVEN YOUR BROTHERS AND YOUR FRIENDS...
I PROMISE. NO ONE WILL KNOW.

LEAST OF ALL THE GANDHARVAS. I WILL COME, ALL ALONE... AT DEAD OF NIGHT... TO YOUR QUARTERS.
NO, NOT THERE!

COME TO THE NEWLY BUILT DANCE-HALL. IT IS DESERTED AT NIGHT AND THE GANDHARVAS DO NOT KNOW OF THAT PLACE.
THE TRYST FIXED, AN ECSTATIC KEECHAKA WENT AWAY TO PREEN HIMSELF.

THAT NIGHT, DECKED, ORNAMENTED AND PERFUMED, HE STRUTTED INTO THE PITCH-DARK DANCE-HALL...
...FELT HIS WAY TO THE COUCH IN A CORNER...

...AND BEGAN TO CARESS THE FORM LYING THERE.
GREAT WEALTH, A MANSION, AND GORGEOUS YOUNG MAIDS TO SERVE YOU ARE ALREADY SET APART FOR YOU. AND AS I HASTENED TO YOU, WOMEN ADMIRED MY LOOKS AND ATTIRE AS UNEQUALLED.

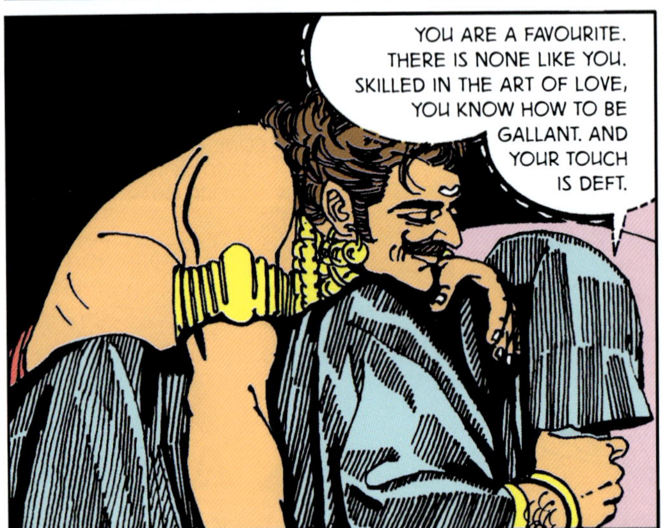
YOU ARE A FAVOURITE. THERE IS NONE LIKE YOU. SKILLED IN THE ART OF LOVE, YOU KNOW HOW TO BE GALLANT. AND YOUR TOUCH IS DEFT.

BUT NEVER BEFORE COULD YOUR TOUCH HAVE GIVEN SO MUCH PLEASURE.
IT WAS BHEEMA DISGUISED AS A WOMAN!

YOUR SISTER, FOUL WRETCH, WILL SEE YOU DRAGGED IN THE DUST AND SLAUGHTERED BY ME.

SAIRANDHRI, AND WE, HER HUSBANDS WILL THEN LIVE IN PEACE.

IN THE VIOLENT SCUFFLE BETWEEN THE TWO GIANTS, BHEEMA'S PUNCHES, POWERED BY HIS PENT-UP RAGE, WERE THE DEADLIER...

...AND KEECHAKA FELL.

COME, O PRINCESS OF PANCHALA, AND SEE THE STATE OF YOUR VILE TORMENTOR!

SUCH WILL BE THE FATE OF ANYONE WHO ATTEMPTS TO VIOLATE YOU.

I HAVE RID YOU OF THE THORN IN YOUR FLESH AND DISCHARGED THE DEBT I OWED MY BROTHERS.
AND BHEEMA WENT BACK TO HIS BED BY THE KITCHEN.

COME! BEHOLD THIS! KEECHAKA IS DEAD. MY GANDHARVA HUSBANDS HAVE SLAIN THE VILLAIN!

DRAUPADI'S LOUD, TRIUMPHANT CALL BROUGHT GUARDS AND KINSMEN INTO THE DANCE-HALL.
ALAS! MIGHTY KEECHAKA LIES DEAD.
HIS DESIRE FOR THIS WOMAN HAS COST HIM HIS LIFE.
SLAY HER!
NO. LET US CREMATE HER WITH HIM AS HE DIED DESIRING HER.
CREMATE HER!

TERROR CHOCKED THE CRY THAT ROSE IN DRAUPADI'S THROAT.

THE MOB SEIZED AND BOUND HER AND...

...PLACING HER ON THE BIER BESIDE THE MANGLED KEECHAKA...
...SET OUT FOR THE CREMATORIUM-

IT WAS ONLY THEN THAT DRAUPADI FOUND HER VOICE.
O JAYA! O JAYANTA! O VIJAYA! O GANDHARVAS! CAN YOU HEAR ME? THEY ARE TAKING ME AWAY!

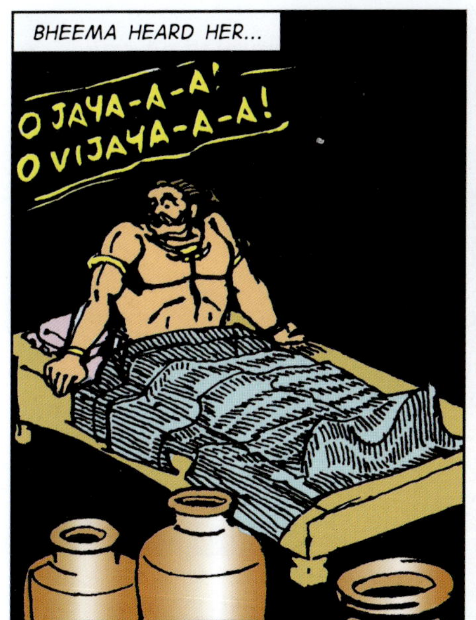
BHEEMA HEARD HER...
O JAYA-A-A!
O VIJAYA-A-A!

...AND FOLLOWED-

SOON -
THE GANDHARVA!

DROP SAIRANDHRI! RUN!
RUN!

BHEEMA SLEW A HUNDRED OF THEM...

...BEFORE GOING TO DRAUPADI.
THEY ARE NO MORE. I HAVE SLAIN THEM ALL.

RETURN TO THE CITY WITHOUT FEAR. I WILL GO BACK TO VIRATA'S KITCHEN.
AND THE TWO TOOK SEPARATE ROUTES BACK TO THE PALACE.

NOT LONG AFTER, THE SPIES SENT OUT BY DURYODHANA TO TRACK AND EXPOSE THE PANDAVAS, RETURNED TO HASTINAPURA.
THEY SEEM TO HAVE VANISHED WITHOUT TRACE.

THEY ARE GONE FOR GOOD.
BUT WE HAVE SOME NEWS FOR YOU AND THE TRIGARTAS.

VIRATA'S COMMANDER, KEECHAKA, IS NO MORE. A GANDHARVA SLEW HIM AND HIS BROTHERS IN THE DEAD OF NIGHT.
SUSHARMAN, THE RULER OF THE TRIGARTAS WAS A STAUNCH ALLY OF THE KAURAVAS.

KEECHAKA HAD FREQUENTLY RAIDED SUSHARMAN'S KINGDOM AND DECIMATED HIS TRIBE.
WITH KEECHAKA DEAD, VIRATA IS POWERLESS. NOW IS THE TIME TO JOIN OUR FORCES AND PLUNDER MATSYA OF ITS IMMENSE CATTLE WEALTH.

THE IDEA APPEALED TO KARNA.

AND SO THE CONSECUTIVE FORAYS ON VIRATA'S KINGDOM WERE MADE.

BUT THERE, THE KAURAVAS TURNED OUT TO BE THE LOSERS AS THE FORAYS WERE ILL-TIMED. WHEN THEY WERE MADE THE THIRTEENTH YEAR HAD JUST ENDED.

AND FOR THE VALOUR AND LOYALTY THE PANDAVAS HAD SEPARATELY SHOWN IN THE BATTLEFIELD...

...VIRATA, WHEN THEY DISCLOSED THEMSELVES, SOUGHT AN ALLIANCE WITH THEM! IT WAS SEALED WITH THE MARRIAGE OF HIS DAUGHTER UTTARAA AND ARJUNA'S SON ABHIMANYU.

FOUR DAYS LATER, KRISHNA, BALARAMA, SATYAKI, DRUPADA, DHRISHTADYUMNA, SHIKHANDI, THE PANDAVAS, VIRATA AND HIS SON, ASSEMBLED AT VIRATA'S COURT.

YET HE, HIS BROTHERS AND ALLIES BEAR THEM NO GRUDGE. THE PANDAVAS WANT ONLY THAT WHICH THEY ESTABLISHED ALL BY THEMSELVES, BATTLING AND SUBDUING VARIOUS KINGS.

SINCE WE DO NOT KNOW DURYODHANA'S MIND, BEFORE WE ACT I THINK WE SHOULD SEND A CLEVER ENVOY TO INDUCE HIM TO RESTORE HALF THE KURU KINGDOM TO THE PANDAVAS.

KRISHNA'S WORDS EVOKED DIVERSE AND DIFFERING OPINIONS. THEN DRUPADA STATED HIS.
I THINK WE SHOULD FIRST SEND OUT MESSENGERS TO OUR FRIENDS TO COME HERE WITH THEIR ARMIES.

AND THEN MY WISE, LEARNED PRIEST COULD GO TO HASTINAPURA WITH OUR DEMAND.

FOR I KNOW DURYODHANA WILL NEVER AGREE AND WILL AT ONCE SEND HIS MESSENGERS OUT. AND THE KINGS WILL HELP THE ONE WHO APPROACHES THEM FIRST.

DRUPADA'S STRATEGY OF PREPARING FOR WAR EVEN WHILE NEGOTIATING FOR PEACE, FOUND FAVOUR WITH KRISHNA. BUT -
I LOOK UPON BOTH FACTIONS WITH EQUAL AFFECTION. YOU ARE PARTIAL TO YUDHISHTHIRA WHICH IS AS IT SHOULD BE.

AND SOON AFTER KRISHNA, BALARAMA AND THE YADAVA ENTOURAGE LEFT, VIRATA AND DRUPADA SENT THEIR ENVOYS OUT TO RALLY THEIR ALLIES.

RESPONDING TO THEIR CALL, THE KINGS TROOPED INTO UPAPLAVYA, THE MATSYA TOWN WHERE THE PANDAVAS NOW LIVED...

...WHILE DRUPADA'S PRIEST LEFT FOR HASTINAPURA AND ARJUNA FOR DWARAKA.

DURYODHANA KNEW OF ALL THEIR MOVES FROM HIS ALERT SPIES.

DURYODHANA AT ONCE SENT OUT HIS ENVOYS TO FRIENDLY KINGS AND SPED TO DWARAKA. THERE HE FOUND KRISHNA FAST ASLEEP. SO HE WAITED.

A LITTLE LATER ARJUNA, TOO CAME THERE.

WHEN KRISHNA AT LAST OPENED HIS EYES, DURYODHANA CRIED OUT –
I SEEK YOUR HELP IN OUR DISPUTE WITH THE PANDAVAS. TRADITION DEMANDS THAT THE GREAT HELP HIM WHO SEEKS IT FIRST.

YOU, DURYODHANA, WERE THE FIRST TO COME AND SPEAK, HOWEVER, I SAW ARJUNA FIRST. SO I AM DUTY-BOUND TO HELP BOTH.

BUT TRADITION DICTATES THAT THE WANTS OF THE YOUNGEST SHOULD BE ATTENDED TO FIRST.

WHAT DO YOU WANT, ARJUNA? A CONTINGENT OF MIGHTY WARRIORS OR MYSELF AS A COUNSELLOR WHO WILL NOT WIELD WEAPONS?
I CHOOSE YOU.

ARJUNA HAD THE INSIGHT TO DISCRIMINATE BETWEEN THE ESSENCE AND THE IMAGE.
COME WITH ME TO UPAPLAVYA. AND BE MY CHARIOTEER.
FOOL!
WHILE KRISHNA AND ARJUNA WENT TO YUDHISHTHIRA...

...DURYODHANA STAYED BACK AND APPROACHED BALARAMA. BUT -
I CANNOT OPPOSE KRISHNA. SO I HAVE DECIDED NOT TO FIGHT. YOU ARE THE DESCENDANTS OF GREAT KING BHARATA. FIGHT YOUR BATTLE BY THE KSHATRIYA CODE.

WITH NEITHER BALARAMA NOR KRISHNA FIGHTING, VICTORY IS SURE TO BE MINE!
AND HE WENT TO KRITAVARMAN WHO WAS TO LEAD THE CONTINGENT OF WARRIORS PROMISED BY KRISHNA.

WHEN HE REACHED HASTINAPURA, HE LEARNT THAT SHALYA,THE MATERNAL UNCLE OF NAKULA AND SAHADEVA, WAS ON HIS WAY TO UPAPLAVYA WITH A HUGE ARMY.
PAVE HIS PATH WITH MAGNIFICENT REST-HOUSES. LAVISH THE KING OF MADRA WITH EVERY HOSPITALITY.

SO EFFECTIVELY WERE THE ORDERS EXECUTED THAT SHALYA WAS OVERWHELMED.
I WOULD GIVE UP MY VERY LIFE FOR THE MAN WHO HAS ARRANGED SUCH A ROYAL RECEPTION IN MY HONOUR.

THEN BE THE COMMANDER OF MY ARMIES AND LEAD US TO VICTORY. FOR I, DURYODHANA AM THE MAN.
UH?
THE ELDEST KAURAVA WAS HARDLY THE HOST HE HAD IN MIND WHEN SHALYA HAD MADE HIS DECLARATION!

BUT RETAINING HIS COMPOSURE, HE GRACIOUSLY HONOURED HIS WORD.
SO BE IT. BUT I WOULD LIKE TO SEE YUDHISHTHIRA BEFORE I JOIN YOU.
GO BY ALL MEANS. BUT DO NOT FORGET YOUR PROMISE.

WHEN SHALYA TOLD YUDHISHTHIRA HOW HE HAD BEEN TRAPPED -
IT IS GOOD YOU AGREED. BECOME KARNA'S CHARIOTEER AND PROTECT ARJUNA BY DEMORALIZING HIM WHEN THEY ENGAGE IN SINGLE COMBAT.

IT SHALL BE DONE. I SHALL MISLEAD HIM WITH CONFUSING COUNSEL AND SHAKE HIS SELF CONFIDENCE BY ERODING HIS SELF-ESTEEM.
AND SHALYA RETURNED TO DURYODHANA.

MEANWHILE DRUPADA'S PRIEST REACHED HASTINAPURA AND COMMENCED HIS TASK.
THOUGH WRONGED BY THE KAURAVAS TIME AND AGAIN, THE PANDAVAS HOLD NO GRUDGE. THEY ONLY WANT THEIR SHARE OF THE PATRIMONIAL KINGDOM WITHOUT WAR.

IF DURYODHANA WITH HIS ELEVEN CONTINGENTS BELIEVES THAT FEAR MAKES THEM SUE FOR PEACE, LET HIM REMEMBER THAT THOUGH THEY HAVE ONLY SEVEN CONTINGENTS, THEY HAVE ARJUNA AND KRISHNA.

WOULD ANYONE SEEK A CONFRONATION WITH THOSE TWO? CONSIDER ALL THIS AND GIVE ME YOUR REPLY.

BHEESHMA WAS ALL FOR THE PANDAVAS.
IT IS FORTUNATE THAT THE PANDAVAS FORGIVE THEIR COUSINS AND SEEK PEACE WITH THEM. FOR INDRA HIMSELF COULD NOT...
ENOUGH!

THEIR EXPLOITS ARE KNOWN TO ALL. THERE IS NO NEED TO RECITE THEM HERE. DURYODHANA WILL NOT PART WITH EVEN A FOURTH OF HIS KINGDOM.

IF THEY TRY TO WREST IT FROM HIM, THEY WILL REPENT.
WHY DO YOU BRAG KARNA? HAVE YOU FORGOTTEN HOW ARJUNA, ALONE, ROUTED THE SIX OF US IN VIRATA'S KINGDOM?

IF WE DO NOT HEED THIS BRAHMANA, IT IS WE WHO WILL HAVE TO REPENT.

DHRITARASHTRA REBUKED KARNA AND LAUDED BHEESHMA.
THE SON OF SHANTANU HAS SPOKEN WELL. FOR THE GOOD OF ALL A WAR MUST BE AVERTED.
HE THEN SENT THE PRIEST BACK TO THE PANDAVAS...

...AND SUMMONED HIS COUNSELLOR SANJAYA TO THE ASSEMBLY.
O SANJAYA, THE PANDAVAS ARE POWERFUL AND GENEROUS. THEY HAVE GIVEN US ALL THE WEALTH THEY HAD WON BY THE MIGHT OF THEIR ARMS. THEY HAVE NO ENEMIES SAVE MY FOOLISH SON AND KARNA.

DURYODHANA IS A FOOL TO THINK HE CAN USURP THEIR KINGDOM WHEN THE PANDAVAS HAVE KRISHNA FOR THEIR COUNSELLOR.

AND YET IT IS YUDHISHTHIRA'S ANGER I FEAR MOST. HE IS AN ASCETIC. IF HE HAD SO CHOSEN, HE COULD HAVE DESTROYED US ALL AT THE GAMBLING BOUT. IT WOULD BE WISE TO AVERT A WAR.

GO TO YUDHISHTHIRA, SANJAYA. PRAISE THE PANDAVAS AND PRAISE KRISHNA. TELL THEM THAT DHRITARASHTRA DESIRES PEACE WITH THEM.
AND SO SANJAYA SET OUT FOR UPAPLAVYA.

AT UPAPLAVYA, SANJAYA MET YUDHISHTHIRA AND AFTER THE CUSTOMARY FORMALITIES, CAME TO THE POINT.
FEAR FOR THE LIVES OF HIS SONS CONSUMES WISE, OLD DHRITARASHTRA. IF THE KURUS DO NOT YIELD YOUR SHARE, FORGO IT.

DO NOT PRECIPITATE A WAR. FOR, WITH ARJUNA AND KRISHNA IN ONE CAMP AND DRONA AND BHEESHMA IN THE OTHER...

...THAT WAR CAN ONLY RESULT IN A WANTON LOSS OF VALUABLE LIVES ON EITHER SIDE.
WOULD ANYONE WANT WAR IF JUSTICE COULD BE ACHIEVED BY PEACEFUL MEANS, O SANJAYA?

THE CHOICE, SANJAYA, LIES WITH THE KAURAVAS. WE ARE READY FOR EITHER - A PEACEFUL SETTLEMENT OR WAR.

TO KILL YOUR KINSMEN FOR THE SAKE OF WEALTH WOULD BE AGAINST DHARMA. AND YOU, YUDHISHTHIRA ARE RENOWNED FOR NEVER STRAYING FROM IT.

NEITHER AM I DEVIATING FROM MY KSHATRIYA DHARMA NOW. IF YOU HAVE ANY DOUBTS, LET KRISHNA AN IMPARTIAL AUTHORITY ON THE SUBJECT DECIDE. I WILL BE GUIDED BY HIM.

THEN KRISHNA SPOKE UP.
I WISH BOTH TO PROSPER. SO I DESIRE PEACE BETWEEN THEM. BUT THE KAURAVAS COVET WHAT IS NOT THEIRS. THE PANDAVAS HAVE FULFILLED THE PLEDGE MADE AT THE GAMBLING BOUT.

IT WAS SETTLED THAT THEY WOULD GET BACK THEIR KINGDOM AFTER DOING SO. THUS IF DHRITARASHTRA AND HIS SONS STILL RETAIN IT, THE PANDAVAS ARE JUSTIFIED IN FIGHTING FOR IT.

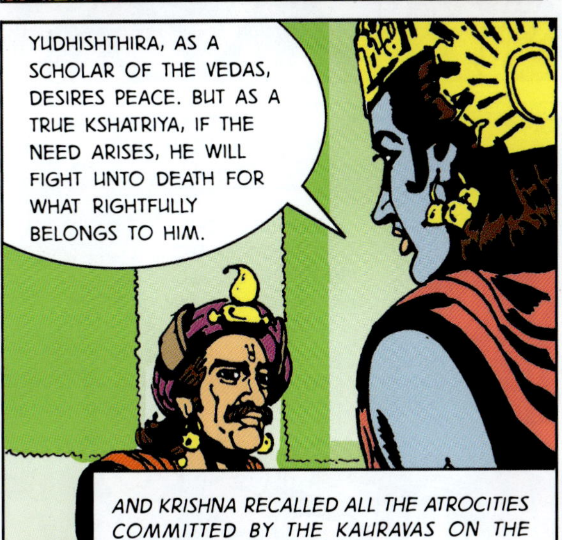
YUDHISHTHIRA, AS A SCHOLAR OF THE VEDAS, DESIRES PEACE. BUT AS A TRUE KSHATRIYA, IF THE NEED ARISES, HE WILL FIGHT UNTO DEATH FOR WHAT RIGHTFULLY BELONGS TO HIM.
AND KRISHNA RECALLED ALL THE ATROCITIES COMMITTED BY THE KAURAVAS ON THE PANDAVAS AND DRAUPADI.

WHEN SANJAYA ROSE TO LEAVE, YUDHISHTHIRA SOFTENED HIS STAND.
YOU ARE AN IMPARTIAL ENVOY AND AS DEAR TO US AS VIDURA IS. SO DO NOT TAKE OUR UNPLEASANT WORDS TO HEART.

TELL DHRITARASHTRA THAT IT WAS HE WHO ONCE INSTALLED ME ON THE THRONE. SO HE SHOULD NOT IGNORE OUR CLAIM NOW.

BUT WE DESIRE PEACE. SO, EVEN IF HE GIVES US FIVE VILLAGES, ONE FOR EACH BROTHER, WE SHALL BE CONTENT. BUT GIVE HE MUST OR FACE A WAR.

WHEN SANJAYA RETURNED TO HASTINAPURA AND DHRITARASHTRA -
YUDHISHTHIRA SENDS YOU HIS GREETINGS AND ASKS AFTER YOUR HEALTH AND THAT OF YOUR DEPENDANTS AND SUBJECTS.

IN ENDURING ALL THE WRONGS INFLICTED ON HIM BY YOU, HE HAS ROBBED YOU OF YOUR GLORY, AND ENHANCED HIS OWN.

AND NOW IF YOU DO NOT YIELD HIM HIS KINGDOM, YOU, NOT THE PANDAVAS, WILL BE RESPONSIBLE FOR THE ANNIHILATION OF THE KURUS!

WHAT DID YUDHISHTHIRA SAY, SANJAYA?
I WILL TELL YOU TOMORROW IN THE PRESENCE OF ALL THE KAURAVAS. I AM TIRED NOW.
GIVING HIM LEAVE TO RETIRE...

...THE TROUBLED KING SUMMONED VIDURA AND TOLD HIM OF SANJAYA'S RETURN AND OF HIS DISPLEASURE.
SLEEP ELUDES ME, WONDERING WHAT TOMORROW WILL BRING. SPEAK TO ME, WISE VIDURA THAT I MAY KNOW PEACE.

VIDURA SPOKE TO HIM AT LENGTH ON THE WISE AND ON WISDOM. THEN -
YUDHISHTHIRA IS WORTHY OF RULING THE UNIVERSE, YET YOU WOULD ENTRUST YOUR KINGDOM TO DURYODHANA AND HIS COUNSELLORS. HOW THEN CAN YOU HOPE FOR PEACE?

YUDHISHTHIRA ENDURED YOUR CRUELTY OUT OF DEFERENCE TO YOUR AGE. THE VIRTUOUS PANDAVAS RESPECT YOU AS THEIR FATHER AND STILL OBEY YOU.

NOT SO, DURYODHANA. HE IS LED BY KARNA, SHAKUNI, AND DUSHASANA. SET HIM ASIDE. LOVE THE PANDAVAS AS YOUR SONS AND...

...LET YUDHISHTHIRA RULE THE KINGDOM.
I KNOW WHAT YOU SAY TO BE TRUE. AND YET...
THUS DID DHRITARASHTRA, WHO HAD ALL THE ROYAL POWER BUT NO FAITH, PASS THAT WAKEFUL NIGHT LISTENING TO VIDURA WHO HAD ALL THE WISDOM BUT NO ROYAL STATUS.

THE NEXT MORNING, WHEN SANJAYA GAVE THE KURUS YUDHISHTHIRA'S MESSAGE AND NAMED THE CHIEF WARRIORS IN THE PANDAVA CAMP -
OF ALL THE WARRIORS YOU MENTION, ARJUNA IS THE MOST FORMIDABLE.

ARJUNA ALWAYS WINS. THIRTY-THREE YEARS AGO TO SATIATE AGNI, HE VANQUISHED THE VERY DEVAS. HE HAS NEVER LOST A BATTLE SINCE.

WE HAVE NEITHER A BOW, NOR A WARRIOR, NOR A CHARIOTEER TO MATCH THE COLLECTIVE IMPACT OF THE GANDEEVA, ARJUNA AND KRISHNA.

NO ONE COULD OVERPOWER BHEEMA EVEN WHEN HE WAS A MERE BOY. WHO WILL BE ABLE TO WITHSTAND HIS MIGHT NOW?

BHEEMA WILL SURELY FELL MY FOOLISH SONS IN BATTLE WITH HIS TERROR-STRIKING MACE.

BHEESHMA, DRONA, KRIPA AND I KNOW HIS MIGHT. THE PANDAVAS ARE BOUND TO BE THE VICTORS. WE KNOW THIS, AND YET WE DO NOT STOP OUR SONS.

YOU DID NOT STOP THEM THEN EITHER, O KING. YOU APPROVED WHEN THE PANDAVAS WERE TRICKED OF THEIR KINGDOM AND YOU APPROVED WHEN THEY WERE EXILED.

VIDURA AND I WARNED YOU THEN THAT YOU WERE STRAYING FROM DHARMA BUT YOU IGNORED US.

IT IS FUTILE TO FEAR THE FATE OF YOUR SONS NOW.
SANJAYA'S WORDS WORKED ON THE KING'S CONSCIENCE.

ALAS! THE DESTRUCTION OF THE KAURAVAS IS IMMINENT AND I SEE NO WAY OUT. I FEAR THE WORDS OF WISE VIDURA WILL PROVE TRUE.

DURYODHANA'S GREED FOR WEALTH AND POWER MADE HIM RESORT TO GAMBLING AND THAT GAMBLE WILL NOW BE THE RUIN OF THE KAURAVAS.

WHAT SHALL I DO? WHERE SHALL I GO?

WE HAVE WANTONLY FANNED THE FIRES OF RIGHTEOUS YUDHISHTHIRA'S WRATH. HE WILL NOT SPARE US NOW.

AND THE SPECTRE OF THE SON OF DHARMA, FLASHED BEFORE DHRITARASHTRA'S UNSEEING EYES.
O KAURAVAS, I DO NOT WANT A WAR WITH THE PANDAVAS. THIS IS THE ONLY DECISION THAT CAN BRING ME PEACE OF MIND AND I MEAN TO KEEP IT.

WE MUST NOT DEVIATE FROM DHARMA. IF WE DO, WE WILL BE UNDONE. OUR LINE WILL BE LOST FOREVER WITHOUT A TRACE.

DHRITARASHTRA SUMMONED DURYODHANA.
DO WHAT THE KURU ELDERS CONSIDER JUST. GIVE BACK TO THE PANDAVAS THEIR SHARE OF THE KINGDOM.

INDEED NONE OF THE ELDERS ON WHOSE MIGHT AND SKILL YOU RELY, APPROVE OF WAR!

IN VAIN DID THE BLIND KING TRY TO MAKE HIS ELDEST SON SEE REASON. BUT-
I WILL NOT CEDE TO THE PANDAVAS EVEN A NEEDLE-POINT OF SPACE OF THE KINGDOM.

AT UPAPLAVYA-
WHAT DO WE DO NOW, KRISHNA?

YUDHISHTHIRA WAS IN A DILEMMA.
WE DO NOT WANT TO GIVE UP OUR KINGDOM. BUT NEITHER DO WE WISH TO SEE THE KURU CLAN RUINED BY A WAR.

HOW DO WE PROTECT OUR INTERESTS AND PRESERVE OUR CLAN?
I WILL GO TO HASTINAPURA AND TRY TO SECURE BOTH.

THE PROSPECT OF A WAR THAT COULD ERASE THE KURUS FROM THE EARTH HAD SOBERED EVEN BHEEMA.
TO LIVE IN PEACE WITH A WRETCH LIKE DURYODHANA WOULD BE HARD FOR ME. YET...

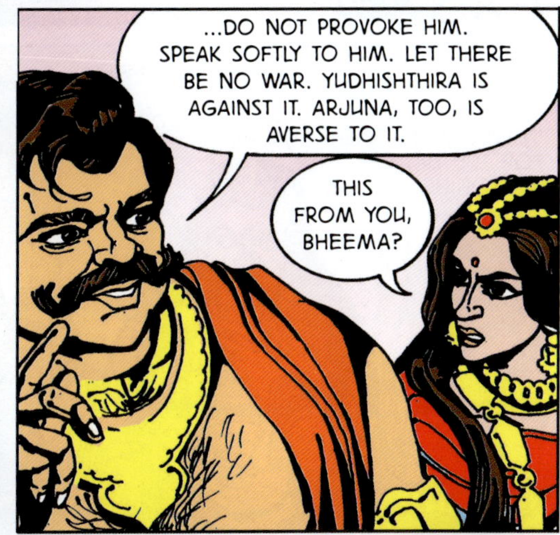
...DO NOT PROVOKE HIM. SPEAK SOFTLY TO HIM. LET THERE BE NO WAR. YUDHISHTHIRA IS AGAINST IT. ARJUNA, TOO, IS AVERSE TO IT.
THIS FROM YOU, BHEEMA?

RACKED BY PAINFUL MEMORIES, DRAUPADI LASHED OUT -
IF I DESERVE YOUR FAVOUR, YOUR COMPASSION, DO NOT SPARE THAT VILE SON OF DHRITARASHTRA.

WHEN YOU SEE HIM, CALL TO MIND THESE TRESSES IN DUSHASANA'S CRUDE GRIP, O KRISHNA!

CAN I EVER KNOW PEACE TILL I SEE THAT ARM OF HIS TORN FROM HIS MANGLED BODY IN THE BATTLEFIELD?

IF VALOROUS BHEEMA AND ARJUNA NOW CRAVE PEACE, MY AGED FATHER, HIS HEROIC SONS, MY OWN FIVE AND ABHIMANYU WILL DO IT.

THIRTEEN LONG YEARS DID I SUPPRESS THE SCORCHING FURY INSIDE ME WAITING FOR THE DAY OF RECKONING.

AND NOW BHEEMA.. BHEEMA SPEAKS OF PEACE!
WIPE THOSE TEARS, DRAUPADI.

ON MY WORD YOU WILL SOON SEE YOUR HUSBANDS SLAY THEIR FOES AND REIGN SUPREME. FOR...

IF THE SONS OF DHRITARASHTRA DO NOT HEED MY WORDS, THEY SHALL END UP AS CARRION-MEAL FOR JACKALS AND VULTURES IN THE WAR OF THEIR MAKING.

AND, UNDER YUDHISHTHIRA'S COMMAND, ALONG WITH BHEEMA, ARJUNA AND THE TWINS, SHALL I ACHIEVE THAT.

I DO NOT TAKE WORDS IN VAIN!
AND KRISHNA LEFT FOR HASTINAPURA.

AT HASTINAPURA, KRISHNA HAVING DISCHARGED ALL THE DEMANDS OF ROYAL PROTOCOL WENT TO VIDURA'S HOUSE WHERE HE LATER MET KUNTI.
KRISHNA!

THE TEARS SHE HAD HELD IN CHECK FOR NEARLY A DECADE AND A HALF NOW BROKE THEIR BOUNDS WITH ABANDON.
OH KRISHNA! FULL FOURTEEN YEARS HAVE GONE BY SINCE MY SONS WERE EXILED BY DURYODHANA.

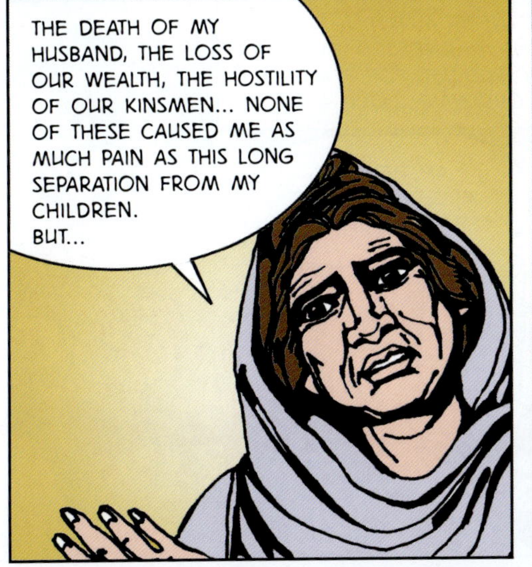
THE DEATH OF MY HUSBAND, THE LOSS OF OUR WEALTH, THE HOSTILITY OF OUR KINSMEN... NONE OF THESE CAUSED ME AS MUCH PAIN AS THIS LONG SEPARATION FROM MY CHILDREN. BUT...

...WHAT HURTS THE MOST IS THE MEMORY OF THE PEERLESS DRAUPADI, DRAGGED INTO THE ASSEMBLY TO BE HUMILIATED LIKE ONE WITH NO PROTECTORS.

KRISHNA GENTLY WIPED KUNTI'S TEARS AND CONSOLED HER. THEN -
THE DAY IS NOT FAR OFF WHEN YOU SHALL SEE HER PROTECTORS VANQUISH THE FOE AND RULE THE EARTH.

I KNOW OF YOUR DEEP CONCERN FOR OTHERS. ANYHOW LET WHAT MUST BE DONE BE DONE STRICTLY IN KEEPING WITH OUR DHARMA.

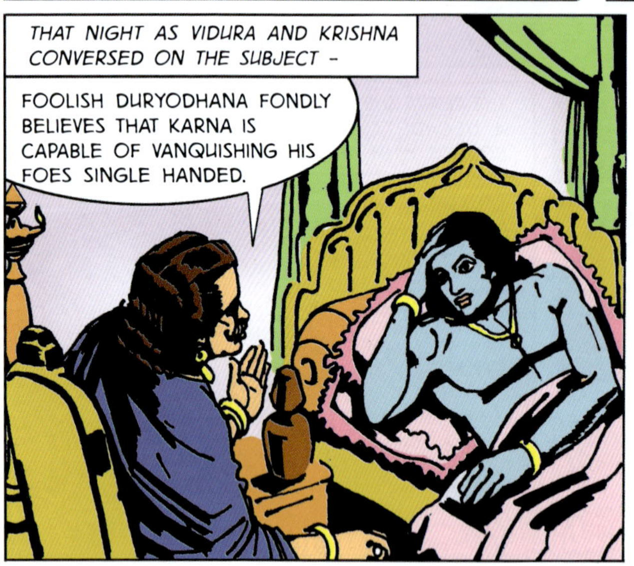
THAT NIGHT AS VIDURA AND KRISHNA CONVERSED ON THE SUBJECT -
FOOLISH DURYODHANA FONDLY BELIEVES THAT KARNA IS CAPABLE OF VANQUISHING HIS FOES SINGLE HANDED.

AND HE COVETS UNRIVALLED SOVEREIGNTY. SO HE WILL NEVER OPT FOR PEACE.
I KNOW DURYODHANA, AND I KNOW WHAT YOU SAY IS TRUE.

YET LET NOT MY DETRACTORS SAY: KRISHNA COULD HAVE PREVENTED KINSMEN FROM KILLING ONE ANOTHER BUT HE MADE NO ATTEMPT TO DO SO.

AND ACCORDINGLY, THE NEXT MORNING AT THE KAURAVA COURT, KRISHNA HARNESSED EVEN HIS SUPERHUMAN POWER, AND PLEADED FOR PEACE. BUT DURYODHANA REMAINED OBSTINATE. LATER -
I AM HELPLESS, KRISHNA! FATE, IT SEEMS, IS SUPREME.

KRISHNA LEFT THE COURT AND GOING BACK TO KUNTI, TOLD HER WHAT HAD HAPPENED AT THE COURT–

KRISHNA THEN LEFT FOR UPAPLAVYA.

THESE WORDS COMING FROM VIDURA CONFOUNDED KUNTI.
I ADMIT THAT VICTORY IN THIS WAR WILL BE NO VICTORY WITH FRIENDS AND KINSMEN SLAIN ON EITHER SIDE. YET... WE SHALL BE THE POORER FOR NOT FIGHTING.

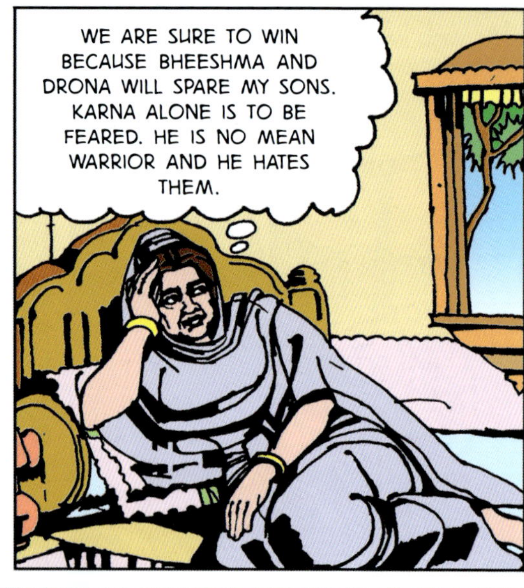
WE ARE SURE TO WIN BECAUSE BHEESHMA AND DRONA WILL SPARE MY SONS. KARNA ALONE IS TO BE FEARED. HE IS NO MEAN WARRIOR AND HE HATES THEM.

AND THEN KUNTI MADE THE HARDEST DECISION OF HER LIFE.
I WILL TELL HIM THE TRUTH TODAY AND TRY TO...

THE SUN BLAZED BRIGHT AS SHE WENT TO THE BANKS OF THE GANGA AND WAITED FOR KARNA TO END HIS MIDDAY WORSHIP.

AT LAST HIS PRAYERS OVER, KARNA TURNED ROUND –

O LADY, WHAT MAY I, THE SON OF ADHIRATHA AND RADHA, DO FOR YOU?
YOU ARE KUNTI'S SON, NOT RADHA'S. NOR IS ADHIRATHA YOUR FATHER.

AND KUNTI TOLD THE HAPLESS KARNA THE SECRET OF HIS BIRTH. THEN -
WHAT ARJUNA ACQUIRED FOR YUDHISHTHIRA, WAS USURPED BY THE KAURAVAS. WREST IT FROM THEM AND ENJOY IT WITH YOUR BROTHERS.

OBSERVE YOUR PRIME DUTY. OBEY YOUR MOTHER. LET THE AVARICIOUS KAURAVAS SEE YOU AND ARJUNA UNITED IN FRATERNAL LOVE.
IT IS TOO LATE, MOTHER.

KARNA GAVE KUNTI HIS REASONS AND THEN -
I WILL BE HONEST WITH YOU. FOR THE LOVE OF DURYODHANA, I WILL FIGHT ALL YOUR SONS WITH ALL MY MIGHT AND SKILL. BUT...

...I WILL SLAY ONLY ARJUNA. YOU WILL STILL HAVE FIVE SONS ALIVE.
THE KAURAVAS WILL BE EXTERMINATED. IT IS SO DESTINED. ALL THE SAME...

...REMEMBER THIS PLEDGE WHEN YOU FIGHT. MAY GOOD HEALTH BE YOURS.
AND MOTHER AND SON WENT THEIR PARALLEL WAYS.

MEANWHILE KRISHNA HAD REACHED UPAPLAVYA.
I TRIED TO REASON WITH DURYODHANA...

DURYODHANA HAD INDEED LOST NO TIME IN MARSHALLING HIS ELEVEN CONTINGENTS UNDER DRONA, KRIPA, ASHWATTHAMA, SHAKUNI, SHALYA, JAYADRATHA, KRITAVARMAN, BHURISHRAVAS, BALHIKA, SUDAKSHINA AND KARNA. THEN HE APPROACHED BHEESHMA TO BE THEIR COMMANDER.

...SINCE THE PANDAVAS ARE INVINCIBLE, I CAN SLAY NEITHER HIM NOR HIS BROTHERS. I PROMISE, HOWEVER, TO SLAY TEN THOUSAND WARRIORS FOR YOU EACH DAY TILL I AM SLAIN. BUT...

AND BHEESHMA STATED HIS CLAUSE.
KARNA WILL NOT FIGHT TILL I FALL. OR LET HIM FIGHT FIRST AND I WILL LEAD YOUR ARMY WHEN HE FALLS.

KARNA PROMPTLY SETTLED THE MATTER.
I WILL NOT TAKE UP ARMS TILL HE FALLS. AND THEN, I WILL SLAY ARJUNA.
AND EVER TRUE TO HIMSELF, KARNA KEPT HIS WORD.

EVEN AS DURYODHANA AND HIS ARMY OF ELEVEN CONTINGENTS, COMMANDED BY BHEESHMA, MARCHED TO KURUKSHETRA...
...YUDHISHTHIRA AND HIS SEVEN CONTINGENTS, LED BY DHRISHTADYUMNA, LEFT UPAPLAVYA.

DURYODHANA THEN SENT FOR SHAKUNI'S SON, ULOOKA.
GO TO THE PANDAVAS AND TELL YUDHISHTHIRA THAT THE TIME HAS COME TO MAKE GOOD THE BOAST HE HURLED AT US THROUGH SANJAYA.

TELL HIM THAT WE REJECTED HIS ABJECT OFFER TO SETTLE FOR FIVE VILLAGES BECAUSE IT WAS WAR WITH THEM THAT WE SOUGHT.

TELL HIM THAT HE SHOULD SHED HIS SAINTLY GARB, ACT LIKE A KSHATRIYA, DECLARE WAR AND BE READY TO ACHIEVE ALL THAT HE HAS PROMISED TO ACHIEVE.
THUS WAS ULOOKA SENT AS AN ENVOY TO TAUNT THE PANDAVAS INTO MAKING THE FIRST MOVE.

YUDHISHTHIRA LET ULOOKA HEAR THE REACTIONS OF THE REST TO THE MESSAGE AND THEN HE SPOKE.
TELL DURYODHANA THAT I DID NOT WANT MY KINSMEN SLAUGHTERED. BUT...

...IT IS NOW BOUND TO HAPPEN BECAUSE OF HIM. FOR...

...I WILL HAVE TO GIVE THESE VALIANT KSHATRIYAS A CHANCE TO FREELY DISPLAY THEIR FULL MIGHT ON THE BATTLEFIELD.

WHEN ULOOKA RETURNED WITH THAT MESSAGE FROM THE PANDAVAS -
BE READY FOR BATTLE BY SUNRISE TOMORROW.

WHILE MESSENGERS RODE THROUGH THE KAURAVA CAMP CRYING...
BE READY BY SUNRISE.
THE BATTLE BEGINS TOMORROW!

...BHEESHMA WAS BUSY EVALUATING THE CHIEF WARRIORS OF BOTH CAMPS AND RATING THEM AS RATHAS, ATIRATHAS, MAHARATHAS.
ASHWATTHAMA IS A MAHARATHA. THERE IS NONE ON EITHER SIDE THAT CAN WITHSTAND HIM. SHALYA, I WOULD CONSIDER...

WHEN KARNA'S TURN CAME -
AS FOR THIS DEAR FRIEND OF YOURS WHO IS FOREVER BRAGGING ABOUT HIS SKILL AND URGING YOU TO FIGHT WITH THE PANDAVAS, I COUNT HIM AS BUT HALF A RATHA.

WITHOUT HIS NATIVE ARMOUR WHICH HE WAS FOOLISH ENOUGH TO GIVE AWAY AND BURDENED BY PARASHURAMA'S CURSE, HE WILL NOT ESCAPE ALIVE IF HE TAKES ON ARJUNA.

DRONA ADDED -
WHAT YOU SAY IS TRUE. A BRAGGART BEFORE EACH BATTLE, HE FLEES THE FIELD WHEN THE FIGHT IS FURIOUS. I, TOO, SEE IN HIM ONLY HALF A RATHA.

KARNA COULD NOT REMAIN SILENT ANY LONGER.
O BHEESHMA, FOR DURYODHANA'S SAKE I HAVE TOLERATED YOUR UNJUST TAUNTS AND BARBS. YOU ARE AN ENEMY OF THE KURUS BUT THE KING DOES NOT KNOW IT.

ABANDON THIS WICKED ONE, O DURYODHANA. HE SEEKS TO HARM YOU BY SOWING SEEDS OF DOUBT AND DISSENSION AMONG YOUR MEN.

ELDERS SHOULD BE RESPECTED SAY THE SCRIPTURES. THEY COULD NOT SURELY MEAN THE VERY AGED FOR THESE BECOME CHILDREN AGAIN, TEND TO BOAST, AND ARE LED BY THEIR WHIMS.

BHEESHMA WAS ENRAGED.
I HAVE REASON TO BOAST. ALONE, IN A SINGLE CHARIOT, I FOUGHT A HORDE OF KINGS AND CAME AWAY WITH THE PRINCESSES OF KASHI FOR THE KURU KING!

NOW MAKE GOOD YOUR BOAST. FIGHT ARJUNA FOR THE KAURAVAS! I WOULD LIKE TO SEE YOU COME AWAY WITH YOUR LIFE FROM THAT ENCOUNTER!

DURYODHANA QUICKLY PACIFIED HIM.
THINK OF ME, O BHEESHMA. GREAT IS THE TASK ON HAND. AT DAWN WE FIGHT THE FOE. TELL ME OF THE TACTICS AND MANOEUVRES.

MEANWHILE VYASA CAME TO DHRITARASHTRA.
THE TIME IS UP FOR YOUR SONS AND MANY KINGS IN EITHER CAMP. DEATH STALKS ALL OF THEM. IF YOU WISH TO SEE THEM FIGHT...
NO!

NO. I DO NOT WANT TO SEE MY KINSMEN KILLING EACH OTHER. BUT I WANT TO BE TOLD OF ALL THAT HAPPENS THERE.

SO VYASA ENTRUSTED THE TASK TO SANJAYA CONFERRING ON HIM THE BOON OF SUPERNATURAL VISION.
SANJAYA SHALL SEE AND KNOW EVERYTHING AND DESCRIBE IT TO YOU.

AND SO THE FATED WAR THAT EVEN KRISHNA COULD NOT AVERT BECAME A REALITY. BY DAWN THE TROOPS HAD ASSEMBLED, RULES WERE SET AND COVENANTS MADE FOR THE CONDUCT OF COMBAT. CONCHES BLARED AND DRUMS THUNDERED AS THE TWO ARMIES WAITED FOR THE SUN TO RISE.

O KRISHNA, TAKE ME CLOSER TO THE WARRIORS ASSEMBLED TO DO WHAT WICKED DURYODHANA WILLS.

THE SIGHT OF HIS GURU AND KINSMEN IN THE HOSTILE CAMP THREW ARJUNA INTO A FIT OF DESPONDENCY.
HOW CAN I SLAY THEM FOR THE SAKE OF A KINGDOM? IT WOULD BE BETTER TO LET THEM SLAY ME!

HOW CAN I AIM TO KILL BHEESHMA AND DRONA WHO ARE WORTHY OF MY WORSHIP? NO I WILL NOT FIGHT.
HIS ACT THREW BOTH ARMIES INTO A SHOCKED SILENCE.

BUT THROUGH THE BHAGAVAD-GITA, A LONG DISCOURSE ON THE NATURE AND ATTRIBUTES OF THE SOUL AND THE PHILOSOPHY OF FINAL EMANCIPATION...

...KRISHNA DISPELLED ARJUNA'S DELUSION AND FINALLY -
I WILL FIGHT!

THE PANDAVA ARMY ROARED FOR JOY AND BLEW THEIR CONCHES AND BEAT THEIR DRUMS TILL THE VERY SKIES REVERBERATED THE UPROAR...

...ONLY TO FALL INTO SILENCE AGAIN. IT WAS YUDHISHTHIRA, THIS TIME. CASTING OFF HIS COAT-OF-MAIL, HE STEPPED DOWN FROM HIS CHARIOT...

...AND WALKED TOWARDS THE ENEMY RANKS TO THE GREAT CONSTERNATION OF HIS BROTHERS.
WHAT ARE YOU DOING?
WHY DO YOU ABANDON US AND WALK TOWARDS THE FOE?

HE GOES TO PAY OBEISANCE TO THE ELDERS, SEEK THEIR PERMISSION TO FIGHT AND OBTAIN THEIR COUNSEL.

HE COMES IN TERROR TO SEEK BHEESHMA'S SHELTER!
FIE ON HIM!
INFAMOUS WRETCH!

THE FEEBLE FELLOW DREADS THE PROSPECT OF A WAR!
HE IS NO KSHATRIYA!

WHEN YUDHISHTHIRA IGNORED THEM AND WALKED ON TOWARDS BHEESHMA –
WHAT WILL HE SAY?
WHAT WILL BHEESHMA SAY IN REPLY?
GREAT INDEED WAS THE CURIOSITY OF BOTH ARMIES.

O INVINCIBLE ONE, IF IT IS TO BE A FIGHT, GRANT US YOUR PERMISSION AND YOUR BLESSINGS.

HAD YOU NOT DONE THIS, I WOULD HAVE CURSED YOU WITH DEFEAT, YUDHISHTHIRA. FIGHT US AND WIN!

WEALTH IS NO ONE'S SLAVE. BUT MAN IS A SLAVE TO WEALTH. OBLIGATED AS I AM TO YOUR FOES, FOR THE WEALTH I ENJOY, I SHALL HAVE TO FIGHT FOR THEM. BUT...

...SEEK A BOON FROM US.
THEN TELL US, O GRANDSIRE, HOW WE MAY OVERPOWER YOU WHO ARE INVINCIBLE.

NOT EVEN INDRA CAN VANQUISH ME AS LONG AS I FIGHT, YUDHISHTHIRA.
THAT IS WHY I ASK YOU HOW YOUR DEATH IN BATTLE CAN BE CONTRIVED.

NOT BEFORE I AM READY FOR IT. SO COME TO ME AGAIN.

YUDHISHTHIRA THEN WENT TO DRONA AND SOUGHT HIS SANCTION AND BLESSINGS. AFTER THEY WERE GRANTED -
AS LONG AS I FIGHT, VICTORY CAN NEVER BE YOURS. SO TRY TO SLAY ME AS QUICKLY AS YOU CAN.

ALAS FOR THIS, BUT TELL US HOW YOU COULD BE SLAIN, O GURU.
IT CAN BE DONE ONLY WHEN I SET ASIDE MY WEAPONS AND AM DEEP IN MEDITATION.

AND THIS WILL HAPPEN IN THE MIDST OF A BATTLE ONLY IF I HEAR BAD TIDINGS FROM ONE WHOM I TRUST.
YUDHISHTHIRA THEN WENT TO KRIPA AND SHALYA.

KRISHNA MEANWHILE WENT TO KARNA.
COME FIGHT ON OUR SIDE, KARNA TILL BHEESHMA IS SLAIN. WHEN HE FALLS YOU MAY AGAIN JOIN DURYODHANA.
BUT KARNA FLATLY REFUSED AND...

...KRISHNA RETURNED TO YUDHISHTHIRA WHO STOOD AMIDST THE KURU WARRIORS PROCLAIMING -
HE WHO WOULD CHOOSE TO JOIN US WILL BE WELCOMED AS OUR ALLY.

YUYUTSU, THE SON OF DHRITARASHTRA AND THE TRADES-WOMAN, CAME FORWARD.
O PRINCE, ACCEPT US AS WE ACCEPT YOU.
ALONG WITH YUYUTSU AND THE REST, YUDHISHTHIRA THEN RETURNED TO HIS ARMY AND DONNED HIS COAT-OF-MAIL.

AND SO THE BATTLE BEGAN AND RAGED FURIOUSLY FOR FULL NINE DAYS WITH THE PANDAVAS AND THE KAURAVAS FIGHTING AS IF THEY WERE POSSESSED BUT RESPECTING ALL THE CODES AND COVENANTS.
ADVANTAGE SEEMED TO SWING FROM ONE SIDE TO THE OTHER UNTIL...

...AT THE END OF THE NINTH DAY'S BATTLE, THE PANDAVA ARMY, UNABLE TO WITHSTAND BHEESHMA'S FURY, WAS ABOUT TO FLEE. WHEN HE SAW THIS.
THE SUN HAS SET. LET FIGHTING CEASE FOR THE DAY.
SO BOTH ARMIES WITHDREW...

...AND ENTERED THEIR TENTS.

IN YUDHISHTHIRA'S TENT-
BHEESHMA HAD SAID THAT THOUGH HE COULD NOT FIGHT FOR US HE WOULD COUNSEL US.

IN HIS GOOD COUNSEL MIGHT LIE OUR VICTORY AND MY SOVEREIGNTY.

LET US GO TO HIM, NOW, AND SEEK IT.
KRISHNA APPROVED.

I WILL NEVER STRIKE DRUPADA'S SON SHIKHANDI WHO WAS ONCE A FEMALE. SO, PLACING SHIKHANDI BETWEEN US, LET ARJUNA ATTACK AND FELL ME FROM MY CHARIOT. VICTORY AND SOVEREIGNTY WILL THEN BE YOURS FOR SURE.

AND SO ON THE TENTH DAY, A LITTLE BEFORE SUNSET, ARJUNA SHIELDED BY SHIKHANDI BROUGHT ABOUT THE FALL OF BHEESHMA.

BATTLE WAS RESUMED ON THE **ELEVENTH** DAY WITH DRONA COMMANDING THE KAURAVA CONTINGENTS.

WITH DRONA ON ONE SIDE AND ARJUNA ON THE OTHER BOTH ARMIES SEEMED TO MAKE NO HEADWAY.

AND THAT DAY'S BATTLE CAME TO AN UNEVENTFUL CLOSE.

ON THE **TWELFTH** DAY, A SUICIDE SQUAD OF WARRIORS SWORE TO EITHER SLAY ARJUNA OR BE SLAIN BY HIM. AND WHILE THEY ENGAGED ARJUNA...

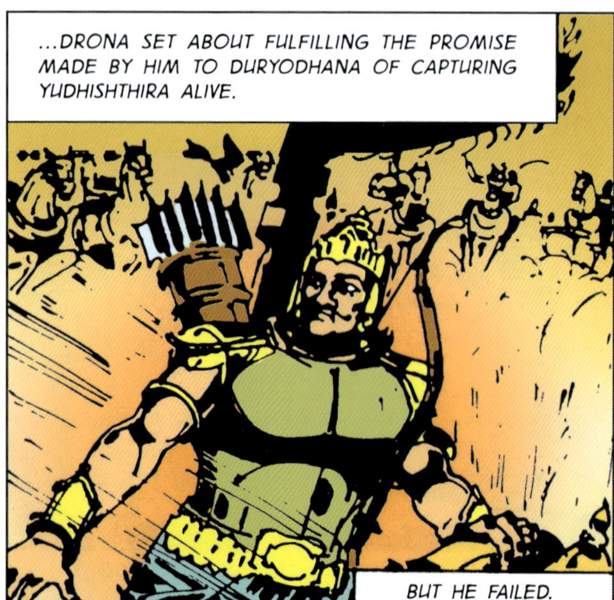
...DRONA SET ABOUT FULFILLING THE PROMISE MADE BY HIM TO DURYODHANA OF CAPTURING YUDHISHTHIRA ALIVE.
BUT HE FAILED.

AND SO DID THE SUICIDE SQUAD.

PIQUED BY THE PREVIOUS DAY'S FIASCO AND DURYODHANA'S CAUSTIC REMARKS, DRONA ON THE MORNING OF THE THIRTEENTH DAY TOOK AN OATH.

SO THAT DAY THE SUICIDE SQUAD ONCE AGAIN CHALLENGED ARJUNA AND LED HIM AWAY TO THE SOUTHERN END OF THE FIELD.

DRONA MEANWHILE ARRAYED HIS MEN IN CONCENTRIC CIRCLES OF MIGHT WITH DURYODHANA IN THE CENTRE, PROTECTED BY THE MIGHTIEST. LED BY BHEEMA, THE PANDAVA HOST ATTACKED.

...BUT DRONA PUSHED THEM BACK WITH A SHOWER OF ARROWS, WHILE HE STEADILY ADVANCED TOWARDS THE SON OF DHARMA.

THE ELDEST PANDAVA TURNED IN ALARM TO ARJUNA'S TEENAGED SON, ABHIMANYU.
O CHILD, TAKE THE LEAD AND SCATTER THAT ARRAY!

ELSE, RETURNING FROM HIS ENCOUNTER YOUR FATHER WILL REPROVE US ALL.
MY FATHER HAS TAUGHT ME HOW TO BREAK AND ENTER THAT ARRAY BUT...

...I DO NOT KNOW HOW TO COME OUT IF I AM SURROUNDED.
DO NOT WORRY! WE WILL FOLLOW CLOSE BEHIND AND PROTECT YOU.

ABHIMANYU'S CHARIOTEER HOWEVER PROTESTED.
HEAVY IS THE BURDEN PLACED ON YOU. MAKE SURE YOU CAN BEAR IT BEFORE YOU PROCEED.

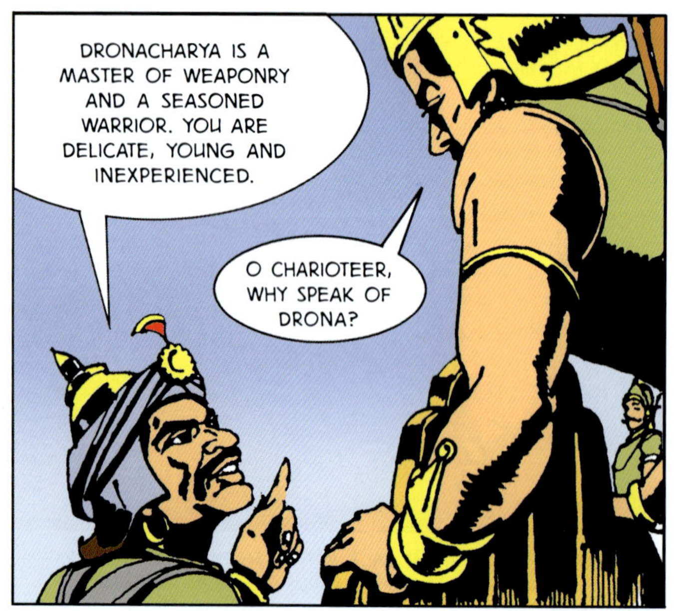
DRONACHARYA IS A MASTER OF WEAPONRY AND A SEASONED WARRIOR. YOU ARE DELICATE, YOUNG AND INEXPERIENCED.
O CHARIOTEER, WHY SPEAK OF DRONA?

HAD I TO TAKE ON EVEN KRISHNA, MY UNCLE, OR ARJUNA, MY FATHER, I WOULD NOT FLINCH! SO SPEED ON TOWARDS HIM!
COMMANDED THUS, THE CHEERLESS CHARIOTEER CHARGED.

WHEN THEY SAW HIM COME, LEADING THE OTHER HEROES, THE KAURAVAS LED BY DRONA TRIED TO STRIKE HIM DOWN. BUT, SKILFULLY DODGING THEIR ARROWS...

...YOUNG ABHIMANYU, UNDER DRONA'S VERY EYE, BROKE THE ARRAY.

AS DURYODHANA RUSHED TOWARDS THE LAD...
STOP THE KING! THE LAD SLAYS ALL HE AIMS AT! ATTACK HIM AND PROTECT THE KURU KING!

ORDERED BY DRONA, MIGHTIER WARRIORS SURROUNDED ABHIMANYU, AND TRIED TO SLAY HIM.

BUT THE SON OF ARJUNA DEFTLY DEFENDED HIMSELF EVEN AS HE WENT DEEPER INTO THE ARRAY WITH THE OTHERS FOLLOWING CLOSE BEHIND.

IT WAS THEN THAT JAYADRATHA REMEMBERED SHIVA'S BOON.
YOU WILL HOWEVER DEFEAT THE OTHER FOUR PANDAVAS AND YUDHISHTHIRA'S ARMY FOR A DAY.
THIS SHALL BE THE DAY.

HE HELD THE PANDAVA ARMY IN CHECK, PREVENTING THEM FROM FOLLOWING ABHIMANYU INTO THE ARRAY.

ABHIMANYU, MEANWHILE, BRUSHED ASIDE CHARIOTS AND ELEPHANTS AND STEEDS AND MEN LEAVING A TRAIL OF HEADLESS TRUNKS AND FLEEING WARRIORS AS HE FOUGHT HIS WAY TO THE INNERMOST RING OF WARRIORS.

INFURIATED AT THE ROUT OF HIS ARMY AND THAT TOO BY A MERE LAD, DURYODHANA ONCE AGAIN CHARGED BUT WAS FORCED TO RETREAT.
IN THE SAME MANNER, ONE BY ONE, ASHWATTHAMA, KRIPA, KRITAVARMAN, KARNA, SHAKUNI AND DRONA HIMSELF WERE BEATEN BACK BY THE HERO.

ONLY ONE WARRIOR, DURYODHANA'S SON, LAKSHMANA, DARED TAKE ABHIMANYU ON.
BUT AFTER A TERRIBLE ENCOUNTER, HE WAS SLAIN BY ONE OF ABHIMANYU'S ARROWS.

DURYODHANA'S GRIEF COMPOUNDED HIS RAGE.
I WILL SLAY HIM! I WILL SLAY THAT FELLOW!

IN SINGLE COMBAT IT IS HE WHO WILL SLAY US. LET US GANG UP AND ATTACK HIM. LET US CONSULT DRONA ON HOW IT CAN BE DONE.

WHEN DURYODHANA, SHAKUNI AND KARNA APPROACHED DRONA -
ABHIMANYU KNOWS ALL THERE IS TO BE KNOWN ABOUT WEAPONS AND WARFARE. I AM DELIGHTED WITH HIM.

EVEN THE MIGHTIEST WARRIORS BRISTLING WITH RAGE CANNOT FIND ANY CHINK IN HIS ARMOUR OR FLAW IN HIS TECHNIQUE. HE TAKES AFTER HIS FATHER, THE WIELDER OF THE GANDEEVA.

KARNA CONCURRED WITH THE VETERAN.
I CONTINUE TO FIGHT ONLY BECAUSE AS A WARRIOR I MUST.

INDEED, MY HEART TURNS FAINT BEFORE THE FIERCE, SURE, ARROWS OF THAT YOUTH.
YOUNG HE IS, BUT IN SKILL, A VETERAN!

I TAUGHT HIS FATHER THE ART OF WEARING ARMOUR. SO HIS COAT OF MAIL IS IMPENETRABLE. BUT...

...YOU COULD CUT OFF HIS BOW, THE REINS OF HIS STEEDS, FELL THE STEEDS THEMSELVES AND THE CHARIOTEER WITH WELL-AIMED ARROWS.

YOU ARE AN ACE BOWMAN, KARNA. DO THIS IF YOU CAN. DEPRIVE HIM OF HIS CHARIOT AND DIVEST HIM OF HIS BOW.

THAT WOULD COMPEL HIM TO RETREAT. SLAY HIM AS HE RETREATS.
AND THUS BEGAN THE END OF ALL DHARMA IN THAT DREADFUL WAR.

WITH THE "SANCTION" OF THE GURU, KARNA BROKE ABHIMANYU'S BOW...

...WHILE KRITAVARMAN SLEW HIS STEEDS AND KRIPA HIS CHARIOTEER.

AND ALONG WITH ASHWATTHAMA, SHAKUNI AND DRONA, THEY RUTHLESSLY SHOT ARROWS AT THE CHARIOTLESS, BOWLESS, YOUTH.

ATTACKED IN THIS VILE MANNER BY SIX VETERANS THE LAD, UNDAUNTED TOOK UP A SWORD AND SHIELD...

...AND LEAPT INTO THE SKY. BUT DRONA DESTROYED THE SWORD AND KARNA, THE SHIELD.

THE LAD, HOWEVER, HOLDING THE CHARIOT WHEEL ALOFT, RUSHED AT DRONA.

BUT THE NEXT MOMENT -

YET THE LAD DID NOT GIVE UP. HE PICKED UP A FALLEN MACE...

...AND ATTACKED ASHWATTHAMA. DRONA'S SON ESCAPED.

...BUT ABHIMANYU SLEW HIS CHARIOTEER AND STEEDS.

SLAYING WARRIORS AND ELEPHANTS LEFT AND RIGHT WITH HIS MACE...

...ABHIMANYU ATTACKED DUSHASANA'S SON, SMASHING HIS CHARIOT AND STEEDS WITH HIS MACE.

BUT THE LATTER TOO PICKED UP A MACE AND...

...SWUNG OUT AT ABHIMANYU.

THE TWO COUSINS FOUGHT LONG AND HARD TILL ABHIMANYU WAS HIT. HE FELL.

ABHIMANYU WAS ABOUT TO DRAG HIMSELF TO HIS FEET WHEN –
THUD!

THE FATIGUED HERO WHO HAD FELLED THOUSANDS IN THAT WAR WAS FATALLY STUNNED BY THAT SINGLE BLOW.

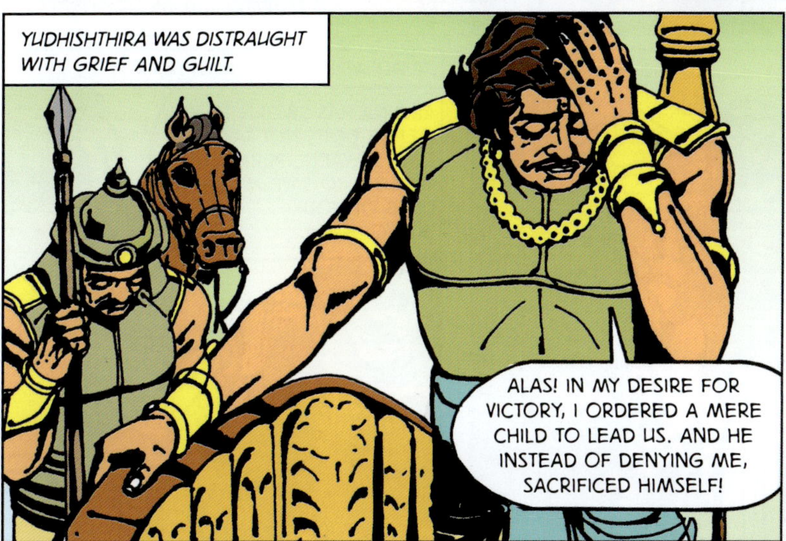
YUDHISHTHIRA WAS DISTRAUGHT WITH GRIEF AND GUILT.
ALAS! IN MY DESIRE FOR VICTORY, I ORDERED A MERE CHILD TO LEAD US. AND HE INSTEAD OF DENYING ME, SACRIFICED HIMSELF!

WHAT WILL I SAY TO ARJUNA? HOW WILL I FACE KRISHNA AND SUBHADRA?

ARJUNA WILL NOW FINISH OFF THE KAURAVAS FOR SURE.

BUT WHEN ARJUNA HEARD THE FACTS FROM YUDHISHTHIRA THAT EVENING, HIS FURY TURNED WHOLLY AGAINST JAYADRATHA.
THAT WRETCH CAUSED THE MURDER OF THE CHILD!

I SWEAR I WILL SLAY HIM BEFORE TOMORROW'S SUN SETS. IF I DO NOT...

...I WILL ENTER A BLAZING FIRE RIGHT HERE IN THIS BATTLEFIELD.
THE DIN OF MARTIAL MUSIC AND JOYOUS ROARS THAT RENT THE PANDAVA CAMP SEEMED A WHIMPER BEFORE THE RESOUNDING BLARE OF ARJUNA'S CONCH.

WHEN THAT UNMISTAKABLE BLARE PIERCED THE KAURAVA CAMP –
THEY REJOICE AT A TIME WHEN THEY SHOULD WEEP!

JAYADRATHA SHOOK WITH FEAR.
ARJUNA HAS SWORN TO KILL ME! HE DOES NOT TAKE AN OATH IN VAIN... PERMIT ME TO GO... TO SAVE MY LIFE... I BEG OF YOU, DURYODHANA.

WHAT ARE YOU AFRAID OF? YOU ARE A PRIME WARRIOR! A HERO! BESIDES, ALL MY CONTINGENTS ARE THERE TO PROTECT YOU.
CONSOLED BUT NOT CONVINCED JAYADRATHA STAYED...

...AND THAT NIGHT WENT WITH DURYODHANA TO DRONA.
O GURU, WHAT ARE MY CHANCES AGAINST ARJUNA? TELL ME THE TRUTH.

YOU HAVE BOTH HAD THE SAME LEVEL OF INSTRUCTION. HOWEVER, BECAUSE OF HIS YOGA AND THE HARD LIFE LED BY HIM...

...ARJUNA IS SUPERIOR. BUT TAKE COURAGE, FOR I WILL PROTECT YOU FROM HIM.
THEN I WILL FIGHT.
LOUD MUSIC AND JOYOUS ROARS NOW EXPRESSED THE DELIGHT OF THE KAURAVAS.

WHEN THEIR DELIGHT WAS HEARD IN THE PANDAVA CAMP IT WAS KRISHNA'S TURN TO BE PERTURBED.
SWEARING ALOUD THAT YOU WOULD SLAY JAYADRATHA BY SUNDOWN OR GIVE UP YOUR LIFE WAS A RASH DEED, ARJUNA.

THEY WILL NOW PROTECT HIM WITH SPECIAL CARE. SIX OF THEIR ABLEST WARRIORS INCLUDING KARNA, KRIPA, SHALYA AND ASHWATTHAMA WILL BE GIVEN THE TASK. AND...

...WHEN FIGHTING TOGETHER AS ONE, THOSE SIX ARE FORMIDABLE. LET US CONSULT...
THEIR COMBINED POWER DOES NOT EQUAL EVEN HALF OF MINE.

ARJUNA WENT ON WITH HIS VAIN BOAST.
KNOWING HOW INVINCIBLE I AM, WHY DO YOU REBUKE ME, KRISHNA?

MY GANDEEVA IS A CELESTIAL BOW. I MYSELF WILL WIELD IT. YOU ARE MY CHARIOTEER. WHO THEN COULD VANQUISH ME?!

KRISHNA WISELY REMAINED SILENT.
SO, SINCE WE HAVE A GRAVE MISSION ON HAND, HAVE OUR CHARIOT WELL-EQUIPPED BEFORE DAWN.
NONE IN THE PANDAVA CAMP SLEPT WELL THAT NIGHT.

AT MIDNIGHT, KRISHNA SPOKE HIS HEART TO DARUKA HIS CHARIOTEER.
DURYODHANA HAS TAKEN MINUTE CARE TO SEE THAT ARJUNA IS THWARTED IN HIS VOW.

HE HAS ORDERED SEVERAL CONTINGENTS TO PROTECT THE SINDHU KING. DRONA AND ASHWATTHAMA WILL ALSO PROTECT HIM... AND ARJUNA CANNOT HOPE TO SLAY ANY WHOM DRONA PROTECTS AND...

...I CANNOT IMAGINE AN EARTH BEREFT OF ARJUNA. I WILL SEE THAT ARJUNA SLAYS JAYADRATHA BEFORE THE SUN SETS TOMORROW.

IT WAS CLOSE TO SUNDOWN THE NEXT DAY WHEN ARJUNA, MAKING HIS WAY THROUGH THE FORMIDABLE KAURAVA ARRAY, AT LAST NEARED JAYADRATHA...

...AND IN ONE SHOT WITH TWO ARROWS CUT OFF THE HEAD OF HIS FOE'S CHARIOTEER AND HIS STANDARD TOO.

AS KRISHNA HAD WARNED, THE SELECT SIX AT ONCE ENCIRCLED JAYADRATHA.

TO SLAY JAYADRATHA, ARJUNA WOULD FIRST HAVE TO VANQUISH THEM.
EXERT YOURSELF AS YOU WILL, YOU WILL NEVER BE ABLE TO VANQUISH THEM AND SLAY HIM BEFORE SUNSET.

KRISHNA WAS RIGHT. SHEER TIME WOULD HINDER ARJUNA.
I WILL CREATE AN ILLUSION OF DARKNESS. BELIEVEING THE SUN HAS SET, JAYADRATHA WILL NO LONGER HIDE AMIDST THEM.

TAKE THAT OPPORTUNITY, ARJUNA AND ANNIHILATE HIM.
SO BE IT.

SOON -
THE SUN HAS SET!
JAYADRATHA LIVES!
ARJUNA WILL NOW LAY DOWN HIS LIFE.

LOOK, ARJUNA! JAYADRATHA GAZES TOWARDS THE WEST WITH RELIEF.

HIS HOUR HAS COME! SLAY THE WRETCH! CUT OFF HIS HEAD AND KEEP YOUR VOW.

KRISHNA'S COMMAND BECAME MORE URGENT, MORE INSISTENT.
QUICK, ARJUNA! THE SUN IS NOW TRULY ABOUT TO SET AT THE MOUNTAIN OF ASTA. CUT OFF HIS HEAD!

TAKE THE HELP OF A CELESTIAL MISSILE AND SLAY JAYADRATHA BEFORE THEY REALIZE WHAT YOU ARE DOING.

ARJUNA PULLED OUT AN ARROW INSPIRED WITH DIVINE POWERS, RAISED HIS GANDEEVA, AND LICKING THE CORNER OF HIS LIPS, TOOK AIM.

THE MISSILE SPED FROM THE GANDEEVA, FLASHED TOWARDS JAYADRATHA...

...SNATCHED HIS HEAD AWAY LIKE A HAWK SNATCHING A SMALL BIRD FROM THE TOP OF A TREE...

...AND CARRIED IT OUT OF THE BOUNDARIES OF KURUKSHETRA...
...TO ITS DESTINATION - THE LAP OF VRIDDHAKSHETRA, THE SINDHU KING'S FATHER.

ONLY WHEN KRISHNA DISPELLED THE ILLUSION WERE DURYODHANA AND HIS ALLIES AWARE THAT THEY HAD BEEN DUPED BY THE YADAVA.

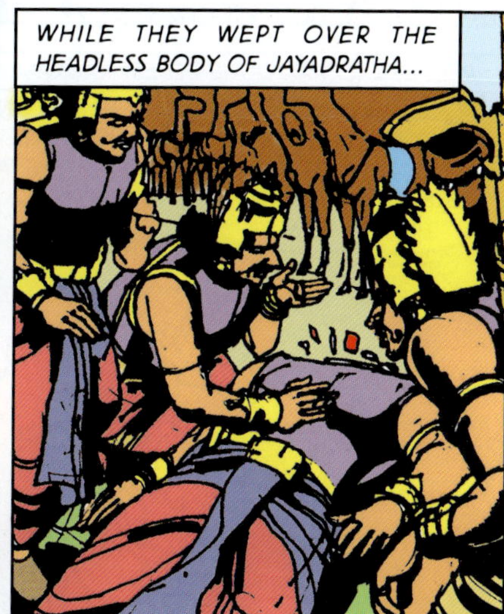
WHILE THEY WEPT OVER THE HEADLESS BODY OF JAYADRATHA...

...KRISHNA RUSHED WITH ARJUNA TO YUDHISHTHIRA.
YOUR FOE HAS BEEN SLAIN! YOUR YOUNGER BROTHER HAS KEPT HIS OATH!

MEANWHILE, DEFEATED AND DEJECTED, DURYODHANA SLID INTO THE SLOUGH OF SELF-PITY.
ARJUNA THE WARRIOR HAS NO PEER. CERTAINLY NONE WHEN HIS ANGER IS AROUSED.

SEVEN CONTINGENTS WIPED OUT, MY PRIME WARRIOR HUMBLED, AND JAYADRATHA SLAIN. NOT ONE OF THEM COULD WITHSTAND HIM.

ALAS! THERE IS NO ONE WHO CAN PROTECT MY ARMY NOW. NO, NOT EVEN INDRA HIMSELF.

REGRET LACERATED THE ELDEST KAURAVA.
DURYODHANA WILL NOT PART WITH EVEN A FOURTH OF HIS KINGDOM.
KARNA ON WHOM I RELIED AND SOUGHT WAR...

...KARNA RELYING ON WHOM I SPURNED KRISHNA'S OFFER OF PEACE AND FRIENDSHIP... KARNA ON WHOM I RELIED AND POOH-POOHED KRISHNA...

...ALAS, THAT KARNA HAS BEEN VANQUISHED AND JAYADRATHA SLAIN.

SUNK IN SUCH SELF PITY DURYODHANA WENT TO DRONA.
YOU HAVE, FOR SURE, ORDAINED OUR DEFEAT. YOU HAVE BEEN PARTIAL TO YOUR DISCIPLE, ARJUNA.

DRONA REFRESHED DURYODHANA'S MEMORY.

THE GURU DID NOT SPARE DURYODHANA.

THOSE VERY ARROWS SPED FROM ARJUNA ARE NOW SLAYING US. THE TERRIBLE CARNAGE, FORETOLD THEN BY VIDURA, AND IGNORED BY YOU HAS COME TRUE NOW.

O GURU, HOW WILL I REPAY THOSE KINGS WHO FOUGHT AND DIED FOR ME?
YOU'RE A FOOL WHO IGNORED THE WORDS OF TRUE FRIENDS AND FOLLOWED HIS OWN FANCIES!

DURYODHANA PLUNGED ONCE AGAIN INTO SELF-LACERATION.
YES MY ACTS ALONE HAVE CAUSED THIS MASSACRE OF HEROIC KINGS. I AM AVARICIOUS, COVETOUS, IGNORANT OF VIRTUE, SINFUL AND A FOMENTOR OF INTERNECINE BATTLES.

I SHALL GO TODAY WHERE ARJUNA HAS SENT THOSE KINGS. PERMIT ME, O GURU OF THE PANDAVAS, TO LAY DOWN MY LIFE. I HAVE NO USE FOR IT.

O WHY DOES THE EARTH NOT GIVE ME A TRENCH TO SINK INTO, SINCE I AM SO SINFUL?

WHEN DURYODHANA TURNED SO WRETCHEDLY ABJECT, DRONA SOFTENED HIS TONE.
PIERCED AS I AM BY YOUR WORDS, O DURYODHANA, I WILL NOT DOFF MY ARMOUR TILL I HAVE SLAIN EVERY SINGLE PANCHALA.

LOOK! THERE THEY COME, CHARGING TOWARDS ME! THE PANDAVAS AND THE PANCHALAS. THEY WOULD FIGHT EVEN BY NIGHT.

GREAT MUST BE THEIR RAGE AT ABHIMANYU'S DEATH. IF YOU CAN, GO DEFEND YOUR TROOPS.
AND DRONA MADE READY FOR THAT BATTLE BY NIGHT.

DURYODHANA, HOWEVER, STILL DOUBTING DRONA'S SINCERITY WENT TO KARNA.
O KARNA, ARJUNA HAS DECIMATED MY VAST ARMY.

HAD I PERMITTED THE SINDHU KING TO GO, SUCH CARNAGE WOULD NEVER HAVE TAKEN PLACE. BUT DRONA PROMISED TO PROTECT HIM...

HOW, INDEED, COULD ARJUNA BREAK THROUGH AND REACH JAYADRATHA IN TIME TO SLAY HIM, WITHOUT DRONA'S CONNIVANCE?
DO NOT BLAME THE GURU, O KING.

AND KARNA DEFENDED DRONA.
DO NOT DOUBT HIM. HE FIGHTS WITH ALL HIS MIGHT AND COURAGE NOT CARING FOR HIS VERY LIFE.

BUT HE IS OLD, SLOW IN HIS MOVEMENTS AND TIRES EASILY. WHEREAS ARJUNA IS YOUNG, AGILE AND HAS KRISHNA FOR HIS CHARIOTEER.

WE FOUGHT ARJUNA WITH ALL OUR MIGHT AND SKILL, YET JAYADRATHA WAS SLAIN. SUCCESS, THUS MUST DEPEND WHOLLY ON FATE.

KARNA CONTINUED HIS MUSINGS OVER FATE.
WHEN THE WAR BEGAN, YOUR ARMY WAS VAST AND MIGHTY. YET WITH THEIR SMALL FORCE, THE PANDAVAS DECIMATED IT.

PROWESS, DECEIT, POISON, FIRE, DICE, EXILE... ALL THESE WE TRIED, IN KEEPING WITH THE DICTATES OF STATECRAFT, WITH MUCH PLANNING AND GREAT CARE.

BUT HOWEVER HARD WE STROVE TO OVERPOWER THE PANDAVAS, OUR EFFORTS BORE NO FRUIT. WHY?

NOT BECAUSE THE PANDAVAS ARE ENDOWED WITH ANY EXTRA INTELLGENCE, OR THAT WE LACK IT, BUT BECAUSE...

...FATE DECREES THE RESULTS OF EFFORT. AND FATE, EVER CONCERNED WITH ITS OWN PURPOSES, IS UNPREDICTABLE.

SO LET US KEEP FIGHTING, O KING WHO KNOWS, BETWEEN THE TWO, PUTTING FORTH THEIR BEST AS WARRIORS, FATE MAY YET SMILE ON THE FACTION THAT EXCELS.

AND FIGHT KARNA DID, IN THAT GORY BATTLE BY NIGHT, EXCELLING ALL BUT -
O KRISHNA, YUDHISHTHIRA DREADS KARNA'S FIGHTING FETTLE TODAY. TAKE ME TO HIM.

I WILL EITHER SLAY KARNA OR BE SLAIN BY HIM TODAY.
NO, NOT YET, ARJUNA. HE STILL HAS INDRA'S MISSILE WITH HIM. SO...

LET GHATOTKACHA TAKE HIM ON. HIDIMBAA'S SON POSSESSES BOTH CELESTIAL MISSILES AND THE WEAPONS OF RAKSHASAS.

GHATOTKACHA, WITH THOSE DUAL ENDOWMENTS, PROVED A FORMIDABLE FOE. SOON -
FLEE! ALL IS LOST!
FLEE!

AND THEN AS KRISHNA HAD FORSEEN -
O KARNA, USE INDRA'S MISSILE AND SLAY THE RAKSHASA BEFORE HE SLAYS US ALL!

KARNA PULLED OUT THE UNIQUE, LETHAL MISSILE HE HAD RESERVED FOR ARJUNA AND HURLED IT AT BHEEMA'S SON.

PIERCING HIS HEART...

AND SEARING HIS BODY...

...GHATOTKACHA FELL TO EARTH CRUSHING A WHOLE CONTINGENT OF DURYODHANA'S ARMY UNDER HIM.
AFTER A BRIEF REST, THE BATTLE WAS RESUMED AND CONTINUED INTO THE FIFTEENTH DAY.

AT DAWN ON THE FIFTEENTH DAY, DRONA SLEW DRUPADA'S THREE GRANDSONS, DRUPADA HIMSELF AND VIRATA, THE MATSYA KING.

SIRE AND SONS SLAIN, DHRISHTADYUMNA STIFLED HIS GRIEF WITH AN ANGRY VOW.
I WILL SLAY DRONA THIS VERY DAY!

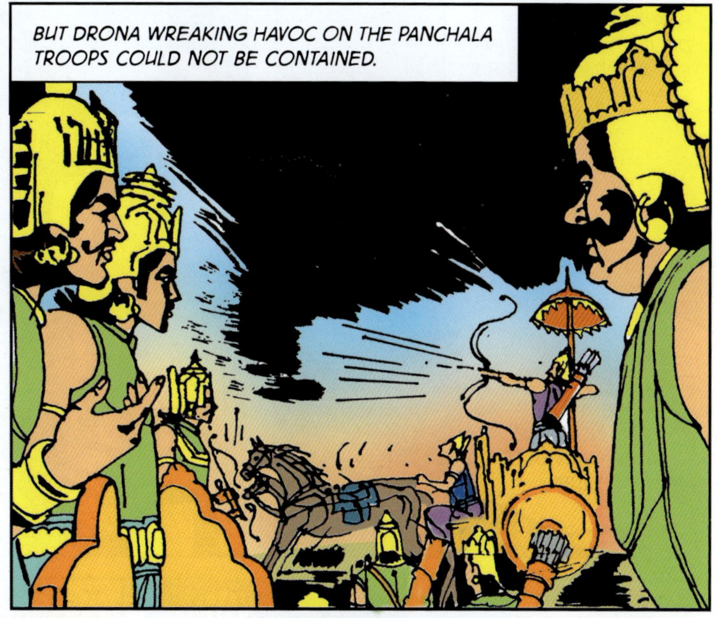
BUT DRONA WREAKING HAVOC ON THE PANCHALA TROOPS COULD NOT BE CONTAINED.

THE PANDAVAS DESPAIRED OF VICTORY.
WE ARE BUT STRAWS TO THE FIRE OF DRONA'S ATTACK.
ARJUNA ALONE CAN COMBAT HIM BUT HE WILL NOT.

AT LAST -
YOU WILL HAVE TO ABANDON VIRTUE AND RESORT TO STRATAGEM, ARJUNA.

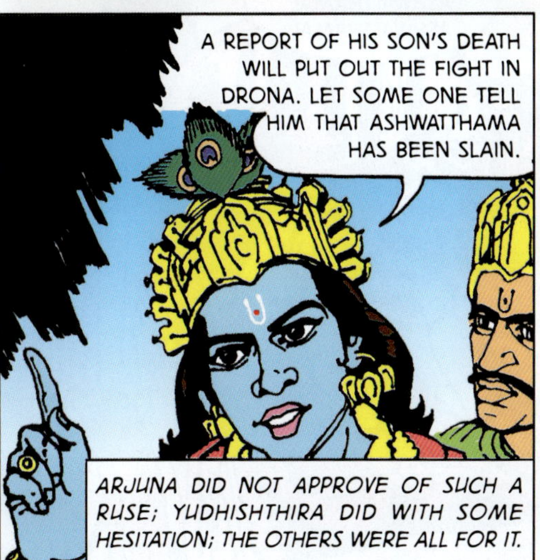
A REPORT OF HIS SON'S DEATH WILL PUT OUT THE FIGHT IN DRONA. LET SOME ONE TELL HIM THAT ASHWATTHAMA HAS BEEN SLAIN.
ARJUNA DID NOT APPROVE OF SUCH A RUSE; YUDHISHTHIRA DID WITH SOME HESITATION; THE OTHERS WERE ALL FOR IT.

BHEEMA SLEW AN ELEPHANT NAMED ASHWATTHAMA, GINGERLY APPROACHED DRONA, AND EXCLAIMED LOUDLY IN HIS HEARING-
ASHWATTHAMA HAS BEEN SLAIN!

FOR AN INSTANT DRONA WAS TAKEN IN, BUT REMEMBERING HIS SON'S PROWESS-
IT IS NOT TRUE! IT CAN NEVER BE TRUE!

I WILL ASK YUDHISHTHIRA. HE IS RENOWNED FOR HIS HONESTY.
O SON OF DHARMA, IS ASHWATTHAMA DEAD OR NOT?

YUDHISHTHIRA'S LOVE OF TRUTH PALED BEFORE HIS DESIRE FOR VICTORY.
YES. ***ASHWATTHAMA*** THE ELEPHANT IS DEAD!

YOUR SON IS DEAD. CEASE FIGHTING, O BRAHMANA. THE MOTIVE FOR YOU, A SEEKER OF BRAHMA, TAKING TO THE VIOLENT PRACTICES OF WARRIORS NO LONGER EXISTS.

DRONA FELT HIS LIMBS DISSOLVE.
O KARNA, O KRIPA, O DURYODHANA! I LAY DOWN MY WEAPONS. MAY NO HARM COME TO YOU FROM THE PANDAVAS.

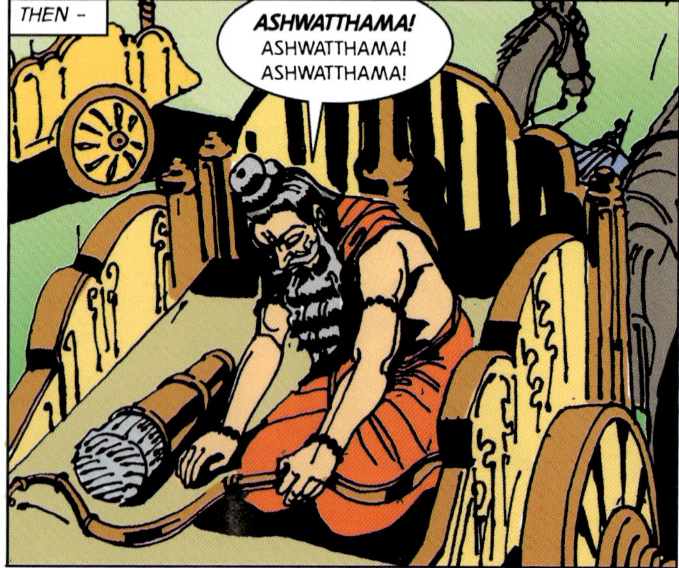
THEN -
ASHWATTHAMA! ASHWATTHAMA! ASHWATTHAMA!

HE SAT IN HIS CHARIOT AND LOST HIMSELF IN MEDITATION. SUDDENLY-

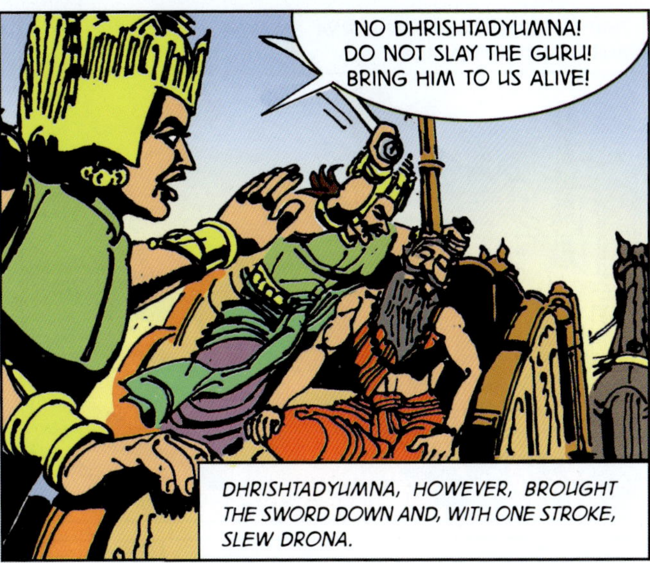
NO DHRISHTADYUMNA! DO NOT SLAY THE GURU! BRING HIM TO US ALIVE!
DHRISHTADYUMNA, HOWEVER, BROUGHT THE SWORD DOWN AND, WITH ONE STROKE, SLEW DRONA.

THE BATTLE WAS RESUMED ON THE SIXTEENTH DAY, WITH KARNA COMMANDING THE PALTRY KAURAVA HOST AND SHALYA MANNING HIS CHARIOT. NO MAJOR WARRIOR WAS SLAIN THAT DAY.

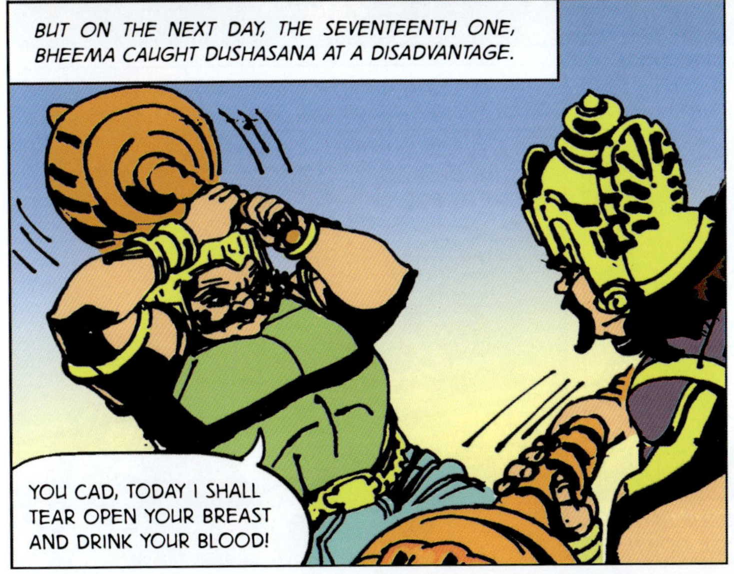
BUT ON THE NEXT DAY, THE SEVENTEENTH ONE, BHEEMA CAUGHT DUSHASANA AT A DISADVANTAGE.
YOU CAD, TODAY I SHALL TEAR OPEN YOUR BREAST AND DRINK YOUR BLOOD!

THE MACE CAME DOWN AND SNUFFED OUT DUSHASANA'S LAST BREATH.
BHEEMA THEN, TO THE HORROR OF ALL, FULFILLED THE BLOODY OATH HE HAD TAKEN AT THAT ILLFATED GAMBLING MATCH.

THAT AFTERNOON, WHEN KARNA WAS AT A DISADVANTAGE...

...KRISHNA PROMPTED ARJUNA TO SEIZE THE OPPORTUNITY.
HIS WHEEL IS STUCK. CUT OFF HIS HEAD BEFORE HE GETS INTO HIS CHARIOT.

EVEN AS HIS FOE WAS DOWN LABOURING WITH HIS CHARIOT WHEEL, ARJUNA TOOK UP A SHARP ARROW AND...

...CUT OFF KARNA'S STANDARD.

THE STANDARD FELL, AND WITH IT FELL THE PRIDE, THE HOPES, AND THE HEARTS OF THE KAURAVAS.
ALAS! ALAS!
BEFORE THE CRIES COULD DIE DOWN...

...ARJUNA PULLED OUT ANOTHER MISSILE FROM HIS LOADED QUIVER AND -
IF I MERIT IT, LET THIS MISSILE OF MINE FINISH MY FOE.
358

THE MISSILE, AIMED AT KARNA'S NECK, HIT ITS MARK AND -

THE LOSS OF KARNA PLUNGED DURYODHANA INTO THE DEPTHS OF GRIEF AND DESPAIR.
ALAS! O KARNA! ALAS! O KARNA!

HE STAGGERED TO HIS CAMP WITH THE HANDFUL OF KINGS LEFT ON HIS SIDE.

ON THE EIGHTEENTH DAY, SHALYA LED THE PITIFUL REMNANTS OF THE ONCE VAST KAURAVA ARMY.

YUDHISHTHIRA'S MISSILE...

...IN A THRICE FELLED THE KAURAVA COMMANDER.

AND BY NOON THAT DAY SAHADEVA CUT OFF SHAKUNI'S HEAD, THE HEAD WHICH HAD FED THE FEUD BETWEEN THE COUSINS.

AS THE BEHEADED SHAKUNI FELL...

...THE DELIGHTED PANDAVAS SURROUNDED SAHADEVA IN JOY.
OUR HERO HAS SLAIN THE EVIL SHAKUNI. OUR WOES ARE OVER.

AFTER THE FALL OF SHAKUNI, DURYODHANA LOST ALL HEART.

ALAS! THE KURU CLAN IS WIPED OUT AS THE WISE VIDURA HAD PREDICTED.
HE FLED ON FOOT TO A SHALLOW LAKE IN THE EAST...

...AND HID THERE IN IT.

MEANWHILE, THE PANDAVAS OUT TO KILL HIM, SEARCHED THE BATTLEFIELD IN VAIN FOR THE ELDEST SON OF DHRITARASHTRA.

AT LAST THEY GAVE UP AND...

...RETURNED TO THEIR CAMPS.

SOMETIME LATER BHEEMA RUSHED INTO YUDHISHTHIRA'S TENT.
O KING, DURYODHANA HAS BEEN SPOTTED BY THE HUNTSMEN WHO BRING ME MEAT.

HE LIES HIDDEN IN THE WATERS OF A LAKE!

YUDHISHTHIRA AND HIS FOLLOWERS AT ONCE SET OUT FOR THE LAKE.
THE SON OF DHRITARASHTRA HAS BEEN FOUND.

WHEN THEY REACHED THE LAKE, YUDHISHTHIRA TAUNTED DURYODHANA.
HOW COULD YOU COME HERE AND HIDE TO SAVE YOUR LIFE, AFTER WIPING OUT YOUR CLAN AND A HOST OF VALIANT, VIRTUOUS KINGS?

IT WAS NOT FEAR, NOR GRIEF, NOR LOVE OF MY LIFE THAT BROUGHT ME HERE.

IT WAS FATIGUE. I WAS ALONE WITHOUT A SINGLE KING TO STAND BY ME IN BATTLE. AND I NEEDED SOME REST.

YUDHISHTHIRA DID NOT SPARE HIM.
RISE THEN. BE A KING AND FIGHT. EITHER SLAY US AND RULE THE LAND OR BE SLAIN BY US AND SLEEP ON THE BARE EARTH.

I HAVE NO DESIRE FOR THE KINGDOM, NOR EVEN FOR LIFE BEREFT AS I AM OF FRIENDS AND ALLIES.

RENOUNCING THE WORLD, I WOULD ENTER THE FORESTS CLAD IN DEER-SKINS.

GO, YUDHISHTHIRA, AND RULE THE LAND DEVOID AS IT IS OF KINGS AND WARRIORS. IT IS ALL YOURS.

NO DURYODHANA. I WOULD NOT ACCEPT THE KINGDOM FROM ONE WHO IS POWERLESS TO RETAIN IT BY MIGHT.

BESIDES ONE OF US HAS TO DIE. PEOPLE MUST KNOW, FOR CERTAIN, WHO, THE VICTOR WAS! SO...

...RISE! RISE AND FIGHT US! FIGHT FOR YOUR OWN HONOUR! IF YOU SLAY EVEN ONE OF US, YOU MAY REMAIN KING.

DURYODHANA EMERGED FROM THE LAKE.
IF I MAY FIGHT ONE OF YOU AT A TIME...

...LET HIM WHO WILL FIGHT ME, TAKE UP A MACE.

BHEEMA TOOK UP THE CHALLENGE OF DURYODHANA.
I WILL FIGHT WITH THIS MACE AND SLAY YOU, YOU VILE DESTROYER OF YOUR CLAN!

EE-E E-A-AH!

A DEADLY COMBAT TOOK PLACE BETWEEN THE TWO. EACH WAS OUT TO ANNIHILATE THE OTHER.

TESTING THEIR SKILLS AND STRETCHING THEIR TACTICS, THE TWO VETERAN MACE FIGHTERS ATTACKED AND DODGED EACH OTHER.

AT LAST -
IF BHEEMA DOES NOT SLAY HIM BY UNFAIR MEANS, IT IS CERTAIN THAT DURYODHANA WILL REMAIN KING!

BHEEMA HAS VOWED TO BREAK DURYODHANA'S THIGHS. LET HIM DO IT NOW!
ARJUNA MOVED CLOSER TO THE COMBATANTS.

THEN, WAITING TO CATCH BHEEMA'S EYE, ARJUNA GAVE THE SIGNAL.

HITTING AT THE THIGHS WAS NOT ALLOWED BUT BHEEMA WAS UNCARING -

THE MACE FRACTURED THE ELDEST KAURAVA'S THIGHS AND...

...HE FELL TO THE EARTH WITH A LOUD THUD.
WE HAVE NO POISON, NO ARSON, NO DECEPTION, NO DICE.

...NO UNDERHAND DEALINGS...

OUR MIGHT, O KING, IS THE SOLE WEAPON WITH WHICH WE QUELL OUR FOES.

HIS HEART BRIMMING WITH JOY, BHEEMA TURNED TO YUDHISHTHIRA.
THE EARTH IS YOURS TODAY WITH ALL THORNS REMOVED.

THE CAUSE OF ALL VIOLENCE LIES HELPLESS. HIS KINSMEN, COUNSELLORS AND FRIENDS ARE SLAIN.

YOU HAVE NO FOES ALIVE.
QUITE SO. GUIDED BY KRISHNA, WE HAVE CONQUERED THE EARTH. YOU HAVE DISCHARGED YOUR DEBT BOTH TO YOUR MOTHER AND YOUR WRATH.

WHEN BHEEMA ONCE AGAIN KICKED THE HEAD OF THE FALLEN KAURAVA -
STOP HIM! WHY DO YOU LET HIM GLOAT IN THIS VULGAR WAY, YUDHISHTHIRA?

IT DOES NOT PLEASE ME. BUT DURYODHANA HAS GIVEN HIM ENOUGH CAUSE.

SO LET HIM DO AS HE WISHES, BE HIS BEHAVIOUR COURTLY OR CRUDE.
SO BE IT.

THIS SHAMELESS, COVETOUS, MAN WAS AS GOOD AS SLAIN...

...THE DAY HE IGNORED THE ADVICE OF VIDURA AND DRONA AND DENIED YOU YOUR SHARE OF THE KINGDOM

DURYODHANA WAS DOWN BUT NOT HIS SPIRIT.
CAN THERE BE ANYONE MORE SHAMELESS THAN YOU, YOU SON OF KAMSA'S SLAVE.

DO YOU THINK I DID NOT SEE YOU ADVISE ARJUNA? DO YOU THINK I DID NOT SEE ARJUNA'S SIGNAL TO BHEEMA?

BY RESORTING TO FOUL MEANS YOU HAVE CAUSED THE DEATH OF MANY A WARRIOR WHO ALWAYS FOUGHT FAIR.

BHEESHMA, DRONA, KARNA, ME... BY FAIR MEANS YOU COULD NEVER HAVE VANQUISHED ANY OF US.
AND DURYODHANA FELL BACK, EXHAUSTED.

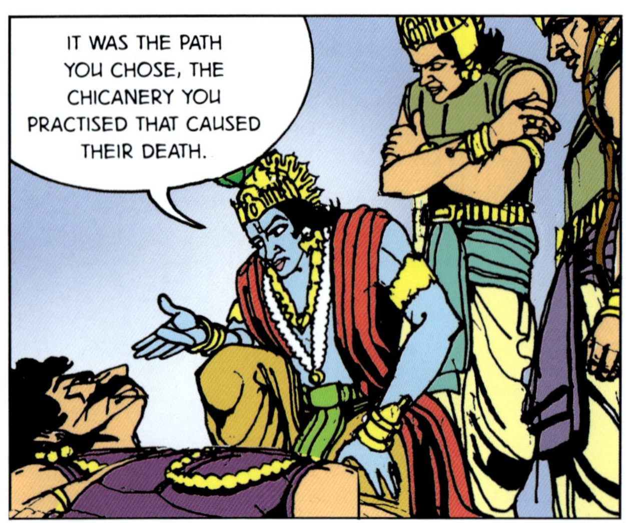
IT WAS THE PATH YOU CHOSE, THE CHICANERY YOU PRACTISED THAT CAUSED THEIR DEATH.

A SLAVE OF GORGING GREED, YOU IGNORED THE WISE WORDS OF YOUR ELDERS AND REVELLED IN SINFUL DEEDS.

REAP NOW THE FRUIT OF THOSE DEEDS.
FRUIT THAT NO OTHER HAS EARNED.

ON EARTH I ATTAINED AND ENJOYED EARTHLY PLEASURES AND PROSPERITY OF THE HIGHEST KIND.

AND NOW, DEATH IN BATTLE, THE END COVETED BY KINGS AND WARRIORS WHO ARE TRUE TO THEIR STATION AND ITS DUTIES, IS ALSO MINE.

WITH ALL MY BROTHERS, FRIENDS AND FOLLOWERS, I AM ABOUT TO ATTAIN THE CELESTIAL STATE OF VIRTUOUS KINGS.

IN YOUR PRIME, YOU COULD NOT ENJOY THIS WORLD. NOW WHEN IT IS YOURS IT IS BARREN WITHOUT WEALTH OR WARRIORS.

THE HEAVENS SHOWERED FLOWERS UPON THE DYING HERO AND DECLARED -
PRAISE BE TO DURYODHANA.
BHEESHMA, DRONA AND KARNA WERE SLAIN BY UNRIGHTEOUS MEANS.

KRISHNA AND THE PANDAVAS HUNG THEIR HEADS IN SHAME.
IT IS TRUE. HAD YOU FOUGHT THEM FAIRLY, YOU COULD NEVER HAVE SLAIN THEM. NO, NOT EVEN WITH ALL YOUR MIGHT AND SKILL.

BUT DO NOT TAKE THAT TO HEART. WHEN VASTLY OUTWEIGHED BY YOUR FOES YOU HAVE TO RESORT TO RUSE. THE DEVAS THEMSELVES DID SO IN THEIR ENCOUNTERS WITH THE ASURAS.

WE HAVE WON. IT IS EVENING. WE HAD BETTER GO BACK TO OUR TENTS WITH OUR ANIMALS AND CHARIOTS AND GET SOME REST.

WHEN THEY REACHED THEIR CAMP, HOWEVER -
FOR AUSPICIOUS REASONS WE SHOULD STAY OUT OF OUR CAMP TONIGHT.
AND THEY PROCEEDED TOWARDS THE BANKS OF THE RIVER OGHAVATI.

ON THE WAY YUDHISHTHIRA TOOK KRISHNA ASIDE.
VICTORY IS OURS, AND YET I DREAD GANDHARI'S WRATH...WHEN SHE HEARS HOW WE...VANQUISHED DURYODHANA...

GO TO HASTINAPURA, KRISHNA AND SPEAK TO HER LEST SHE SHOULD BURN US TO ASHES WITH THE FIRE OF HER AUSTERE PENANCES.
SO KRISHNA WENT TO HASTINAPURA, WHILE THE PANDAVAS SPENT THE NIGHT ON THE BANKS OF THE RIVER.

MEANWHILE HEARING ABOUT DURYODHANA'S FALL, ASHWATTHAMA, KRIPA AND KRITAVARMAN, THE ONLY SURVIVORS OF HIS ELEVEN CONTINGENTS CAME THERE.
MY FATHER WAS SLAIN... CRUELLY SLAIN BY THOSE FIENDS.

BUT MORE PAINFUL IS THIS... THIS PLIGHT TO WHICH YOU HAVE BEEN REDUCED.

I SHALL SLAY ALL THE PANDAVAS TODAY BY EVERY MEANS IN MY POWER. GRANT ME YOUR CONSENT, O KING.

DURYODHANA'S SPIRITS ROSE. HOPE ENLIVENED THE DYING KING'S HEART.
O KRIPACHARYA, BRING ME A POT OF WATER AT ONCE.

WHEN THE ABLUTIONARY WATER WAS BROUGHT -
INSTALL THE SON OF DRONA AS THE COMMANDER OF MY FORCES!

THE COMMAND WAS SOLEMNLY CARRIED OUT.
AND THE THREE LEFT THE SPOT.

LEAVING THE OTHER TWO TO GUARD THE GATE, ASHWATTHAMA STOLE INTO THE PANDAVA CAMP LIKE A THIEF.

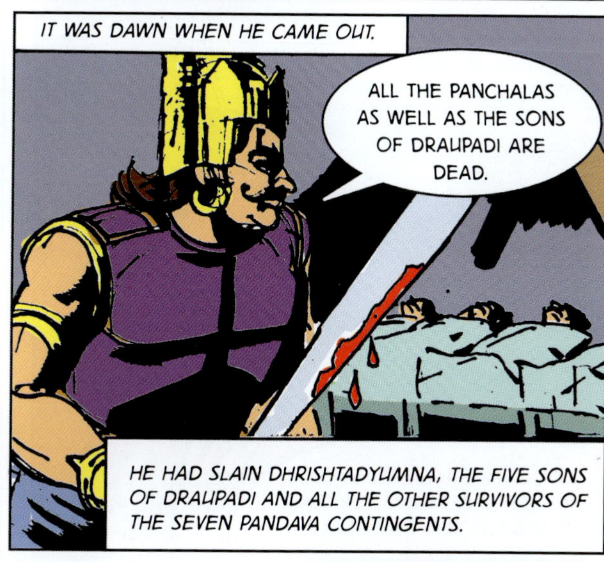
IT WAS DAWN WHEN HE CAME OUT.
ALL THE PANCHALAS AS WELL AS THE SONS OF DRAUPADI ARE DEAD.
HE HAD SLAIN DHRISHTADYUMNA, THE FIVE SONS OF DRAUPADI AND ALL THE OTHER SURVIVORS OF THE SEVEN PANDAVA CONTINGENTS.

YUYUTSU, THE SON OF DHRITARASHTRA BY THE TRADESWOMAN ALONE ESCAPED BECAUSE WITH YUDHISHTHIRA'S CONSENT AND BLESSINGS HE WAS ALREADY AT HASTINAPURA CONFERRING WITH VIDURA.

DURYODHANA WAS STILL ALIVE WHEN THE THREE RUSHED TO HIM.
IF YOU HAVE LIFE IN YOU, HEAR THIS O KING!

I HAVE SLAIN ALL THE SONS OF DRAUPADI. I HAVE SLAIN DHRISHTADYUMNA!

ONLY SEVEN ARE LEFT. THE FIVE PANDAVAS, KRISHNA AND SATYAKI.

DURYODHANA SMILED WEAKLY THROUGH HIS PAIN –
YOU HAVE ACHIEVED WHAT NEITHER BHEESHMA, NOR YOUR FATHER NOR KARNA COULD.

GOOD BE TO YOU...MAY ALL PROSPERITY BE YOURS... WE SHALL ALL BE TOGETHER AGAIN... IN... IN...

THE ELDEST KAURAVA'S VOICE FADED AWAY FOREVER AS HIS BODY FELL LIFELESS...
...AND HIS SOUL ASCENDED THE REALMS OF BYGONE HEROES.

AT THAT MOMENT, DHRISHTADYUMNA'S CHARIOTEER HAD JUST GIVEN THE NEWS OF THE GHASTLY MASSACRE TO THE PANDAVAS.
ALAS! THEY WHO ESCAPED THE LETHAL WEAPONS OF BHEESHMA, DRONA AND KARNA HAVE LOST THEIR LIVES TO NEGLIGENCE!

ALAS! OUR VICTORY HAS ENDED IN DEFEAT. THE FOES WE SLEW HAVE EMERGED THE VICTORS.

THEY WHO WERE SLAIN BY THE VINDICTIVE WRETCHES HAVE FOR SURE ATTAINED THE REALMS OF HEROES SLAIN IN BATTLE. BUT WHAT WILL BE DRAUPADI'S PLIGHT?

ALAS! SHE WILL DIE OF GRIEF WHEN SHE HEARS OF THE SLAUGHTER OF HER SONS AND HER BROTHERS.

SUCH FUTILE LAMENTATIONS OVER, YUDHISHTHIRA TURNED TO NAKULA.
GO TO UPALAVYA AND BRING THE UNFORTUNATE PRINCESS HERE.

HAVING DONE THAT, YUDHISHTHIRA PROCEEDED TO THEIR CAMP WEEPING AND LAMENTING ALL THE WAY.

WHEN DRAUPADI WAS BROUGHT BEFORE YUDHISHTHIRA, SHE SWOONED.

REVIVING IN THE WARMTH OF BHEEMA'S ARMS, SHE WEPT HER HEART OUT.

THEN COLLECTING HERSELF SHE CONFRONTED YUDHISHTHIRA.
IF DRONA'S SON IS NOT MADE TO PAY WITH HIS LIFE FOR HIS FOUL DEED... I SHALL SIT HERE AND GIVE UP MINE!

SLAY HIM AND BRING THE GEM ON HIS FOREHEAD TO ME. WILL YOU?

ONLY AFTER I HAVE PLACED THAT GEM ON YOURS, CAN I BEAR TO LIVE.
WHEN YUDHISHTHIRA REMAINED SILENT...

DRAUPADI APPEALED TO BHEEMA.
COME TO MY RESCUE AS YOU HAVE ALWAYS DONE, BHEEMA. SLAY THE SON OF DRONA FOR ME.
AND BHEEMA COULD NOT RESIST THAT APPEAL.

DETERMINED, TO PLEASE HER BHEEMA RODE OUT WITH NAKULA AS HIS CHARIOTEER, EVEN AS KRISHNA RETURNED FROM HASTINAPURA.
FOLLOW THE TRACKS OF ASHWATTHAMA'S CHARIOT!

NO! ASHWATTHAMA KNOWS THE MYSTERIES OF THE BRAHMASHIRAS MISSILE! BHEEMA SHOULD BE PROTECTED FROM HIM. COME, YUDHISHTHIRA.
TAKING YUDHISHTHIRA INTO HIS CHARIOT...

...KRISHNA AND ARJUNA FOLLOWED BHEEMA AND SOON CAUGHT UP WITH HIM.
THERE HE IS!

WHEN ASHWATTHAMA SAW KRISHNA, ARJUNA AND BHEEMA-
MY HOUR IS COME. WHAT SHALL I DO?

THE BRAHMASHIRAS! I'LL USE IT!

HE PICKED UP A BLADE OF GRASS WITH HIS LEFT HAND...

...EMPOWERED IT WITH THE PROPER CHANTS TO CONVERT IT INTO THAT DEADLY SUPERNATURAL MISSILE AND CRYING...
...FOR THE DESTRUCTION OF THE PANDAVAS...

...SENT IT SAILING IN THE AIR TOWARDS BHEEMA.
QUICK ARJUNA! NEUTRALIZE ASHWATTHAMA'S WEAPON WITH YOUR OWN. SAVE YOUR BROTHERS AND YOURSELF.

AS THE FIERY MISSILE CAME TOWARDS THEM, ARJUNA'S COUNTER-MISSILE HAD ALREADY LEFT HIS GANDEEVA.
MAY ASHWATTHAMA'S MISSILE BE NEUTRALIZED!

SPEEDING RELENTLESSLY TOWARDS EACH OTHER, THE MISSILES SCORCHED AND SHOOK THE EARTH.

WHEN THEY WERE ABOUT TO COLLIDE THERE APPEARED, BLOCKING THE MISSILES...

...THE INDESTRUCTIBLE SAGES, NARADA AND VYASA.
THIS IS A RASH ACT INDEED!

AND BETWEEN THEM, THE SAGES MADE THE MISSILES INERT. THEN -
WHEN ONE BRAHMASHIRAS IS BAFFLED BY ANOTHER THERE IS DROUGHT FOR TWELVE YEARS! THE EARTH AND ITS TREES AND WATERS ARE SCORCHED AND THE CLOUDS DRY UP!

GIVE THEM THE GEM ON YOUR HEAD, ASHWATTHAMA AND THE PANDAVAS WILL SPARE YOUR LIFE.

THE SON OF DRONA RELUCTANTLY SURRENDERED THE GEM TO THE PANDAVAS.
THIS GEM FOREVER RIDS THE WEARER OF ANY FEAR OF HUNGER, DISEASES, WEAPONS, DEVAS, ASURAS, RAKSHASAS AND ROBBERS.

HE THEN GLUMLY WALKED AWAY INTO THE FORESTS...

...WHILE THE PANDAVAS AND KRISHNA MADE THEIR WAY BACK TO THEIR CAMP AND DRAUPADI.

ASHWATTHAMA HAS BEEN DIVESTED OF HIS GEM AND OF HIS FAME. BUT...

...WE HAVE SET HIM FREE... OUT OF REGARD FOR OUR GURU, DRAUPADI...
THE GURU'S SON IS AS WORTHY OF OUR RESPECT AS THE GURU HIMSELF.

"WHEN KRISHNA WAS SETTING OUT FOR UPAPLAVYA ON HIS MISSION OF PEACE YOU HAD SAID:"
I HAVE NO HUSBANDS. I HAVE NO SONS NOR BROTHERS. NOR DO YOU EXIST, KRISHNA, SINCE THE KING DESIRES PEACE.

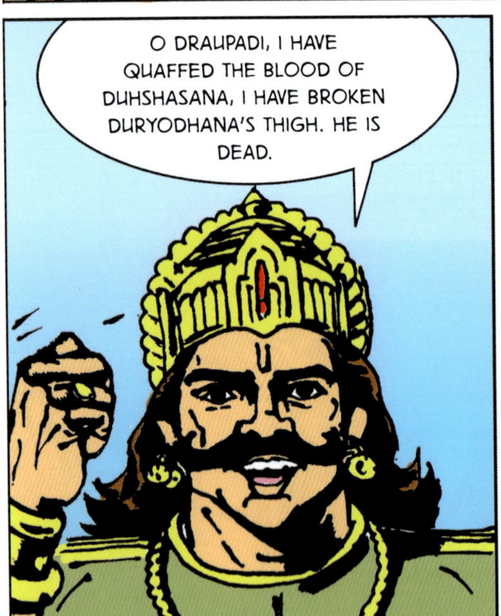
O DRAUPADI, I HAVE QUAFFED THE BLOOD OF DUHSHASANA, I HAVE BROKEN DURYODHANA'S THIGH. HE IS DEAD.

BHEEMA HELD OUT THE GEM.
THIS, FAIR LADY, IS YOURS. THE SLAYER OF YOUR SONS HAS BEEN VANQUISHED.

I ONLY WANTED THE WRONG DONE TO US AVENGED. LET THE KING BIND THIS GEM ON HIS HEAD.

YUDHISHTHIRA TOOK THE GEM AND DID AS DRAUPADI BID.

MEANWHILE SANJAYA, NOW DEPRIVED OF HIS CELESTIAL VISION, CAME TO DHRITARASHTRA WHO WAS INDULGING IN GRIEF.
YOUR SON, TO SETTLE HIS DISSENSIONS WITH THE PANDAVAS CHOSE WAR AND NOT PEACE. HE THUS CAUSED THE DEATH OF COUNTLESS WARRIORS, KNOWN AND UNKNOWN.

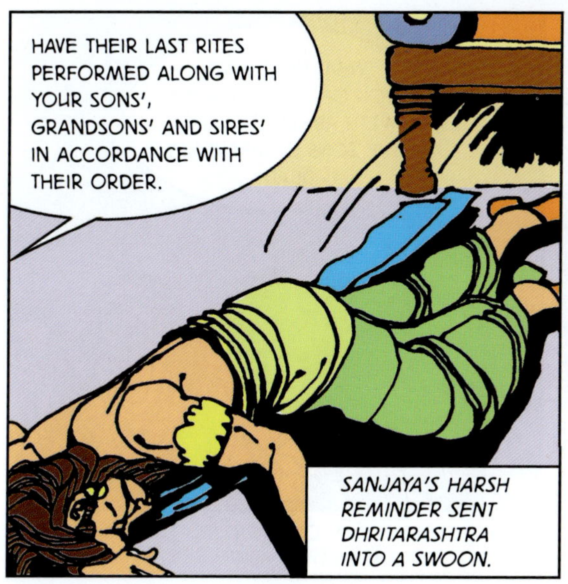
HAVE THEIR LAST RITES PERFORMED ALONG WITH YOUR SONS', GRANDSONS' AND SIRES' IN ACCORDANCE WITH THEIR ORDER.
SANJAYA'S HARSH REMINDER SENT DHRITARASHTRA INTO A SWOON.

VIDURA GENTLY HELPED HIM UP. THEN -
O KING, DO NOT LET YOUR GRIEF OVERWHELM YOU. DO WHAT MUST BE DONE NOW.

DHRITARASHTRA STOOD UP AND SQUARED HIS SHOULDERS.
YOKE MY CHARIOT. BRING GANDHARI, KUNTI AND THE OTHER LADIES HERE, AT ONCE.

AND SURROUNDED BY THOUSANDS OF WAILING WOMEN, THE KING AND HIS ENTOURAGE SLOWLY CAME OUT OF HASTINAPURA.

WHEN YUDHISHTHIRA LEARNT OF THIS, HE SET OUT WITH DRAUPADI, HIS BROTHERS AND KRISHNA TO MEET HIM.

AS THEY NEARED THE GANGES -
WHERE IS RIGHTEOUSNESS FLED TO? AND TRUTH? AND COMPASSION?
HOW CAN YOUR HEART KNOW PEACE, O KING?

WHAT PRICE SOVEREIGNITY GAINED AT SUCH COST? SIRES... BROTHERS...GURUS... FRIENDS... SONS ALL SLAIN... SLAIN O KING!

WHAT NEED HAVE YOU OF SOVEREIGNITY WITH ABHIMANYU AND THE SONS OF DRAUPADI DEAD?
SUPPRESSING HIS OWN GRIEF, YUDHISHTHIRA DROVE PAST THE WOMEN AND...

...MADE HIS WAY TO DHRITARASHTRA.
UNCLE! IT IS I, YUDHISHTHIRA.

DHRITARASHTRA RELUCTANTLY EMBRACED THE ELDEST SON OF PANDU. THEN -
WHERE IS BHEEMA?

BHEEMA WAS ABOUT TO STEP FORWARD WHEN...

...KRISHNA DEFTLY PUSHED AN IRON STATUE FORWARD-

DHRITARASHTRA'S ARMS CLOSED OVER THE IRON STATUE....

...ALL HIS PENT-UP RAGE INTO HIS EMBRACE, AND -

THE NEXT MOMENT HE BROKE DOWN AND WEPT LIKE A BABE.
ALAS! O BHEEMA! ALAS! O BHEEMA!
KRISHNA WAS CONVINCED.

DHRITARASHTRA WAS CONTRITE FOR HAVING, AS HE BELIEVED, KILLED BHEEMA.
DO NOT GRIEVE, O KING. IT WAS NOT BHEEMA BUT AN IRON IMAGE OF HIM THAT YOU CRUSHED TO BITS.

THE SLAYING OF BHEEMA WOULD DO YOU NO GOOD. YOUR SONS WILL NOT BE REVIVED BY IT. SO CONTROL YOUR ANGER.

WHAT WAS DONE WAS DONE TO END HOSTILITIES, AND BRING ABOUT PEACE. APPROVE OF IT.

YOU DID NOT HEED OUR ADVICE BEFORE THE BATTLE BUT PREFERRED DURYODHANA'S PERVERSE PATH.

SO WHY DO YOU SEEK TO SLAY BHEEMA WHEN YOU ARE THE CAUSE OF ALL THAT HAS VISITED YOU?

DHRITARASHTRA KNEW THAT KRISHNA HAD UTTERED NOTHING BUT THE BITTER TRUTH.
YES. IT IS ATTACHMENT FOR MY SON THAT MADE ME STRAY FROM THE PATH OF DHARMA.

I AM FORTUNATE THAT BHEEMA WAS SAVED BY YOU. FOR, MY HAPPINESS NOW DEPENDS UPON THE SONS OF PANDU.

THE WEARY OLD KING THEN EMBRACED BHEEMA AND THE OTHER PANDAVAS AND WEPT HIS HEART OUT.

LATER, THE LAST RITES OF THOUSANDS OF WARRIORS, FRIENDS AND FOES, KINSMEN AND ALIENS WERE PERFORMED.

THEN THE LADIES OFFERED OBLATIONS OF WATER TO THEIR FRIENDS AND KINSMEN.

THE NEXT MOMENT -
THAT HERO WHOM YOU SLEW, ARJUNA... THE HERO WHOM YOU BHEEMA, TOOK FOR A CHARIOTEER'S SON...WAS YOUR ELDEST BROTHER.

KUNTI WENT ON WITH HER REVELATION TO THE STUNNED HEROES.
YES. OFFER OBLATIONS TO HIM. HE WAS BORN TO ME OF SURYA HIMSELF.

AND YOU CONCEALED THIS FROM US! ALAS! WE ARE UNDONE!
ALAS!
ALAS!
ALAS!
ALAS!

ALAS! THE PAIN I FEEL NOW IS GREATER BY FAR THAN THE PAIN I FELT AT THE DEATH OF ABHIMANYU AND THE SONS OF DRAUPADI.
INDULGING IN SUCH LAMENTS...

...YUDHISHTHIRA OFFERED OBLATIONS TO KARNA, HIS ELDER BROTHER.

AFTER COMPLETING THE CEREMONY HE ROSE FROM THE WATER...

...AND DECIDED TO PASS THE MONTH-LONG PERIOD OF RITUAL POLLUTION ON THE BANKS OF THE GANGA WITH THE REST OF THE KURUS AND THE LADIES.

AND THERE YUDHISHTHIRA CONFRONTED HIMSELF BEFORE HIS BROTHERS.
THROUGH GREED I HAVE CAUSED THE DEATH OF ABHIMANYU... OF THE SONS OF DRAUPADI... OF KARNA MY ELDER BROTHER...

I HAVE SLAIN THOSE I SHOULD NEVER HAVE SLAIN AND WON THE CONTEMPT OF THE WORLD. LIKE A PACK OF DOGS FIGHTING ONE ANOTHER FOR A CHUNK OF MEAT.

THAT PIECE OF MEAT IS NOW GALL TO ME. I SHALL THROW IT UP AND RETIRE TO THE FOREST.

ARJUNA TURNED TO KRISHNA.
ONCE MORE WE HAVE FALLEN INTO GRAVE DANGER. THE SON OF DHARMA IS DISTRAUGHT WITH GRIEF. DISPEL IT O, KRISHNA. COMFORT HIM.

EXHORTED BY KRISHNA, THE ELDEST PANDAVA ROSE, CAST OFF HIS GRIEF AND DOUBT AND...

...ALONG WITH DRAUPADI, HIS BROTHERS AND THE REST, FOLLOWED DHRITARASHTRA AND GANDHARI TO HASTINAPURA.

WHEN THEY ENTERED THE CITY THOUSANDS UPON THOUSANDS CAME TO BEHOLD THE SIGHT.
MOST WORTHY OF PRAISE ARE YOU O PRINCESS OF PANCHALA!

YOUR DEEDS AND DEVOTION HAVE BORNE FRUIT, O LADY!

YUDHISHTHIRA THEN ENTERED THE PALACE...

...AND WORSHIPPED THE HOUSEHOLD DEITIES.

AND THEN ON AN AUSPICIOUS DAY YUDHISHTHIRA, THE GRANDSON OF SATYAVATI'S SON VYASA, THOUGH NOT OF THEIR LINE, WAS INSTALLED ON THE THRONE OF HASTINAPURA AS ITS SOVEREIGN RULER.

SUCH WAS THE OUTCOME OF THE LONG WAR THAT CULMINATED IN AN EIGHTEEN-DAY BATTLE - THE GORY BATTLE THAT EVEN KRISHNA COULD NOT AVERT - BETWEEN FEUDING COUSINS OF THE SAME HOUSE CAUGHT IN THE WEB OF ATTACHMENT AND JEALOUS ANGER.